GRADE 1

COMPREHENSIVE CURRICULUM
of Basic Skills

American Education Publishing™
An imprint of Carson-Dellosa Publishing LLC
Greensboro, North Carolina

American Education Publishing™
An imprint of Carson-Dellosa Publishing LLC
P.O. Box 35665
Greensboro, NC 27425 USA

Printed in the USA • All rights reserved.   ISBN 978-1-60996-330-9

08-069141151

R ADING

R ADING COMPREHENSION

ENGLISH

SPELLING

Name: _____

Name, Address, Phone

This book belongs to Lucy Robinson

- .

I live at

- .

The city I live in is

- .

The state I live in is

- .

My phone number is

- .

Name: _____

Review the Alphabet

Directions: Practice writing the letters.

 Aa AaAaAaAaAaAa

 Bb

Cc

 *Dd*

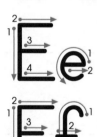 *Ee*

Ff

Gg

Hh

Ii

Name: _____

Review the Alphabet

Directions: Practice writing the letters.

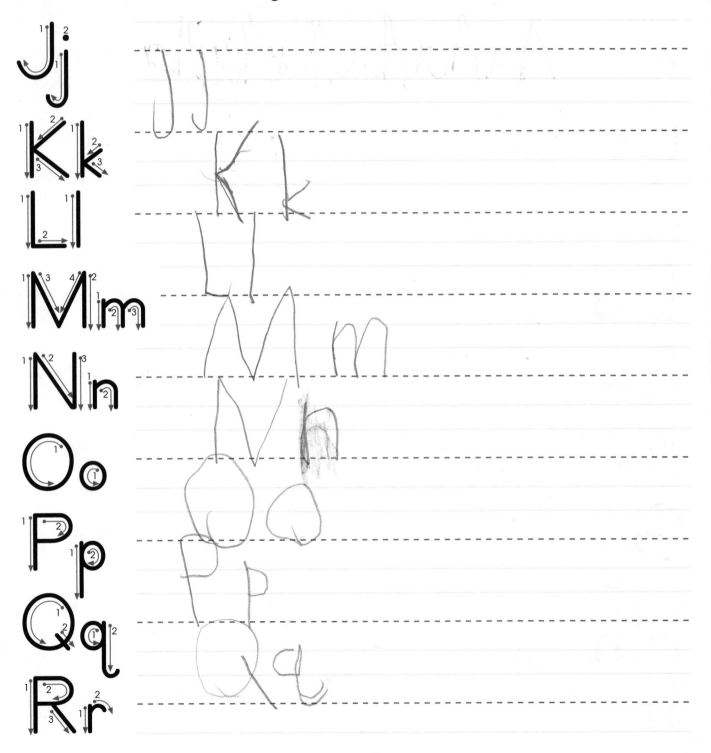

Review the Alphabet

Directions: Practice writing the letters.

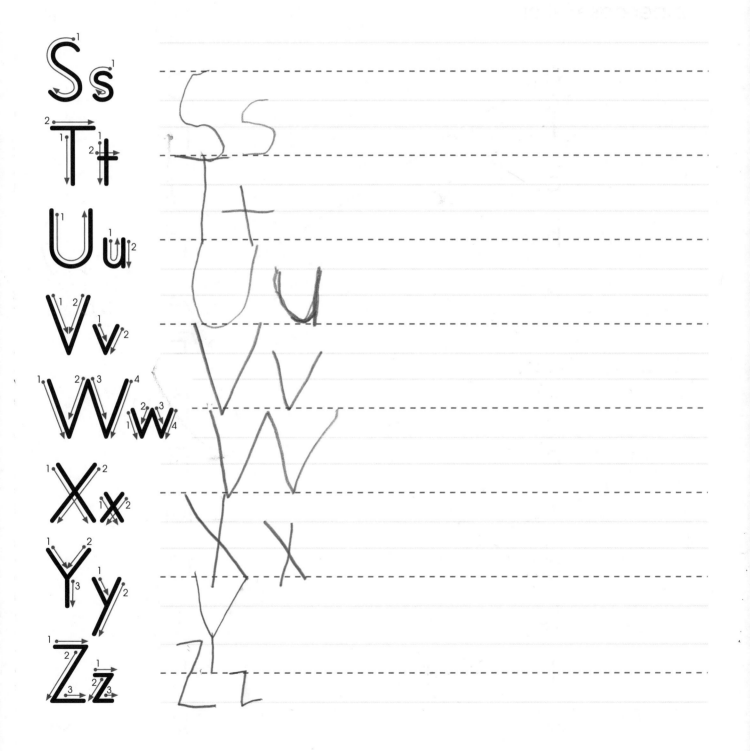

Grade 1 - Comprehensive Curriculum

Name: _____

Letter Recognition

Directions: In each set, match the lower-case letter to the upper-case letter.

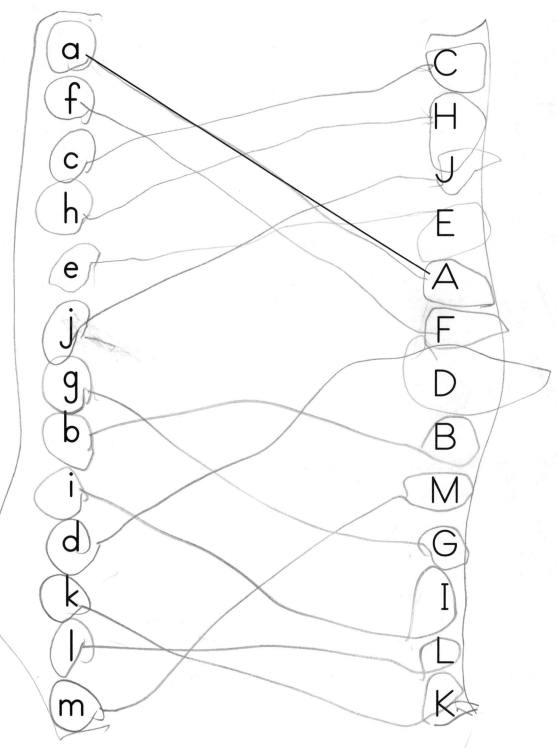

Name: _____

Letter Recognition

Directions: In each set, match the lower-case letter to the upper-case letter.

Grade 1 - Comprehensive Curriculum

Name: _____

Beginning Consonants: Bb, Cc, Dd, Ff

Beginning consonants are the sounds that come at the beginning of words. Consonants are the letters b, c, d, f, g, h, j, k, l, m, n, p, q, r, s, t, v, w, x, y and z.

Directions: Say the name of each letter. Say the sound each letter makes. Circle the letters that make the beginning sound for each picture.

Name: _____

Beginning Consonants: Bb, Cc, Dd, Ff

Directions: Say the name of each letter. Say the sound each letter makes. Draw a line from each letter to the picture which begins with that sound.

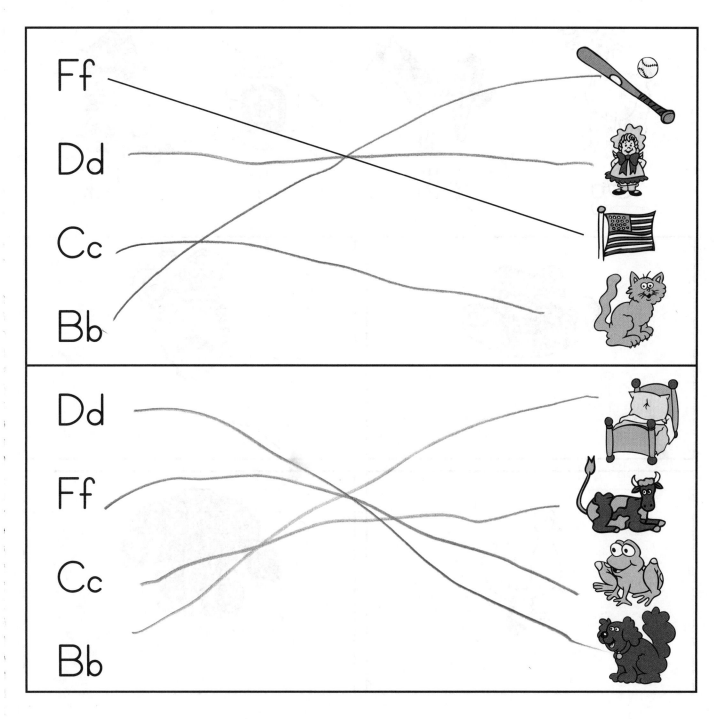

Grade 1 - Comprehensive Curriculum

Name: _____

Beginning Consonants: Gg, Hh, Jj, Kk

Directions: Say the name of each letter. Say the sound each letter makes. Trace the letter pair that makes the beginning sound in each picture.

Gg   Hh   Jj   Kk

Name: _____

Beginning Consonants: Gg, Hh, Jj, Kk

Directions: Say the name of each letter. Say the sound each letter makes. Draw a line from each letter pair to the picture which begins with that sound.

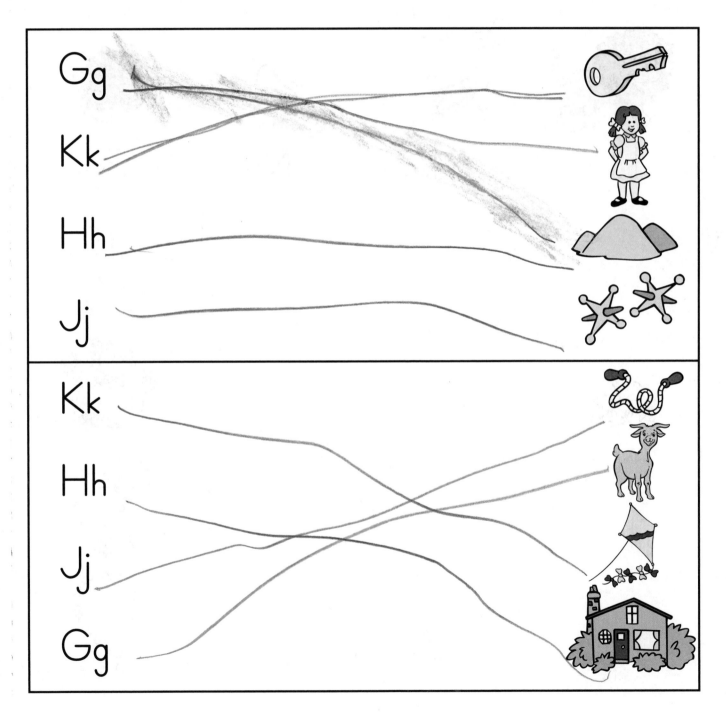

Beginning Consonants: Ll, Mm, Nn, Pp

Directions: Say the name of each letter. Say the sound each letter makes. Trace the letters. Then draw a line from each letter pair to the picture which begins with that sound.

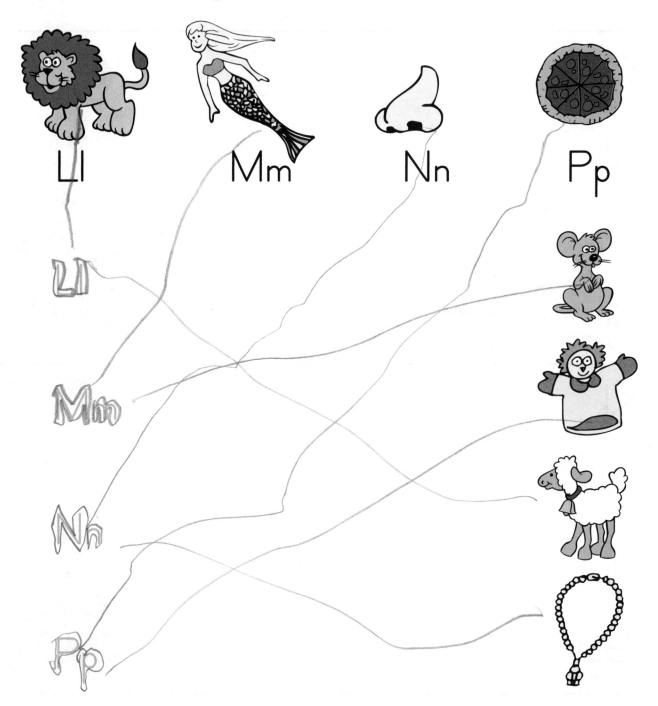

Beginning Consonants: Ll, Mm, Nn, Pp

Directions: Say the name of each letter. Say the sound each letter makes. Trace the letter pair that makes the beginning sound in each picture.

Ll   Mm   Nn   Pp

Mm Ll

Mm Pp

Ll Nn

Pp Mm

Name: _____

Beginning Consonants: Qq, Rr, Ss, Tt

Directions: Say the name of each letter. Say the sound each letter makes. Trace the letter pair in the boxes. Then color the picture which begins with that sound.

Qq   Rr   Ss   Tt

Name: _____

Beginning Consonants: Qq, Rr, Ss, Tt

Directions: Say the name of each letter. Say the sound each letter makes. Draw a line from each letter pair to the picture which begins with that sound.

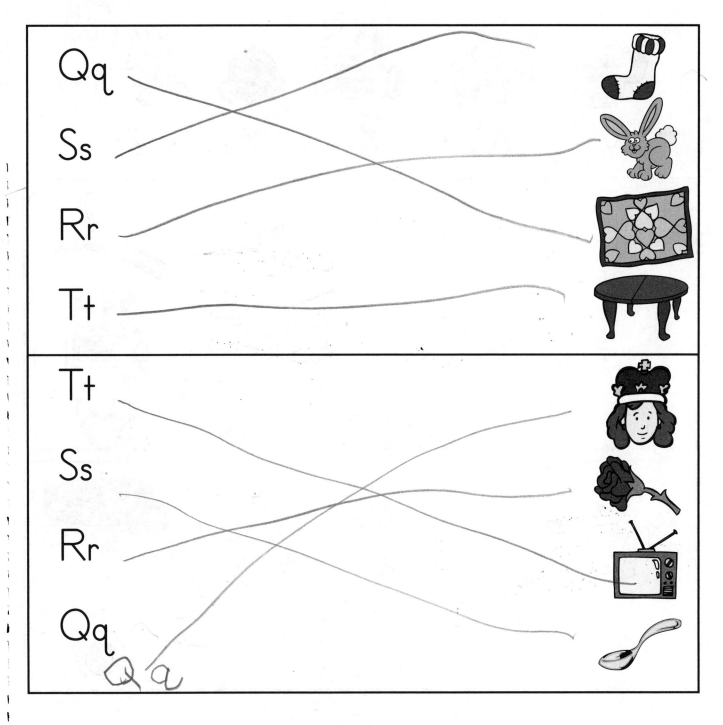

Grade 1 - Comprehensive Curriculum

Name: _____

Beginning Consonants: Vv, Ww, Xx, Yy, Zz

Directions: Say the name of each letter. Say the sound each letter makes. Trace the letters. Then draw a line from each letter pair to the picture which begins with that sound.

Vv   Ww   Xx   Yy   Zz

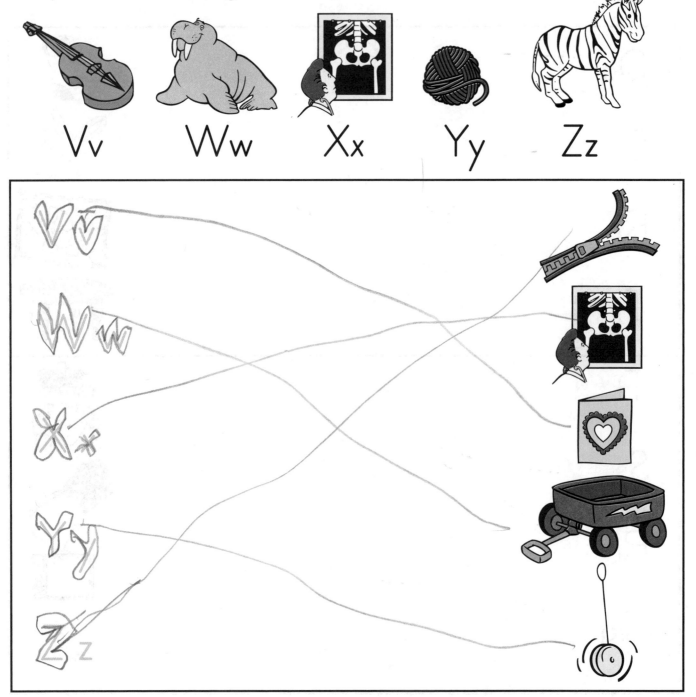

Name: _____

Beginning Consonants: Vv, Ww, Xx, Yy, Zz

Directions: Say the name of each letter. Say the sound each letter makes. Then draw a line from each letter pair to the picture which begins with that sound.

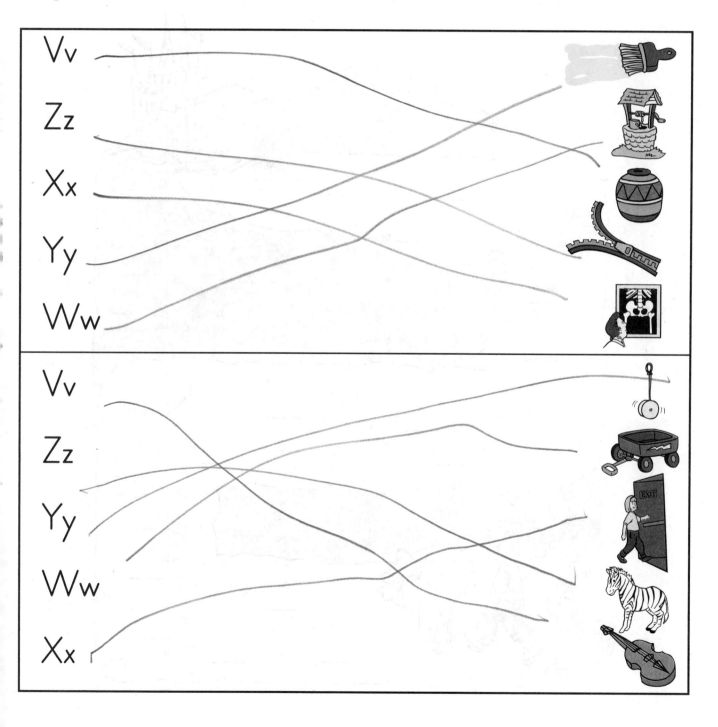

Name: _____

Review

Directions: Help Meg, Kent and their dog, Sam, get to the magic castle. Trace each capital consonant letter and write the lower-case consonant next to it. Say the sound each consonant makes.

Review

Directions: Write the letter that makes the beginning sound for each picture.

C ar

Z ipper

K ite

L etter

B oat

R ose

S un

H ouse

T urtle

G lasses

J ar

D og

Ending Consonants: b, d, f

Ending consonants are the sounds that come at the end of words.

Directions: Say the name of each picture. Then write the letter which makes the **ending** sound for each picture.

Name: _____

Ending Consonants: g, m, n

Directions: Say the name of each picture. Draw a line from each letter to the pictures which end with that sound.

g   m   n

g

m

n

Grade 1 - Comprehensive Curriculum

Name: _____

Ending Consonants: k, l, p

Directions: Trace the letters in each row. Say the name of each picture. Then color the pictures in each row which end with that sound.

Name: _____

Ending Consonants: r, s, t, x

Directions: Say the name of each picture. Then circle the ending sound for each picture.

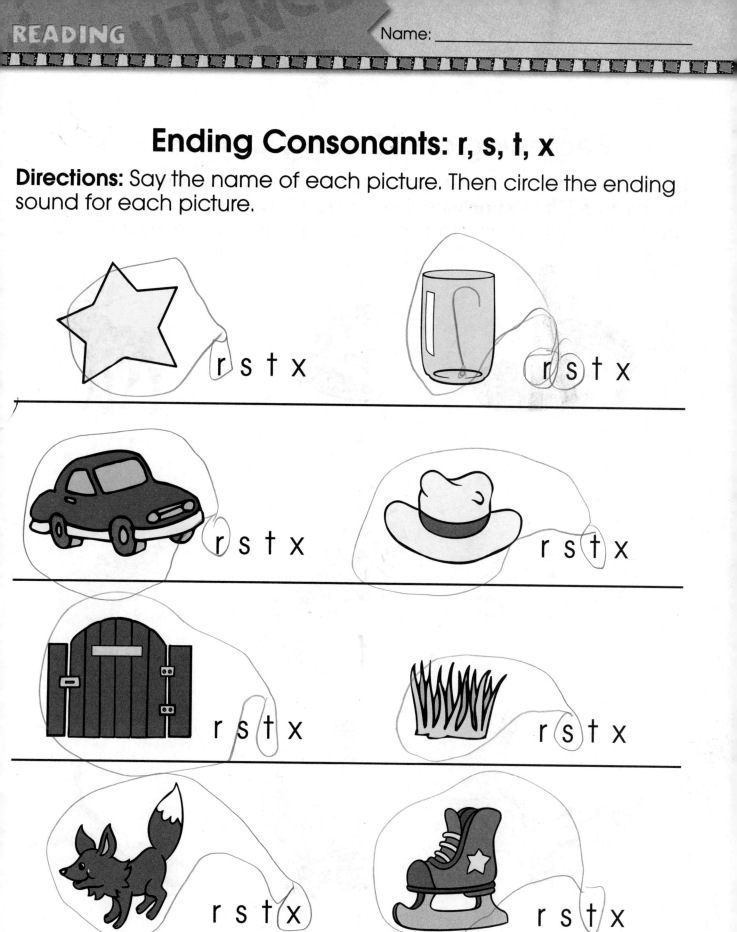

r s t x

r s t x

r s t x

r s t x

r s t x

r s t x

r s t x

r s t x

Grade 1 - Comprehensive Curriculum

Name: _____

Beginning and Ending Consonants

Directions: Say the name of each picture. Draw a **blue** circle around the picture if it **begins** with the sound of the letter below it. Draw a **green** triangle around the picture if it **ends** with the sound of the letter below it.

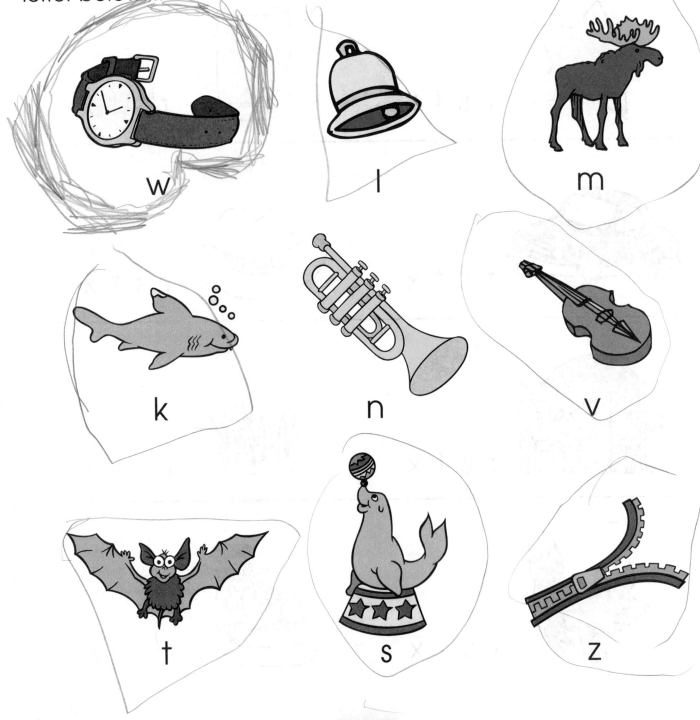

w

l

m

k

n

v

t

s

z

Beginning and Ending Consonants

Directions: Say the name of each picture. Draw a triangle around the letter that makes the **beginning** sound. Draw a square around the letter that makes the **ending** sound. Color the pictures.

o   r   t

f   d   w

v   t   b

x   c   r

t   g   d

d   a   k

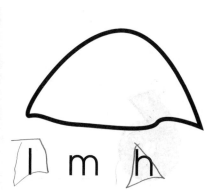

l   m   h

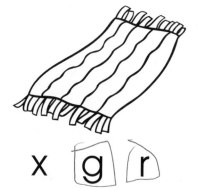

x   g   r

p   t   v

Grade 1 - Comprehensive Curriculum

Name: _____

Beginning and Ending Consonants

Directions: Say the name of each picture. Write the beginning and ending sounds for each picture.

Name: _____

Short Vowels

Vowels are the letters **a, e, i, o** and **u**. Short **a** is the sound you hear in **ant**. Short **e** is the sound you hear in **elephant**. Short **i** is the sound you hear in **igloo**. Short **o** is the sound you hear in **octopus**. Short **u** is the sound you hear in **umbrella**.

Directions: Say the short vowel sound at the beginning of each row. Say the name of each picture. Then color the pictures which have the same short vowel sounds as that letter.

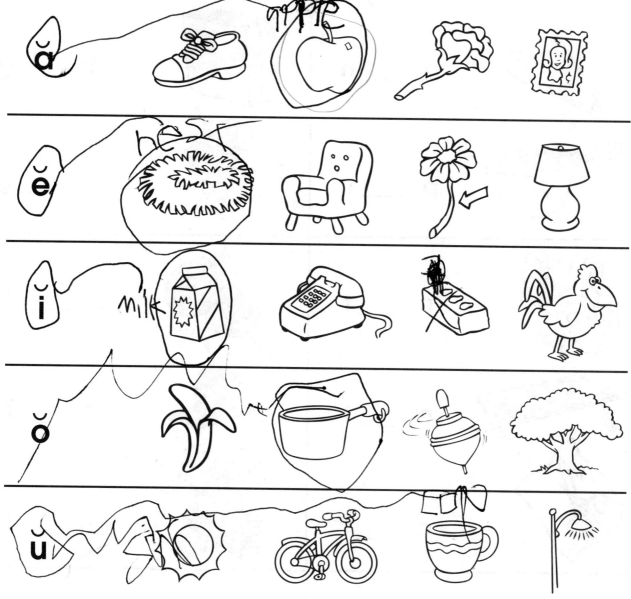

Grade 1 - Comprehensive Curriculum

Name: _____

Short Vowel Sounds

Directions: In each box are three pictures. The words that name the pictures have missing letters. Write **a, e, i, o** or **u** to finish the words.

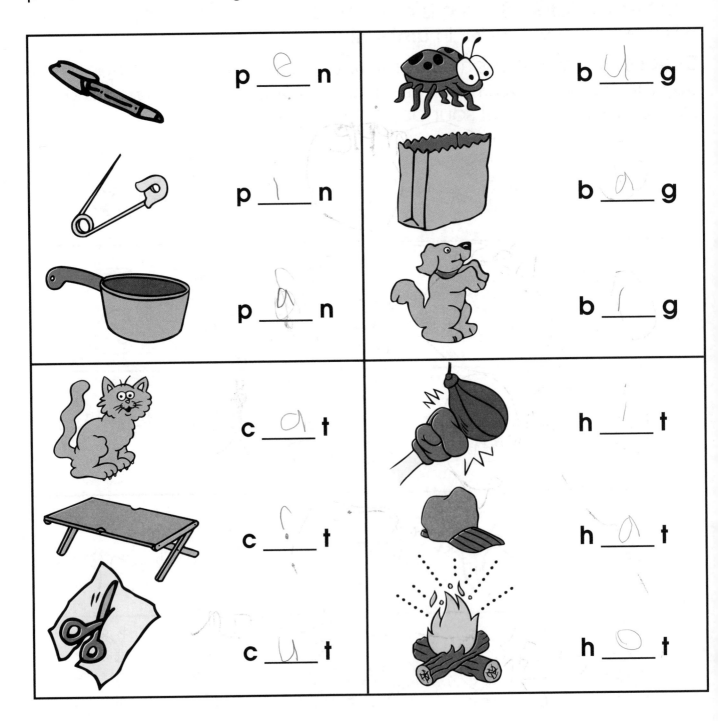

p _e_ n

p _i_ n

p _a_ n

b _u_ g

b _a_ g

b _i_ g

c _a_ t

c _i_ t

c _u_ t

h _i_ t

h _a_ t

h _o_ t

Name: _____

Long Vowels

Vowels are the letters **a, e, i, o** and **u**. Long vowel sounds say their own names. Long **a** is the sound you hear in **hay**. Long **e** is the sound you hear in **me**. Long **i** is the sound you hear in **pie**. Long **o** is the sound you hear in **no**. Long **u** is the sound you hear in **cute**.

Directions: Say the long vowel sound at the beginning of each row. Say the name of each picture. Color the pictures in each row that have the same long vowel sound as that letter.

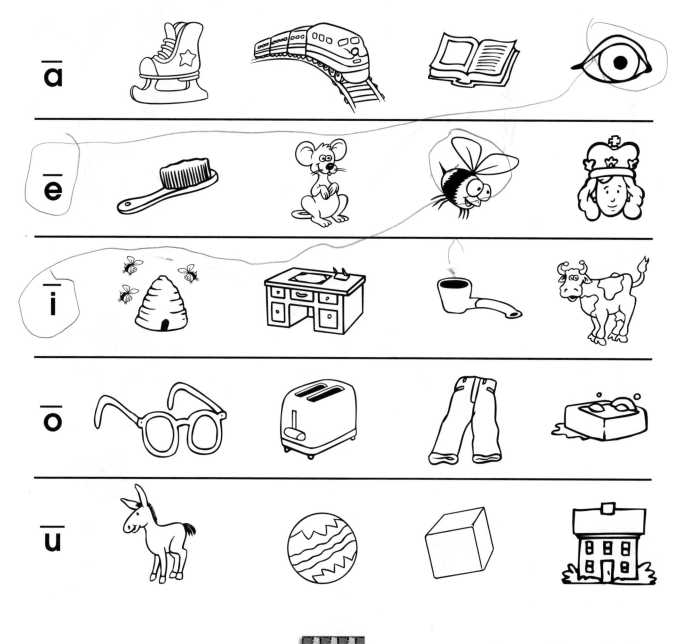

Grade 1 - Comprehensive Curriculum

Long Vowel Sounds

Directions: Write **a, e, i, o** or **u** in each blank to finish the word. Draw a line from the word to the picture.

c a ke

r o se

k i te

f ee t

m a le

Name: _____

Words With a

Directions: Each train has a group of pictures. Write the word that names the pictures. Read your rhyming words.

These trains use the short **a** sound like in the word cat:

These trains use the long **a** sound like in the word lake:

Short and Long Aa

Directions: Say the name of each picture. If it has the short **a** sound, color it **red**. If it has the long **a** sound, color it **yellow**.

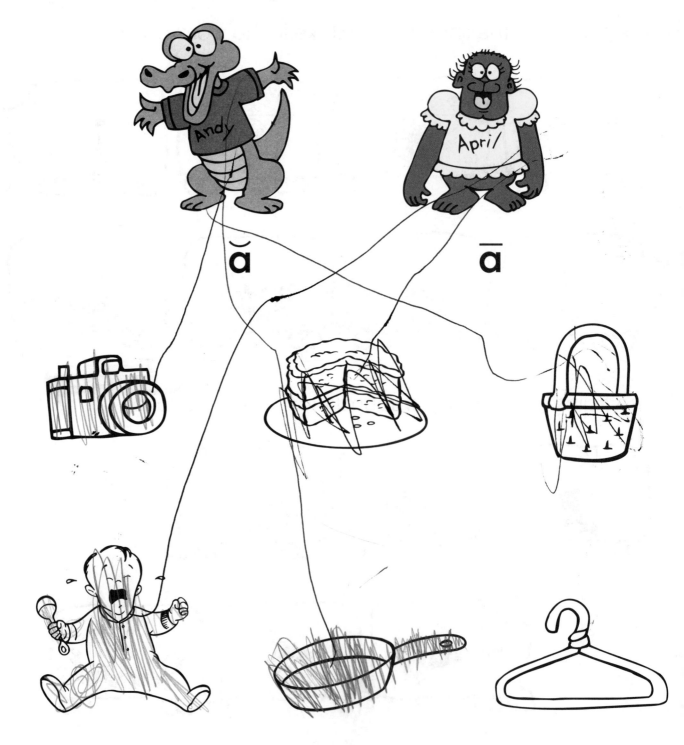

Name: _____

Words With e

Directions: Short **e** sounds like the **e** in hen. Long **e** sounds like the **e** in bee. Look at the pictures. If the word has a short **e** sound, draw a line to the **hen** with your **red** crayon. If the word has a long **e** sound, draw a line to the **bee** with your **green** crayon.

hen   bee

Name: _____

Short and Long Ee

Directions: Say the name of each picture. Circle the pictures which have the short **e** sound. Draw a triangle around the pictures which have the long **e** sound.

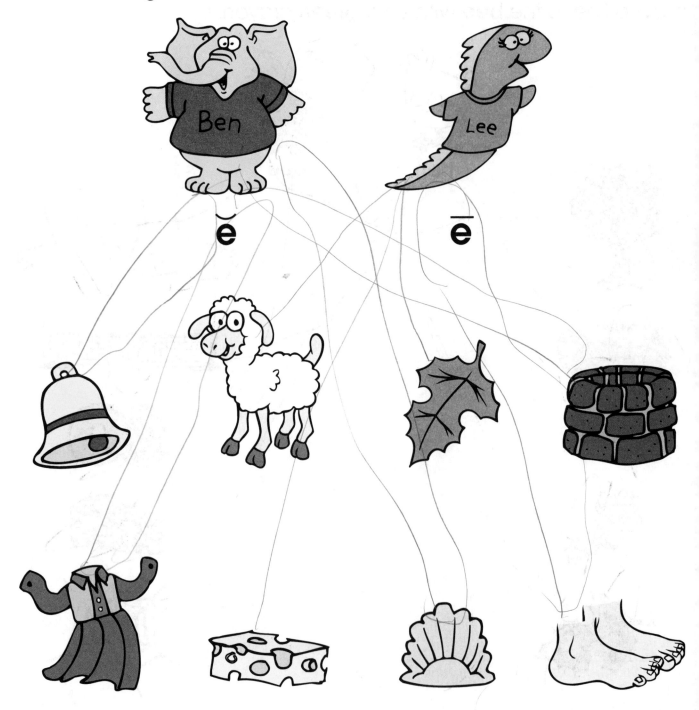

Words With i

Directions: Short **i** sounds like the **i** in pig. Long **i** sounds like the **i** in kite. Draw a circle around the words with the short **i** sound. Draw an **X** on the words with the long **i** sound.

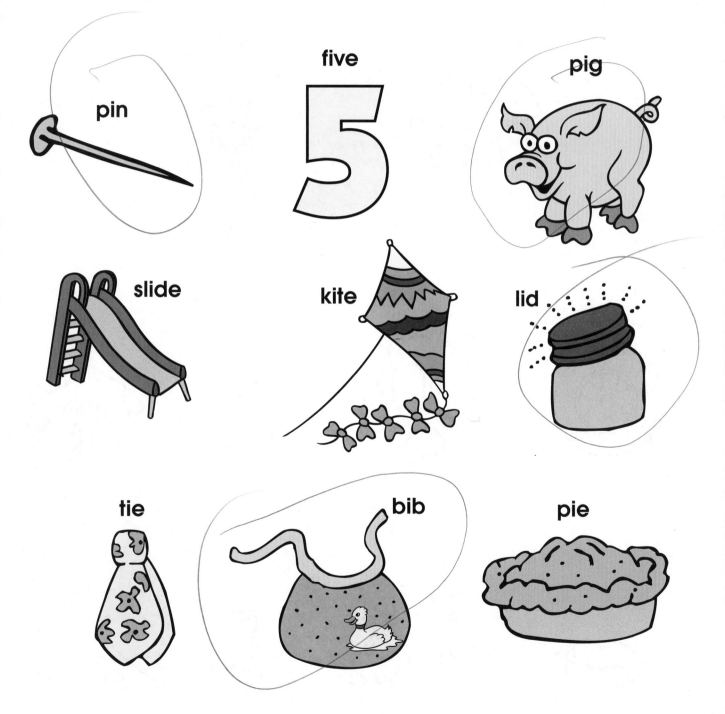

pin

five

pig

slide

kite

lid

tie

bib

pie

Name: _____

Short and Long Ii

Directions: Say the name of each picture. If it has the short **i** sound, color it **yellow**. If it has the long **i** sound, color it **red**.

ĭ

ī

Name: _____

Words With o

Directions: The short **o** sounds like the **o** in dog. Long **o** sounds like the **o** in rope. Draw a line from the picture to the word that names it. Draw a circle around the word if it has a short **o** sound.

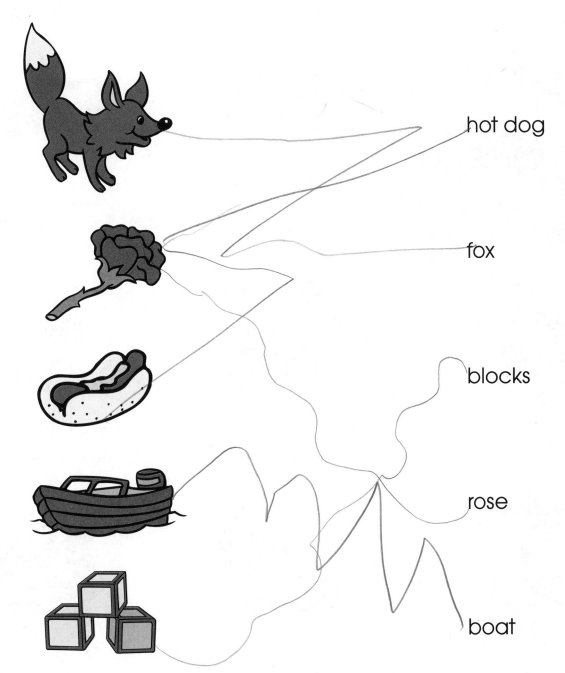

hot dog

fox

blocks

rose

boat

Grade 1 - Comprehensive Curriculum

Name: _____

Short and Long Oo

Directions: Say the name of each picture. If the picture has the long **o** sound, write a **green L** on the blank. If the picture has the short **o** sound, write a **red S** on the blank.

Name: _____

Words With u

Directions: The short **u** sounds like the **u** in bug. The long **u** sounds like the **u** in blue. Draw a circle around the words with short **u**. Draw an **X** on the words with long **u**.

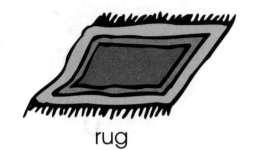

rug

cup

music

tub

suit

glue

bug

puppy

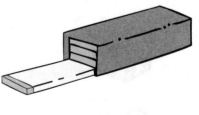

gum

Short and Long Uu

Directions: Say the name of each picture. If it has the long **u** sound, write a **u** in the **unicorn** column. If it has the short **u** sound, write a **u** in the **umbrella** column.

ū

ŭ

Name: _____

Super Silent E

When you add an **e** to the end of some words, the vowel changes from a short vowel sound to a long vowel sound. The **e** is silent.

Example: rip + **e** = ripe.

Directions: Say the word under the first picture in each pair. Then add an **e** to the word under the next picture. Say the new word.

pet   _____

tub   _____

man   _____

kit   _____

pin   _____

cap   _____

Name: _____

Short and Long Vowels

Directions: Say the name of each picture. Write the vowel on each line that completes the word. Color the short vowel pictures. Circle the long vowel pictures.

a e i o u

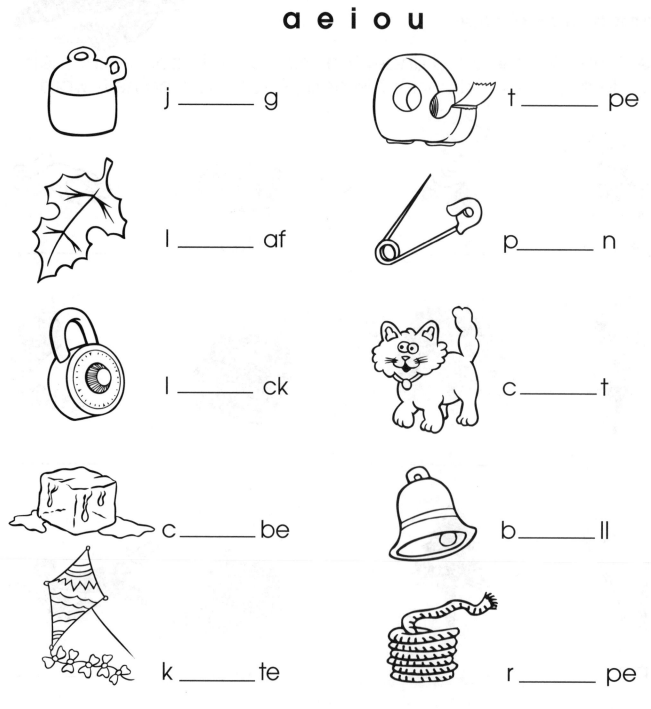

j _____ g

t _____ pe

l _____ af

p _____ n

l _____ ck

c _____ t

c _____ be

b _____ ll

k _____ te

r _____ pe

Name: _____

Short and Long Vowel Sounds

Directions: Cut out the pictures below. If the vowel has a **long** sound glue it on the **long** vowel side. If the vowel has a **short** sound, glue it on the **short** vowel side.

Short | Long

cut ✂ -

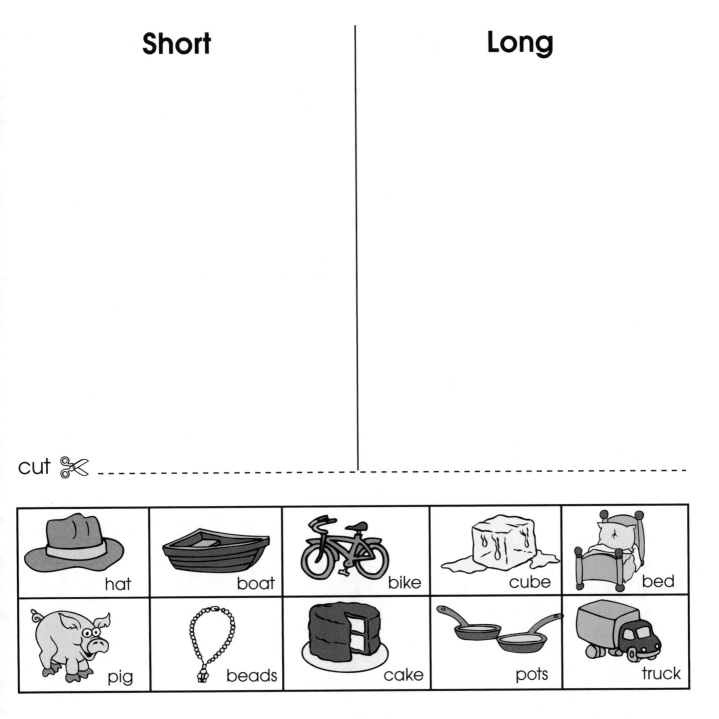

hat	boat	bike	cube	bed
pig	beads	cake	pots	truck

Page is blank for cutting exercise on previous page.

Name: _____

Review

Directions: Color all of the vowels black to discover something hidden in the puzzle.

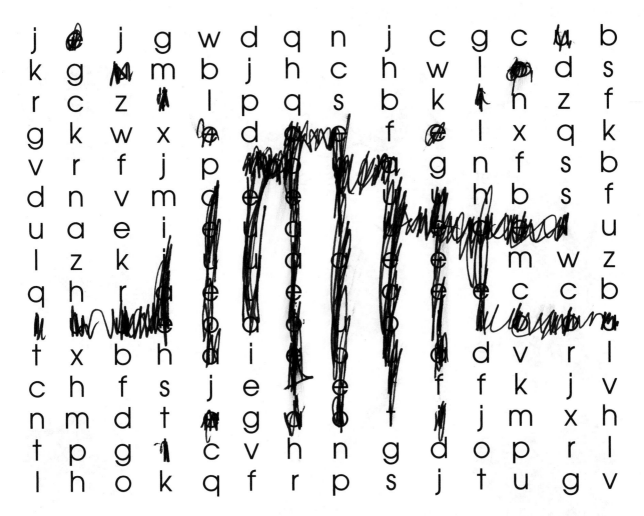

What was hidden?

_____

Review

Directions: Circle the word if it has a long vowel sound.

Remember: A long vowel says its name.

feet

snake

cup

hose

tie

hat

dog

rake

bug

bone

bib

net

Name: _____

Review

Directions: Write the vowel on each line that completes the word.

a   e   i   o   u

c___t

b___k___

sm___k___

tr_____

c___b

p___n

m___m

b___b

d___d

d___ck

Grade 1 - Comprehensive Curriculum

Review

Directions: Circle the **long vowel** words with a **red** crayon.
Underline the **short vowel** words with a **blue** crayon.

Remember: The vowel is long if:
- There are two vowels in the word. The first vowel is the sound you hear.
- There is a "super silent e" at the end.

cub	red	coat
bite	cube	cage
cat	mean	rake
bit	cot	hen
leaf	feet	key
pen	web	bee
nest	boat	fox
rose	dog	pig

Name: _____

My Vowel List

Keep this list handy and add more words to it.

short a
(ă as in cat)

_____   _____

- - - - - - - -   - - - - - - - -

_____   _____

long a
(ā as in train)

_____   _____

- - - - - - - -   - - - - - - - -

_____   _____

short e
(ĕ as in get)

_____   _____

- - - - - - - -   - - - - - - - -

_____   _____

long e
(ē as in tree)

_____   _____

- - - - - - - -   - - - - - - - -

_____   _____

short i
(ĭ as in pin)

_____   _____

- - - - - - - -   - - - - - - - -

_____   _____

long i
(ī as in ice)

_____   _____

- - - - - - - -   - - - - - - - -

_____   _____

short o
(ŏ as in cot)

_____   _____

- - - - - - - -   - - - - - - - -

_____   _____

long o
(ō as in boat)

_____   _____

- - - - - - - -   - - - - - - - -

_____   _____

short u
(ŭ as in cut)

_____   _____

- - - - - - - -   - - - - - - - -

_____   _____

long u
(ū as in cube)

_____   _____

- - - - - - - -   - - - - - - - -

_____   _____

Grade 1 - Comprehensive Curriculum

This page intentionally left blank.

Consonant Blends

Consonant blends are two or more consonant sounds together in a word. The blend is made by combining the consonant sounds.

Example: floor

Directions: The name of each picture begins with a **blend**. Circle the beginning blend for each picture.

bl fl cl

gloves

cl fl gl

fl bl pl

fl cl gl

pl gl cl

gl fl sl

gl fl cl

sl fl cl

cl gl sl

Consonant Blends

Directions: The beginning blend for each word is missing. Fill in the correct blend to finish the word. Draw a line from the word to the picture.

- -

ain

- - - - - - - - - - - - - - - - - - - -

og

- - - - - - - - - - - - - - - - - - - -

ab

- - - - - - - - - - - - - - - - - - - -

um

- - - - - - - - - - - - - - - - - - - -

ush

- - - - - - - - - - - - - - - - - - - -

esent

Name: _____

Consonant Blends

Directions: Draw a line from the picture to the blend that begins its word.

sk

sl

sm

sn

sp

st

sw

Grade 1 - Comprehensive Curriculum

Consonant Blends

Directions: Look at the first picture in each row. Circle the pictures in the row that begin with the same sound.

Name: _____

Beginning Blends

Directions: Say the blend for each word as you search for it.

```
b  l  o  s  l  e  d  a  b  f  t  k  a  i  n
l  b  r  e  a  d  x  s  t  o  p  i  x  a  p
o  l  g  u  f  e  n  p  s  p  i  d  e  r  i
c  l  o  w  n  a  w  l  p  z  j  c  r  a  b
k  t  c  e  n  t  h  s  t  e  g  l  q  c  r
d  h  b  r  e  a  e  j  w  k  x  o  w  h  y
h  u  s  n  a  k  e  m  d  j  l  c  m  a  j
v  m  i  u  k  l  l  s  k  u  n  k  c  i  f
i  b  g  l  o  b  e  m  h  n  o  q  t  r  r
b  f  l  j  x  s  y  a  z  s  l  e  d  o  o
s  h  e  l  l  w  k  l  f  s  s  v  u  p  g
h  a  r  l  c  a  d  l  l  v  w  k  z  s  n
o  z  y  q  s  n  l  t  a  h  n  r  u  m  q
e  f  l  o  w  e  r  a  g  l  o  v  e  e  r
w  g  m  b  c  e  n  m  o  p  d  o  f  l  g
p  r  e  s  e  n  t  r  a  i  n  b  p  l  i
```

Words to find:

block	sled	globe	crab
clock	frog	present	flower
train	glove	skunk	snake
swan	flag	smell	spider
bread	small	chair	shell
stop	sled	shoe	
thumb	wheel	clown	

Grade 1 - Comprehensive Curriculum

Ending Consonant Blends

Directions: Write **lt** or **ft** to complete the words.

be ----------------------------

ra ----------------------------

sa ----------------------------

qui ----------------------------

le ----------------------------

Name: _____

Ending Consonant Blends

Directions: Draw a line from the picture to the blend that ends the word.

lf

lk

sk

st

Grade 1 - Comprehensive Curriculum

Ending Consonant Blends

Directions: Every juke box has a word ending and a list of letters. Add each of the letters to the word ending to make rhyming words.

___and

b _____
h _____
l _____
s _____

___ent

b _____
d _____
t _____
w _____

___ump

b _____
d _____
j _____
p _____

___ink

p _____
s _____
l _____
th _____

___ing

r _____
s _____
st _____
k _____

___ank

b _____
r _____
s _____
t _____

Name: _____

Ending Consonant Blends

Directions: Say the blend for each word as you search for it.

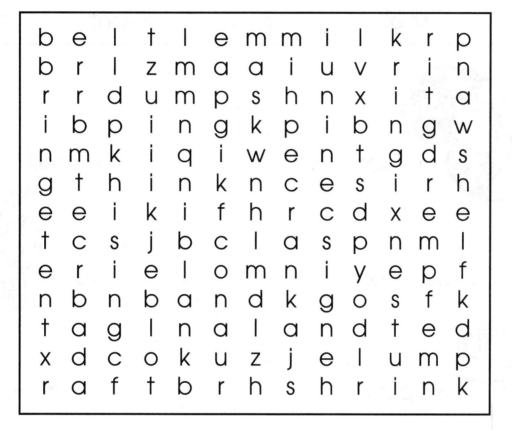

```
b  e  l  t  l  e  m  m  i  l  k  r  p
b  r  l  z  m  a  a  i  u  v  r  i  n
r  r  d  u  m  p  s  h  n  x  i  t  a
i  b  p  i  n  g  k  p  i  b  n  g  w
n  m  k  i  q  i  w  e  n  t  g  d  s
g  t  h  i  n  k  n  c  e  s  i  r  h
e  e  i  k  i  f  h  r  c  d  x  e  e
t  c  s  j  b  c  l  a  s  p  n  m  l
e  r  i  e  l  o  m  n  i  y  e  p  f
n  b  n  b  a  n  d  k  g  o  s  f  k
t  a  g  l  n  a  l  a  n  d  t  e  d
x  d  c  o  k  u  z  j  e  l  u  m  p
r  a  f  t  b  r  h  s  h  r  i  n  k
```

Words to find:

belt	raft	milk	shelf
mask	clasp	nest	band
think	went	lump	crank
ring	blank	shrink	land
bring	tent	dump	sing

Review

Directions: Finish each sentence with a word from the word box.

| sting | shelf | drank | plant | stamp |

1. Tom _____ his milk.

2. A bee can _____ you.

3. I put a _____ on my letter.

4. The _____ is green.

5. The book is on the _____ .

Name _____

Rhyming Words

Rhyming words are words that sound alike at the end of the word. **Cat** and **hat** rhyme.

Directions: Draw a circle around each word pair that rhymes. Draw an **X** on each pair that does not rhyme.

Example:

(soap
rope)

red
dog

book
hook

cold
rock

cat
hat

yellow
black

one
two

rock
sock

rat
flat

good
nice

you
to

meet
toy

old
sold

sale
whale

word
letter

Grade 1 - Comprehensive Curriculum

Rhyming Words

Rhyming words are words that sound alike at the end of the word.

Directions: Draw a line to match the pictures that rhyme. Write two of your rhyming word pairs below.

- -

- -

Name: _____

ABC Order

Directions: Abc order is the order in which letters come in the alphabet. Draw a line to connect the dots. Follow the letters in **abc** order. Then color the picture.

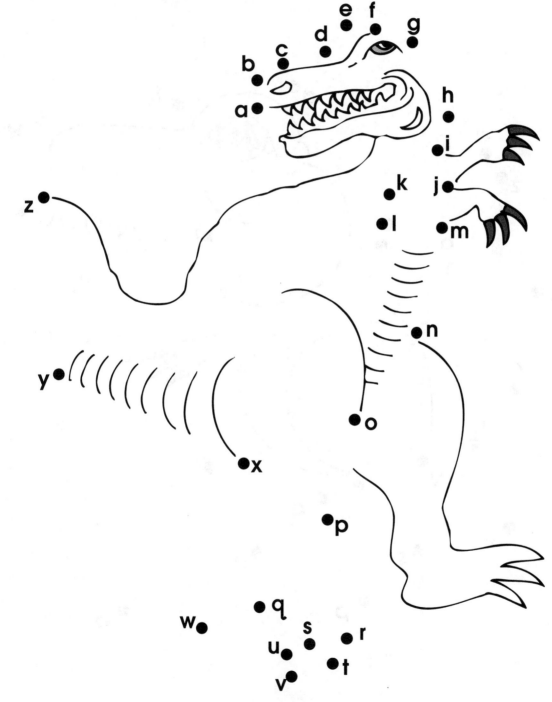

ABC Order

Directions: Draw a line to connect the dots. Follow the letters in abc order. Then color the picture.

Name: _____

ABC Order

Directions: Circle the first letter of each word. Then put each pair of the words in abc order.

ⓒar   ⓑird   moon   two   nest   fan

bird

car

card   dog   pig   bike   sun   pie

Grade 1 - Comprehensive Curriculum

ABC Order

Directions: Look at the words in each box. Circle the word that comes first in abc order.

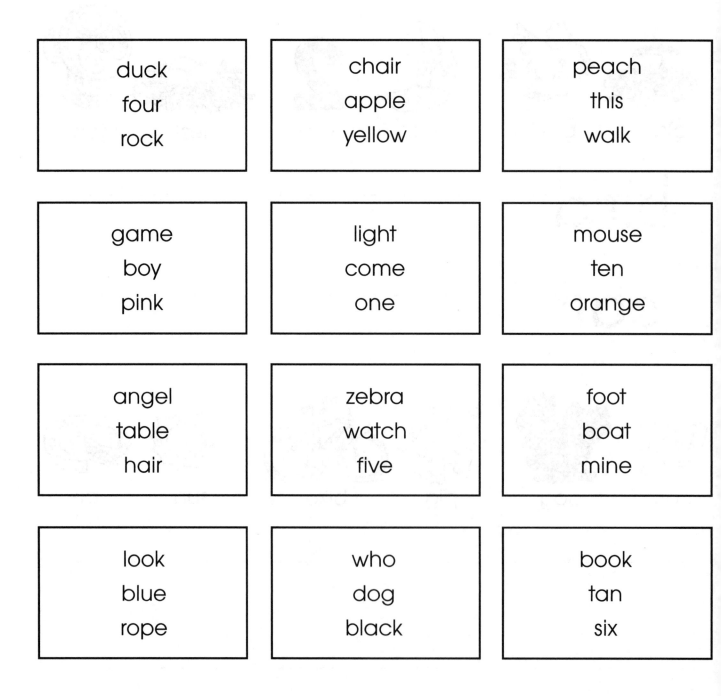

duck four rock	chair apple yellow	peach this walk
game boy pink	light come one	mouse ten orange
angel table hair	zebra watch five	foot boat mine
look blue rope	who dog black	book tan six

Name: _____

ABC Order

Directions: Cut out the foods Mom wants to buy when she goes shopping. Glue the words in abc order on the shopping list.

Shopping List

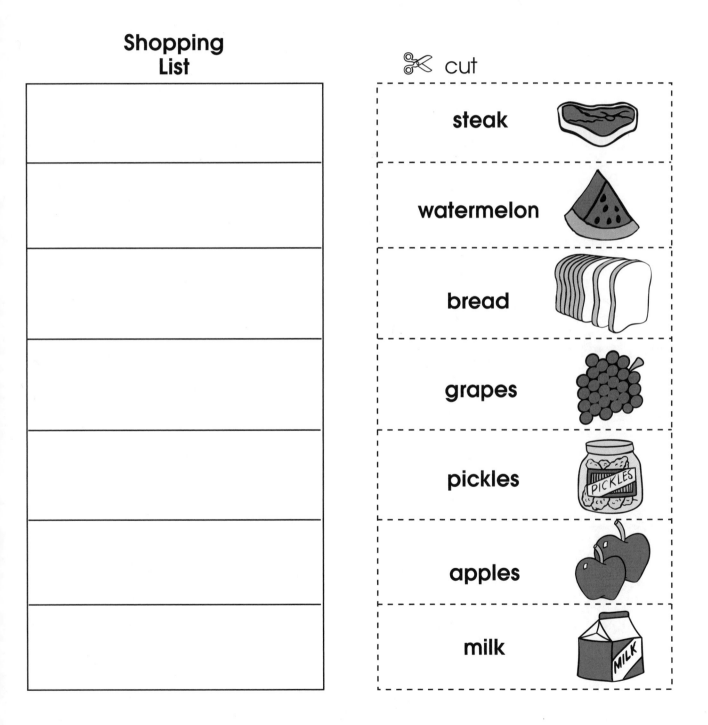

✂ cut

steak

watermelon

bread

grapes

pickles

apples

milk

Grade 1 - Comprehensive Curriculum

Page is blank for cutting exercise on previous page.

Name: _____

Sequencing: ABC Order

Directions: Put each group of words in ABC order by numbering them 1, 2, 3.

Example:

cold   **w**arm   **h**ot

___1___   ___3___   ___2___

small   **b**ig   **c**ute

_____   _____   _____

doll

_____

truck   **b**all

_____

baby

_____

sister   **f**amily

_____

man

_____

boy   **g**randma

_____

Name: _____

ABC Order

Directions: Put the words in abc order. Circle the first letter of each word. Then write 1, 2, 3, 4, 5 or 6 on the line next to each animal's name.

skunk _____

dog _____

butterfly _____

zebra _____

tiger _____

fish _____

Name: _____

Compound Words

Compound words are two words that are put together to make one new word.

Directions: Look at the pictures and the two words that are next to each other. Put the words together to make a new word. Write the new word.

Example:

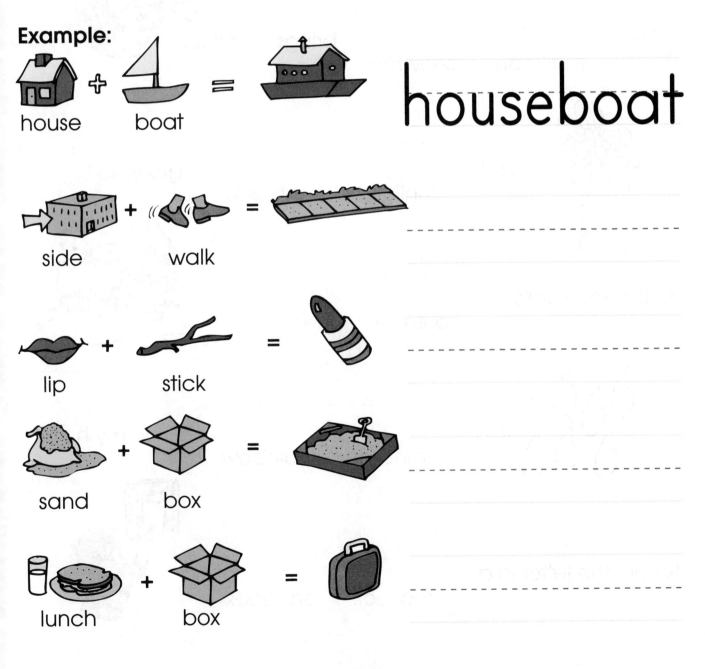

house + boat = houseboat

side + walk = _____

lip + stick = _____

sand + box = _____

lunch + box = _____

Name: _____

Compound Words

Directions: Circle the compound word which completes each sentence. Write each word on the lines.

1. The _____ brings us letters.

    mailman   snowman

2. A _____ grows tall.

    sunlight   sunflower

3. The snow falls _____ .

    outside   inside

4. A _____ fell on my head.

    raindrop   rainbow

5. I put the letter in a _____ .

    mailbox   shoebox

Name: _____

Compound Words

Directions: Cut out the pictures and words at the bottom of the page. Put two words together to make a compound word. Write the new word.

☐ + ☐ = _

☐ + ☐ = _

☐ + ☐ = _

☐ + ☐ = _

cut ✂ -

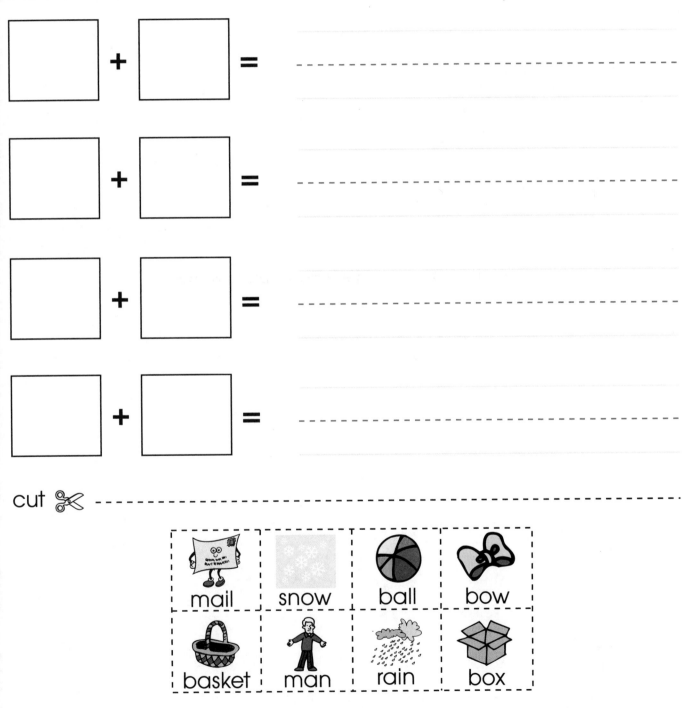

| mail | snow | ball | bow |
| basket | man | rain | box |

Page is blank for cutting exercise on previous page.

Compound Words

Directions: Cut out the cards below. Turn them over. Take turns trying to make compound words. When a compound word is made, the player gets to keep the word.

Cut ✂ -

flash	snow	ball	sun
mail	house	plant	room
light	bow	light	card
base	shine	dog	box
rain	flake	thing	post
family	house	in	house
any	side	day	birth

Grade 1 - Comprehensive Curriculum

Page is blank for cutting exercise on previous page.

Names

You are a special person. Your name begins with a capital letter. We put a capital letter at the beginning of people's names because they are special.

Directions: Write your name. Did you remember to use a capital letter?

_____

- -

Directions: Write each person's name. Use a capital letter at the beginning.

Ted

- -

Katie

- -

Mike

- -

Tim

- -

Write a friend's name.
Use a capital letter at
the beginning.

- -

Grade 1 - Comprehensive Curriculum

Names: Days of the Week

The days of the week begin with capital letters.

Directions: Write the days of the week in the spaces below. Put them in order. Be sure to start with capital letters.

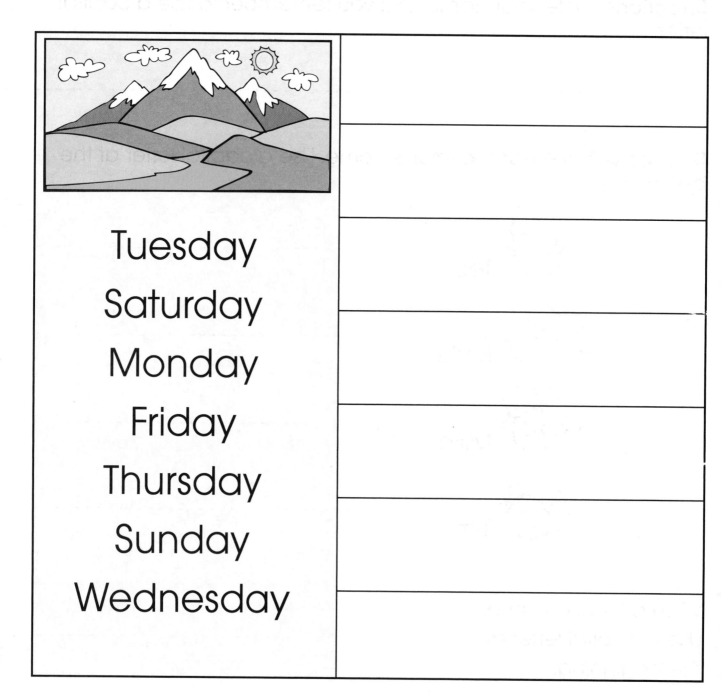

Tuesday

Saturday

Monday

Friday

Thursday

Sunday

Wednesday

Names: Months of the Year

The months of the year begin with capital letters.

Directions: Write the months of the year in order on the calendar below. Be sure to use capital letters.

January September	December February	April July	May March	October November	June August

_____

_____

_____

_____

_____

_____

_____

_____

_____

_____

_____

_____

Name: _____

More Than One

Directions: An **s** at the end of a word often means there is more than one. Look at each picture. Circle the correct word. Write the word on the line.

two

dog   dogs

- - - - - - - - - - - - - - - - -

four

flower   flowers

- - - - - - - - - - - - - - - - -

one

bikes   bike

- - - - - - - - - - - - - - - - -

three

toys   toy

- - - - - - - - - - - - - - - - -

a

lamb   lambs

- - - - - - - - - - - - - - - - -

two

cat   cats

- - - - - - - - - - - - - - - - -

Name: _____

More Than One

Directions: Read the nouns under the pictures. Then write each noun under **One** or **More Than One**.

One

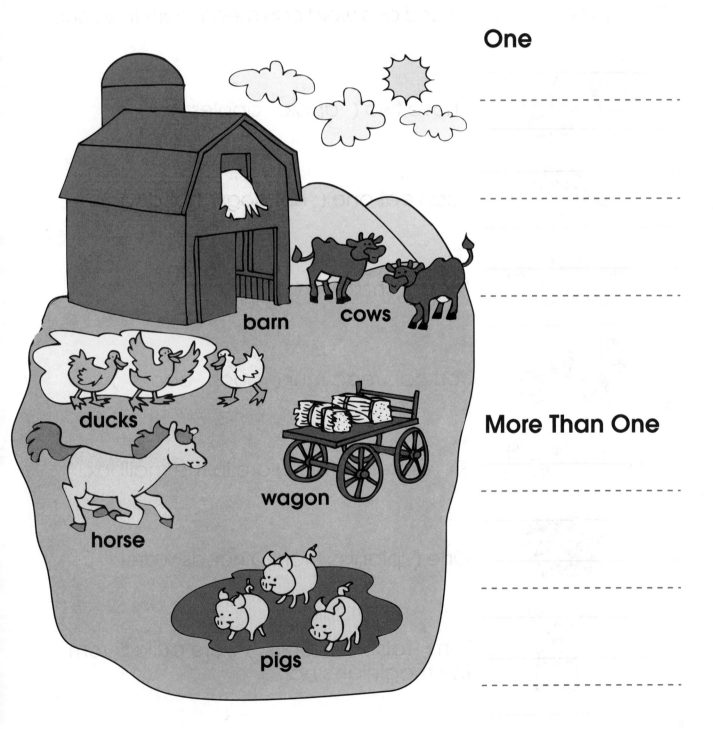

barn

cows

ducks

wagon

horse

pigs

More Than One

Grade 1 - Comprehensive Curriculum

Name: _____

More Than One

Directions: Circle the correct word to complete each sentence.

Remember: An **s** at the end of a word can mean more than one.

I have two (apple, apples) .

I can eat one (hot dogs, hot dog) .

My dad has five (hats, hat) .

You can read four (book, books) .

Six (letter, letters) are in the mailbox.

One (plants, plant) needs water.

Ten (rabbit, rabbits) were pulled from the magician's hat.

More Than One

Directions: Choose the word which completes each sentence. Write each word on the line.

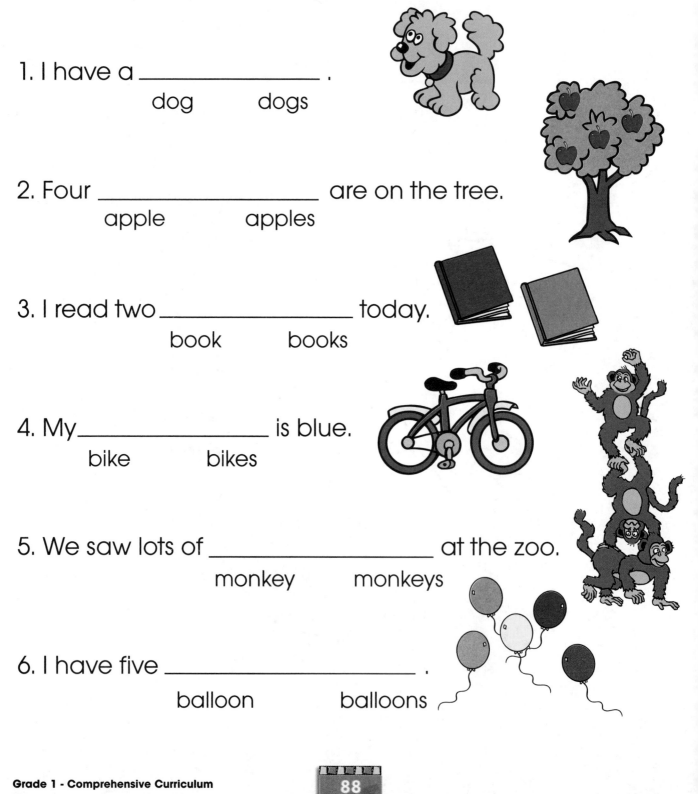

1. I have a _____ .

   dog   dogs

2. Four _____ are on the tree.

   apple   apples

3. I read two _____ today.

   book   books

4. My _____ is blue.

   bike   bikes

5. We saw lots of _____ at the zoo.

   monkey   monkeys

6. I have five _____ .

   balloon   balloons

Riddles

Directions: Read the word. Trace and write it on the line. Then draw a line from the riddle to the animal it tells about.

long long _____

I am very big.
I lived a long, long time ago.
What am I?

giraffe

My neck is very long.
I eat leaves from trees.
What am I?

rabbit

I have long ears.
I hop very fast.
What am I?

dinosaur

Riddles

Directions: Read the word and write it on the line. Then read each riddle and draw a line to the picture and word that tells about it.

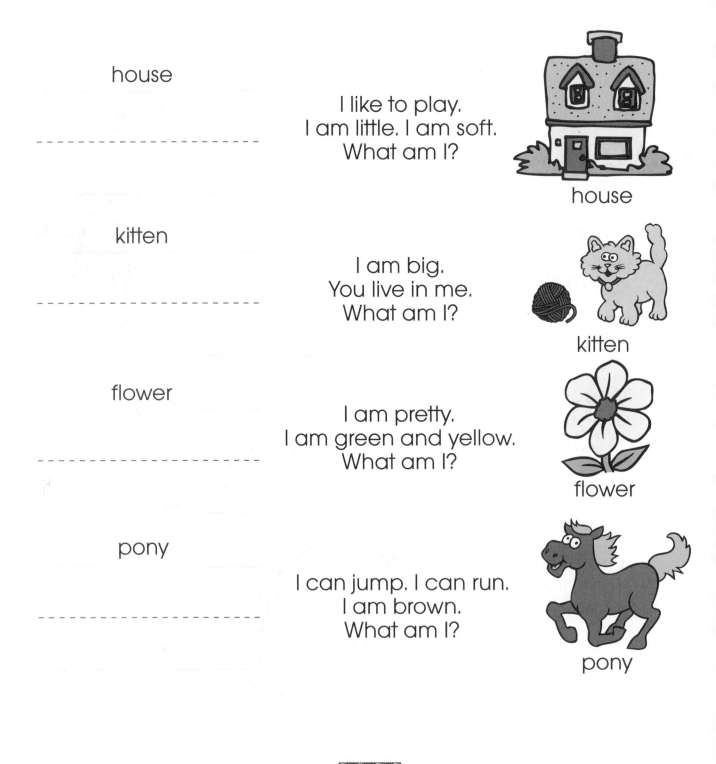

house

_____

I like to play.
I am little. I am soft.
What am I?

house

kitten

_____

I am big.
You live in me.
What am I?

kitten

flower

_____

I am pretty.
I am green and yellow.
What am I?

flower

pony

_____

I can jump. I can run.
I am brown.
What am I?

pony

Name: _____

Riddles

Directions: Write a word from the box to answer each riddle.

ice cream	book	chair	sun

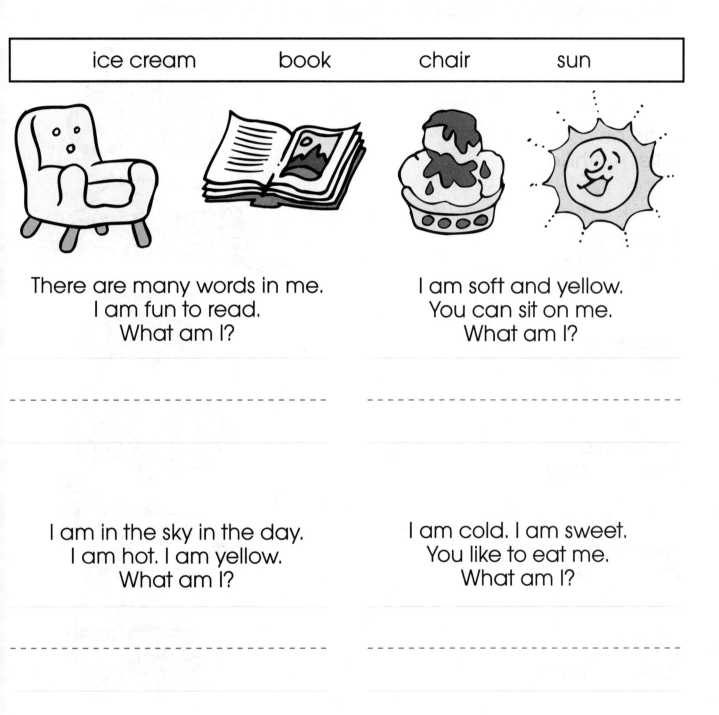

There are many words in me.
I am fun to read.
What am I?

- - - - - - - - - - - - - - -

I am soft and yellow.
You can sit on me.
What am I?

- - - - - - - - - - - - - - - - - -

I am in the sky in the day.
I am hot. I am yellow.
What am I?

- - - - - - - - - - - - - - - - -

I am cold. I am sweet.
You like to eat me.
What am I?

- - - - - - - - - - - - - - - - -

Grade 1 - Comprehensive Curriculum

Picture Clues

Directions: Read the sentence. Circle the word that makes sense. Use the picture clues to help you. Then write the word.

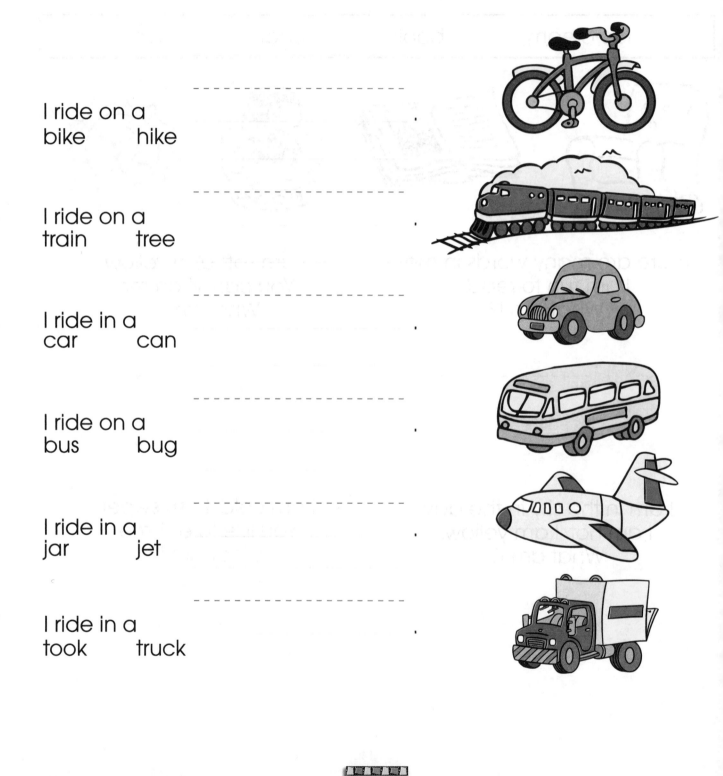

I ride on a
bike   hike

- - - - - - - - - - - - - - - - - - - .

I ride on a
train   tree

- - - - - - - - - - - - - - - - - - - .

I ride in a
car   can

- - - - - - - - - - - - - - - - - - - .

I ride on a
bus   bug

- - - - - - - - - - - - - - - - - - - .

I ride in a
jar   jet

- - - - - - - - - - - - - - - - - - - .

I ride in a
took   truck

- - - - - - - - - - - - - - - - - - - .

Name: _____

Picture Clues

Directions: Read the sentence. Circle the word that makes sense. Use the picture clues to help you. Then write the word.

I see the
bird   book
- .

I see the
fish   fork
- .

I see the
dogs   dig
- .

I see the
cats   coat
- .

I see the
snake   snow
- .

I see the
rat   rake
- .

Grade 1 - Comprehensive Curriculum

Picture Clues

Directions: Draw a line from the picture to its sentence.

The ducks like to swim.

The bear eats honey.

The cat is under the table.

The bee is on a flower.

Picture Clues

Directions: Cut out the pictures below. Glue them next to the sentences.

The sun is yellow.

It is raining.

I can grin.

The bed is broken.

My pen and paper are here.

Cut -

Page is blank for cutting exercise on previous page.

Comprehension

Directions: Look at the picture. Write the words from the box to finish the sentences.

frog	log	bird	fish	ducks

The _____ can jump.

The turtle is on a _____ .

A _____ is in the tree.

The boy wants a _____ .

I see three _____ .

Comprehension

Directions: Read the poem. Write the correct words in the blanks.

A Poem

The hat was on a mat.
A cat sat on the hat.
Now the hat is flat.

The hat was on _____ .

Who sat on the hat? _____

Now the hat is _____ .

Following Directions: Color the Path

Directions: Color the path the girl should take to go home. Use the sentences to help you.

1. Go to the school and turn left.

2. At the end of the street, turn right.

3. Walk past the park and turn right.

4. After you pass the pool, turn right.

Following Directions

Directions: Look at the pictures. Follow the directions in each box.

Draw a circle around the caterpillar.
Draw a line under the stick.

Draw an **X** on the mother bird.
Draw a triangle around the baby birds.

Draw a box around the rabbit.

Color the flowers. Count the bees.
There are _____ bees.

Classifying

Directions: Classifying is sorting things into groups. Draw a circle around the pictures that answer the question.

What Can Swim?

What Can Fly?

Name: _____

Classifying: These Keep Me Warm

Directions: Color the things that keep you warm.

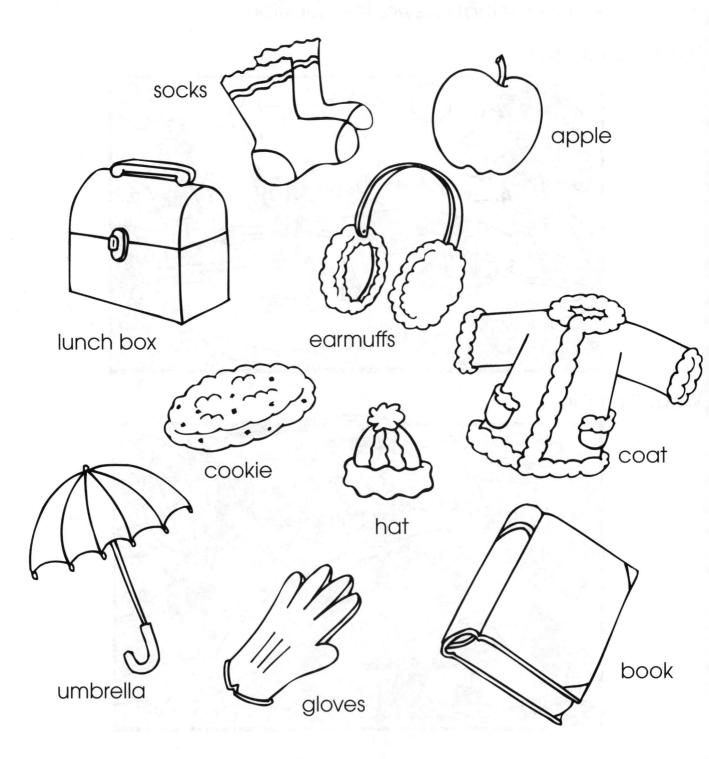

socks

apple

lunch box

earmuffs

coat

cookie

hat

book

umbrella

gloves

Name: _____

Classifying: Objects

Help Dan clean up the park.

Directions: Circle the litter. Underline the coins. Draw a box around the balls.

Classifying: Things to Drink

Directions: Circle the pictures of things you can drink. Write the names of those things in the blanks.

milk

ice

soup and crackers

juice

soda

ice-cream bar

- -

-        -

Classifying: Leaves

Directions: Cut out the leaves. Put them into two groups. Glue each group in a box on the top of the page. Write a name for each group.

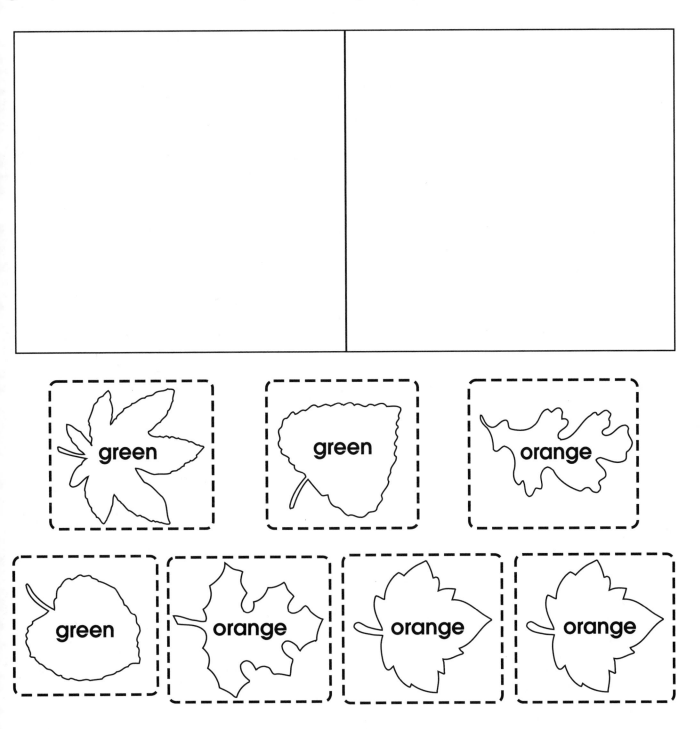

Grade 1 - Comprehensive Curriculum

Page is blank for cutting exercise on previous page.

Name: _____

Classifying: Things to Chew

Directions: Draw a line from the pictures of things you chew to the plate.

soup

ice-cream bar

pizza

carrot

GULP!

soda

macaroni

corn on the cob

milk

gum

Vocabulary

Directions: Read the words. Trace and write them on the lines. Look at each picture. Write **hot** or **cold** on the lines to show if it is hot or cold.

hot

hot ----------------------------------

cold

cold ----------------------------------

Name: _____

Vocabulary

Directions: Read the words. Trace and write them on the lines. Look at each picture and write **day** or **night** on the lines to show if they happen during the day or night.

day

day

night

night

Grade 1 - Comprehensive Curriculum

Classifying: Night and Day

Directions: Write the words from the box under the pictures they describe.

stars	sun	moon	rays	dark	light	night	day

Name: _____

Classifying: Clowns and Balloons

Some words describe clowns. Some words describe balloons.

Directions: Read the words. Write the words that match in the correct columns.

float	laughs	hat	string
air	feet	pop	nose

clown   balloons

-------------------------------   -------------------------------

-------------------------------   -------------------------------

-------------------------------   -------------------------------

-------------------------------   -------------------------------

Grade 1 - Comprehensive Curriculum

Name: _____

Similarities: Objects

Directions: Circle the picture in each row that is most like the first picture.

Example:

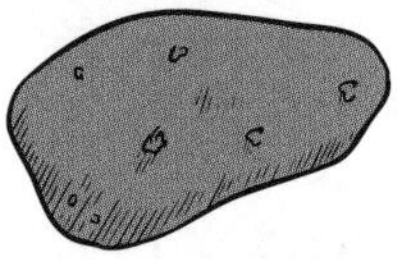

| potato |  rose |  tomato |  tree |

| shirt |  mittens |  boots | 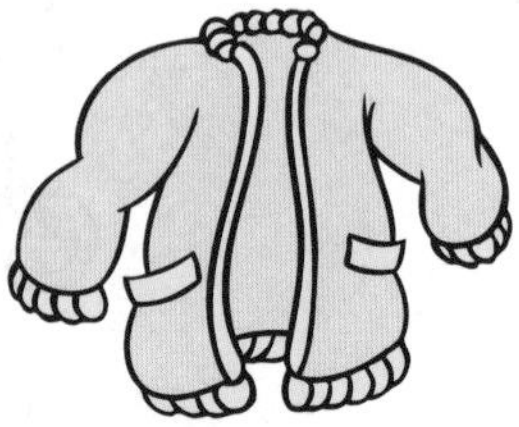 jacket |

| whale |  cat |  dolphin |  monkey |

| tiger |  giraffe |  lion |  zebra |

Similarities: Objects

Directions: Circle the picture in each row that is most like the first picture.

Example:

| carrot | jacks | bread | pea |

| baseball | sneakers | basketball | bat |

| store | school | home | bakery |

| kitten | dog | fox | cat |

Grade 1 - Comprehensive Curriculum

Name: _____

Classifying: Food Groups

Directions: Color the meats and eggs brown. Color the fruits and vegetables green. Color the breads tan. Color the dairy foods (milk and cheese) yellow.

fish   bread   apple   cheese

crackers   carrot   orange   eggs

steaks   pear   milk   yogurt

ice cream   chicken   potato   pretzel

Same and Different: These Don't Belong

Directions: Circle the pictures in each row that go together.

Row 1   cookies   cake   beans   ice cream

Row 2   apple   banana   orange   cookies

Row 3   kite   dice   checkers   chess

Directions: Write the names of the things that do not belong.

Row 1 -

Row 2 -

Row 3 -

     Grade 1 - Comprehensive Curriculum

Classifying: What Does Not Belong?

Directions: Draw an **X** on the picture that does not belong in each group.

fruit

| apple |  peach |  corn |  watermelon |

wild animals

| bear |  kitten |  gorilla |  lion |

pets

| cat |  fish |  elephant |  dog |

flowers

| grass |  rose |  daisy |  tulip |

Name: _____

Classifying: What Does Not Belong?

Directions: Draw an **X** on the word in each row that does not belong.

1. flashlight   candle   radio   fire

2. shirt   pants   coat   bat

3. cow   car   bus   train

4. beans   hot dog   ball   bread

5. gloves   hat   book   boots

6. fork   butter   cup   plate

7. book   ball   bat   milk

8. dogs   bees   flies   ants

Grade 1 - Comprehensive Curriculum

Classifying: Objects

Directions: Write each word in the correct row at the bottom of the page.

airplane   drum   radio   plate   car   pencil

spoon   crayon   chalk   fork   television   boat

Things we ride in:

_____

_____

Things we eat with:

_____

_____

Things we draw with:

_____

_____

Things we listen to:

_____

_____

Classifying: Names, Numbers, Animals, Colors

Directions: Write the words from the box next to the words they describe.

Joe	cat	blue	Tim
two	dog	red	ten
Sue	green	pig	six

Name
Words

Number
Words

Animal
Words

Color
Words

Name: _____

Classifying: Things That Belong Together

Directions: Circle the pictures in each row that belong together.

Row 1   knife   key   fork   spoon

Row 2   orange   apple   candy   banana

Row 3   beach ball   soccer ball   baseball   apple

Directions: Write the names of the pictures that do not belong.

Row 1 _____

Row 2 _____

Row 3 _____

Classifying: Why They Are Different

Directions: Look at your answers on page 120. Write why each object does not belong.

Row 1 _____

Row 2 _____

Row 3 _____

Directions: For each object, draw a group of pictures that belong with it.

candy bar

lettuce

Classifying: What Does Not Belong?

Directions: Circle the two things that do not belong in the picture. Write why they do not belong.

1. _____

_____

_____

2. _____

_____

Name: _____

Sequencing: Fill the Glasses

Directions: Follow the instructions to fill each glass. Use crayons to draw your favorite drink in the ones that are full and half-full.

full   **half-full**   **empty**

empty   **half-full**   **full**

Grade 1 - Comprehensive Curriculum

Sequencing: Raking Leaves

Directions: Write a number in each box to show the order of the story.

Sequencing: Make a Snowman!

Directions: Write the number of the sentence that goes with each picture in the box.

1. Roll a large snowball for the snowman's bottom.

2. Make another snowball and put it on top of the first.

3. Put the last snowball on top.

4. Dress the snowman.

Sequencing: A Recipe

Directions: Look at the recipe below. Put each step in order. Write **1, 2, 3** or **4** in the box.

HOW TO MAKE BREAD BUDDIES

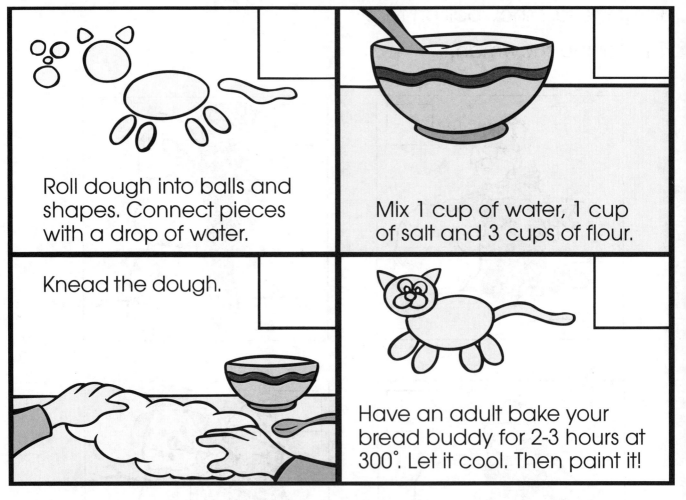

Roll dough into balls and shapes. Connect pieces with a drop of water.

Mix 1 cup of water, 1 cup of salt and 3 cups of flour.

Knead the dough.

Have an adult bake your bread buddy for 2-3 hours at 300°. Let it cool. Then paint it!

What kind of bread buddy did you make?

_____

Sequencing: How Flowers Grow

Directions: Read the story. Then write the steps to grow a flower.

First find a sunny spot. Then plant the seed. Water it. The flower will start to grow. Pull the weeds around it. Remember to keep giving the flower water. Enjoy your flower.

1. _____ .

2. _____ .

3. _____ .

4. _____ .

5. _____ .

Sequencing: Make an Ice-Cream Cone

Directions: Number the boxes in order to show how to make an ice-cream cone.

Name: _____

Sequencing: Eating a Cone

What if a person never ate an ice-cream cone? Could you tell them how to eat it? Think about what you do when you eat an ice-cream cone.

Directions: Write directions to teach someone how to eat an ice-cream cone.

How to Eat an Ice-Cream Cone

1. _____

2. _____

3. _____

4. _____

 Name: ____________________

Comprehension: Apples

Directions: Read about apples. Then write the answers.

I like  . Do you?

Some  are red.

Some  are green.

Some  are yellow.

1. How many kinds of apples does the story tell about?

2. Name the kinds of apples.

------------------ ------------------ ------------------

3. What kind of apple do you like best?

Comprehension: Crayons

Directions: Read about crayons. Then write your answers.

Crayons come in many colors. Some crayons are dark colors. Some crayons are light colors. All crayons have wax in them.

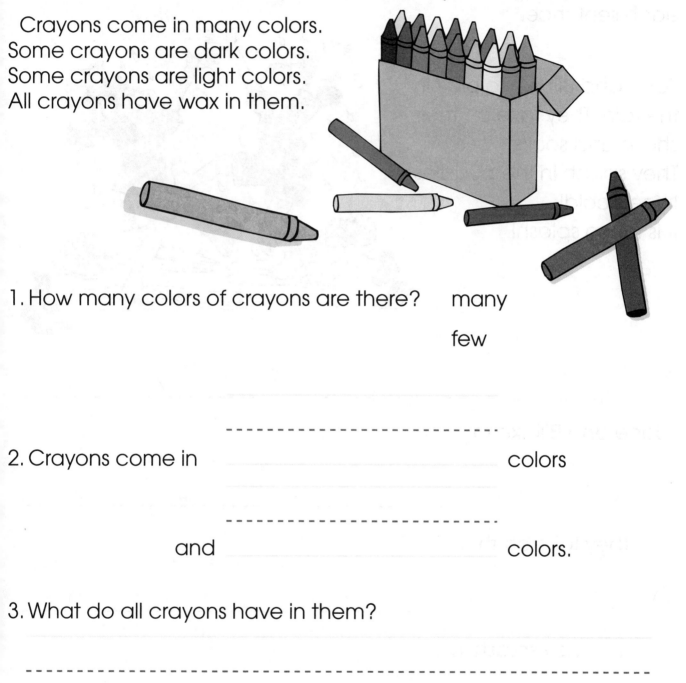

1. How many colors of crayons are there?　　many

　　　　　　　　　　　　　　　　　　　　few

2. Crayons come in _____ colors

　　　　and _____ colors.

3. What do all crayons have in them?

_____

Grade 1 - Comprehensive Curriculum

Comprehension

Directions: Read the story. Write the words from the story that complete each sentence.

Jane and Bill like to play in the rain. They take off their shoes and socks.
They splash in the puddles.
It feels cold!
It is fun to splash!

Jane and Bill like to _____ .

They take off their _____ .

They splash in _____ .

Do you like to splash in puddles?   Yes   No

Comprehension

Directions: Read the story. Write the words from the story that complete each sentence.

Ben and Sue have a bug.
It is red with black spots.
They call it Spot.
Spot likes to eat green
leaves and grass.
The children keep Spot in a box.

Ben and Sue have a _____ .

It is _____ with black spots.

The bug's name is _____ .

The bug eats _____ .

133

Grade 1 - Comprehensive Curriculum

Comprehension: Snow Is Cold!

Directions: Read about snow. Circle the answers.

When you play in snow, dress warmly. Wear a coat. Wear a hat. Wear gloves. Do you wear these when you play in snow?

1. Snow is

warm.

cold.

2. When you play in snow, dress

warmly.

quickly.

Directions: List three things to wear when you play in snow.

- -

- -

- -

Comprehension: Growing Flowers

Directions: Read about flowers. Then write the answers.

Some flowers grow in pots. Many flowers grow in flower beds. Others grow beside the road. Flowers begin from seeds. They grow into small buds. Then they open wide and bloom. Flowers are pretty!

1. Name two places flowers grow.

----

2. Flowers begin from

-- .

3. Then flowers grow into small

-- .

4. Flowers then open wide and

-- .

Name: _____

Comprehension: Raking Leaves

Directions: Read about raking leaves. Then answer the questions.

I like to rake leaves. Do you? Leaves die each year. They get brown and dry. They fall from the trees. Then we rake them up.

1. What color are leaves when they die?

----

2. What happens when they die?

----

3. What do we do when leaves fall?

Name: _____

Comprehension: Clocks

Directions: Read about clocks. Then answer the questions.

Ticking Clocks

Many clocks make two sounds. The sounds are tick and tock. Big clocks often make loud tick-tocks. Little clocks often make quiet tick-tocks. Sometimes people put little clocks in a box with a new puppy. The puppy likes the sound. The tick-tock makes the puppy feel safe.

1. What two sounds do many clocks make?

-        -

                           and

2. What kind of tick-tocks do big clocks make?

- -

3. What kind of clock makes a new puppy feel safe?

- -

Comprehension: Soup

Directions: Read about soup. Then write the answers.

I Like Soup

Soup is good! It is good for you, too. We eat most kinds of soup hot. Some people eat cold soup in the summer. Carrots and beans are in some soups. Do you like crackers with soup?

1. Name two ways people eat soup.

---------------------------------   ---------------------------------

2. Name two things that are in some soups.

---------------------------------   ---------------------------------

3. Name the kind of soup you like best.

Review

Directions: Read about cookies. Then write your answers.

Cookies are made with many things. All cookies are made with flour. Some cookies have nuts in them. Some cookies do not. Some cookies have chocolate chips. Some do not. Cookbooks give directions on how to make cookies.

First, turn on the oven. Then get out all the things that go in the cookies. Mix them together. Roll them out, and cut the cookies. Bake the cookies. Now eat them!

1. Tell one way all cookies are the same.

- -

2. Name one different thing in cookies.

- -

3. Where do you find directions for making cookies?

- -

Grade 1 - Comprehensive Curriculum

Review

Directions: Read the story. Then circle the pictures of things that are wet.

Some things used in baking are dry. Some things used in baking are wet. To bake a cake, first mix the salt, sugar and flour. Then add the egg. Now, add the milk. Stir. Put the cake in the oven.

Directions: Tell the order to mix things when you bake a cake.

1. _____   4. _____

2. _____   5. _____

3. _____

Directions: Circle the answers.

6. The first things to mix are   dry.   wet.

7. Where are cakes baked?   oven   grill

Review

Directions: Read how to make no-cook candy. Then answer the questions.

Some candy needs to be cooked on a stove. You do not need to cook this kind of candy. It is easy to make. You will need a large bowl for mixing. You will need five things to make this candy.

No-Cook Candy

$\frac{1}{2}$ cup peanut butter

4 cups powdered sugar

1 cup cocoa

pinch of salt

4 tablespoons milk

Mix everything in the bowl. Roll it into small balls. (A pinch of salt is just a tiny bit.)

1. What is third on the list of things needed?

_____

2. What is different about no-cook candy?

_____

Directions: Write what to do to make no-cook candy.

3. First, mix everything in a bowl. Then,

_____

Comprehension: The Teddy Bear Song

Do you know the Teddy Bear Song? It is very old!

Directions: Read the Teddy Bear Song. Then answer the questions.

Teddy bear, teddy bear, turn around.

Teddy bear, teddy bear, touch the ground.

Teddy bear, teddy bear, climb upstairs.

Teddy bear, teddy bear, say your prayers.

Teddy bear, teddy bear, turn out the light.

Teddy bear, teddy bear, say, "Good night!"

1. What is the first thing the teddy bear does?

----

2. What is the last thing the teddy bear does?

----

3. What would you name a teddy bear?

Sequencing: Put Teddy Bear to Bed

Directions: Read the song about the teddy bear again. Write a number in each box to show the order of the story.

Comprehension: A New Teddy Bear Song

Directions: Write words to make a new teddy bear song. Act out your new song with your teddy bear as you read it.

- -

Teddy bear, teddy bear, turn   .

- -

Teddy bear, teddy bear, touch the   .

- -

Teddy bear, teddy bear, climb   .

- -

Teddy bear, teddy bear, turn out   .

- -

Teddy bear, teddy bear, say,   .

Comprehension: Balloons

Directions: Read the story. Then answer the questions.

Some balloons float. They are filled with gas. Some do not float. They are filled with air. Some clowns carry balloons. Balloons come in many colors. What color do you like?

1. What makes balloons float?

\- -

2. What is in balloons that do not float?

\- -

3. What shape are the balloons the clown is holding?

\- -

Name: _____

Comprehension: Balloons

Directions: Read the story about balloons again. Draw a picture for the sentence in each box.

The clown is holding red, yellow and blue balloons filled with air.

The clown is holding purple, orange, green and blue balloons filled with gas.

Sequencing: Petting a Cat

Directions: Read the story. Then write the answers.

Do you like cats? I do. To pet a cat, move slowly. Hold out your hand. The cat will come to you. Then pet its head. Do not grab a cat! It will run away.

To pet a cat . . .

1. Move _____ .

2. Hold out your _____ .

3. The cat will come to _____ .

4. Pet the cat's _____ .

5. Do not _____ a cat!

Grade 1 · Comprehensive Curriculum

Name: _____

Comprehension: Cats

Directions: Read the story about cats again. Then write the answers.

1. What is a good title for the story?

----

2. The story tells you how to _____ .

3. What part of your body should you pet a cat with?

----

4. Why should you move slowly to pet a cat?

.

5. Why do you think a cat will run away if you grab it?

Name: _____

Comprehension: Cats

Directions: Look at the pictures and read about four cats. Then write the correct name beside each cat.

Fluffy, Blackie and Tiger are playing. Tom is sleeping. Blackie has spots. Tiger has stripes.

- -

- -

- -

- -

Grade 1 - Comprehensive Curriculum

Same and Different: Cats

Directions: Compare the picture of the cats on page 149 to this picture. Write a word from the box to tell what is different about each cat.

| purple ball | green bow | blue brush | red collar |

1. Tom is wearing a _____ .

2. Blackie has a _____ .

3. Fluffy is wearing a _____ .

4. Tiger has a _____ .

Comprehension: Tigers

Directions: Read about tigers. Then write the answers.

Tigers sleep during the day. They hunt at night. Tigers eat meat. They hunt deer. They like to eat wild pigs. If they cannot find meat, tigers will eat fish.

1. When do tigers sleep?

   -

2. Name two things tigers eat.

   -

   -

   -

3. When do tigers hunt?

Following Directions: Tiger Puzzle

Directions: Read the story about tigers again. Then complete the puzzle.

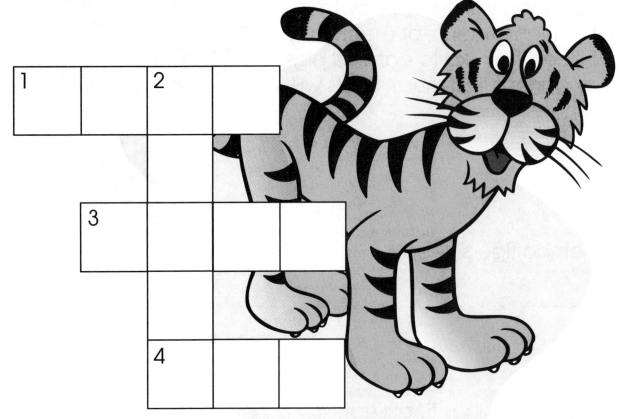

Across:

1. When tigers cannot get meat, they eat _____ .

3. The food tigers like best is _____ .

4. Tigers like to eat this meat: wild _____ .

Down:

2. Tigers do this during the day.

Following Directions: Draw a Tiger

Directions: Follow directions to complete the picture of the tiger.

1. Draw black stripes on the tiger's body and tail.

2. Color the tiger's tongue red.

3. Draw claws on the feet.

4. Draw a black nose and two black eyes on the tiger's face.

5. Color the rest of the tiger orange.

6. Draw tall, green grass for the tiger to sleep in.

Comprehension: How We Eat

Directions: Read the story. Use words from the box to answer the questions.

People eat with spoons and forks. They use a spoon to eat soup and ice cream. They use a fork to eat potatoes. They use a knife to cut their meat. They say, "Thank you. It was good!" when they finish.

fork	ice cream	knife	soup

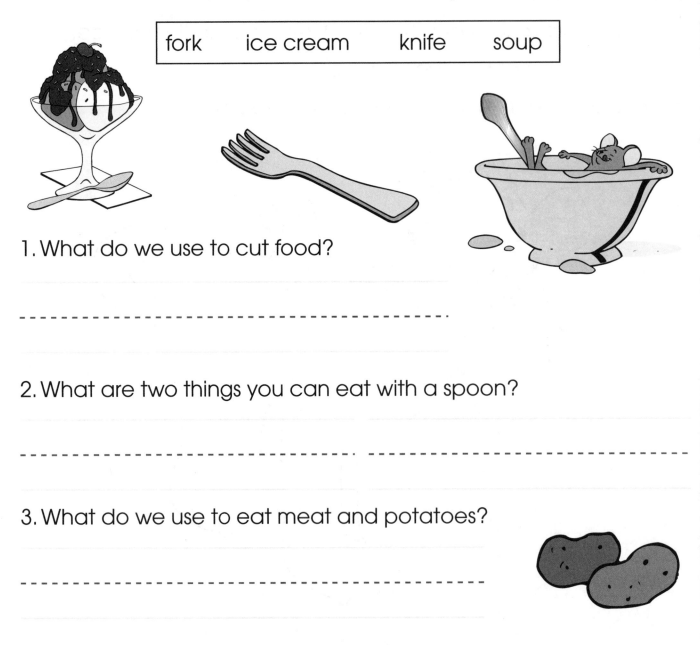

1. What do we use to cut food?

_____

_____

2. What are two things you can eat with a spoon?

_____

3. What do we use to eat meat and potatoes?

_____

Classifying: Foods

Directions: Read the questions under each plate. Draw three foods on each plate to answer the questions.

1. What foods can you cut with a knife?

2. What foods should you eat with a fork?

3. What foods can you eat with a spoon?

Comprehension: Write a Party Invitation

Directions: Read about the party. Then complete the invitation.

The party will be at Dog's house. The party will start at 1:00 P.M. It will last 2 hours. Write your birthday for the date of the party.

Party Invitation

Where: -

Date: -

Time It Begins: -

Time It Ends: -

- -

Directions: On the last line, write something else about the party.

Sequencing: Pig Gets Ready

Directions: Number the pictures of Pig getting ready for the party to show the order of the story.

What kind of party do you
think Pig is going to?   -

Comprehension: An Animal Party

Directions: Use the picture for clues. Write words from the box to answer the questions.

bear	cat
dog	elephant
giraffe	hippo
pig	tiger

1. Which animals have bow ties?

----

2. Which animal has a hat?

3. Which animal has a striped shirt?

Classifying: Party Items

Directions: Draw a ▢ around objects that are food for the party. Draw a △ around the party guests. Draw a ◯ around the objects used for fun at the party.

ice cream

candy

games

tiger

noise makers

cake

garbage can

cat

hat

glasses

candle

bear

juice

balloons

giraffe

pig

potato chips

hippo

Comprehension: Play Simon Says

Directions: Read how to play Simon Says. Then answer the questions.

SIMON SAYS, CLAP YOUR HANDS!

Simon Says

Here is how to play Simon Says: One kid is Simon. Simon is the leader. Everyone must do what Simon says and does but only if the leader says, "Simon says" first. Let's try it. "Simon says, 'Pat your head.'"

"Simon says, 'Pat your nose. Pat your toes.'"

Oops! Did you pat your toes? I did not say, "Simon says," first. If you patted your toes, you are out!

1. Who is the leader in this game? -

2. What must the leader say first each time? -

3. What happens if you do something and the leader did not say, "Simon says?" -

Comprehension: Play Simon Says

Directions: Read each sentence. Look at the picture next to it. Circle the picture if the person is playing Simon Says correctly.

1. Simon says, "Put your hands on your hips."

2. Simon says, "Stand on one leg."

3. Simon says, "Put your hands on your head."

4. Simon says, "Ride a bike."

5. Simon says, "Jump up and down."

6. Simon says, "Pet a dog."

7. Simon says, "Make a big smile."

Following Directions: Play Simon Says

Directions: Read the sentences. If Simon tells you to do something, follow the directions. If Simon does not tell you to do something, go to the next sentence.

1. Simon says: Cross out all the numbers 2 through 9.

2. Simon says: Cross out the vowel that is in the word "sun."

3. Cross out the letter "B."

4. Cross out the vowels "A" and "E."

5. Simon says: Cross out the consonants in the word "cup."

6. Cross out the letter "Z."

7. Simon says: Cross out all the "K's."

8. Simon says: Read your message.

C 3 G U 7 P R U C P E K C P A 8 K K

6 T P U P J C 5 P O K 9 P B U P K K

Comprehension: Rhymes

Directions: Read about words that rhyme. Then circle the answers.

Words that rhyme have the same end sounds. "Wing" and "sing" rhyme. "Boy" and "toy" rhyme. "Dime" and "time" rhyme. Can you think of other words that rhyme?

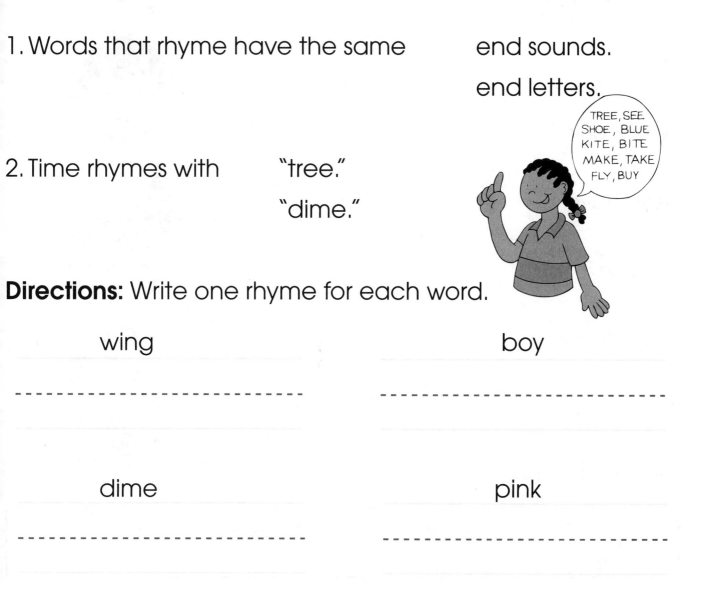

1. Words that rhyme have the same   end sounds.

    end letters.

2. Time rhymes with   "tree."

    "dime."

TREE, SEE
SHOE, BLUE
KITE, BITE
MAKE, TAKE
FLY, BUY

Directions: Write one rhyme for each word.

wing

- - - - - - - - - - - - - - - - - -

boy

- - - - - - - - - - - - - - - - - -

dime

- - - - - - - - - - - - - - - - - -

pink

- - - - - - - - - - - - - - - - - -

Rhyming Words

Many poems have rhyming words. The rhyming words are usually at the end of the line.

Directions: Complete the poem with words from the box.

My Glue

I spilled my _____ .

I felt _____ .

What could I _____ ?

Hey! I have a _____ !

I'll make it _____ .

The cleanest you've _____ .

No one will _____ .

Wouldn't that be _____ ?

blue	clue	scream	seen
glue	do	clean	mean

Classifying: Rhymes

Directions: Cut out the pieces. Read the words. Find two words that rhyme. Put the words together.

Page is blank for cutting exercise on previous page.

Classifying: Rhymes

Directions: Circle the pictures in each row that rhyme.

Row 1

Row 2

Row 3

Directions: Write the names of the pictures that do not rhyme.

These words do not rhyme:

Row 1	Row 2	Row 3

Comprehension: Babies

Directions: Read about babies. Then write the answers.

Babies are small. Some babies cry a lot. They cry when they are wet. They cry when they are hungry. They smile when they are dry. They smile when they are fed.

1. Name two reasons babies cry.

   --------------------------------- ---------------------------------

2. Name two reasons babies smile.

   --------------------------------- ---------------------------------

3. Write a baby's name you like.

Comprehension: Babies

Directions: Read each sentence. Draw a picture of a baby's face in the box to show if she would cry or smile.

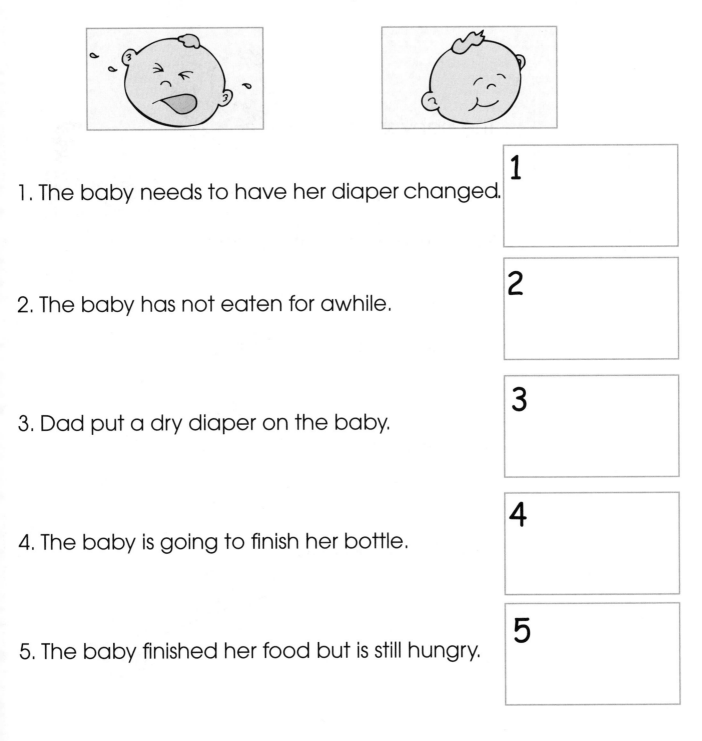

1. The baby needs to have her diaper changed.

    1

2. The baby has not eaten for awhile.

    2

3. Dad put a dry diaper on the baby.

    3

4. The baby is going to finish her bottle.

    4

5. The baby finished her food but is still hungry.

    5

Name: _____

Sequencing: Feeding Baby

Directions: Read the sentences. Write a number in each box to show the order of the story.

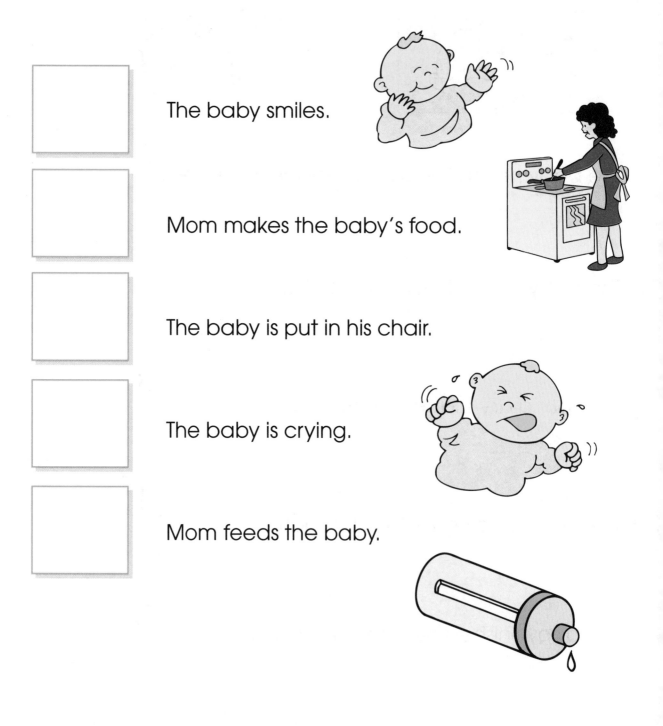

The baby smiles.

Mom makes the baby's food.

The baby is put in his chair.

The baby is crying.

Mom feeds the baby.

Same and Different: Compare the Twins

Directions: Read the story. Then use the words in the box and the picture to write your answers.

Ben and Ann are twin babies. They were born at the same time. They have the same mother. Ben is a boy baby. Ann is a girl baby.

mother	bow	boy	girl	hat	twins

1. Tell one way Ann and Ben are the same. ----------------------------------

   ----

2. Ann and Ben are ----------------------------------.

3. Tell two ways Ann and Ben are different.

   ----------------------   ----------------------
4. Ann is a _____ . Ben is _____ .

5. Ann is   ----------------------   Ben is   ----------------------
   wearing a _____ . wearing a _____ .

Grade 1 - Comprehensive Curriculum

Comprehension: Hats

Directions: Read about hats. Then write your answers.

There are many kinds of hats. Some baseball hats have brims. Some fancy hats have feathers. Some knit hats pull down over your ears. Some hats are made of straw. Do you like hats?

1. Name four kinds of hats.

--------------------------------   --------------------------------

--------------------------------   --------------------------------

Directions: Circle the correct answers.

2. What kind of hats pull down over your ears?

      straw hats

      knit hats

3. What are some hats made of?

      straw

      mud

Sequencing: Choosing a Hat

Directions: Write a number in each box to show the order of the story.

Following Directions: Draw Hats

Directions: Draw a hat on each person. Read the sentences to know what kind of hat to draw.

1. The first girl is wearing a purple hat with feathers.

2. The boy next to the girl with the purple hat is wearing a red baseball hat.

3. The first boy is wearing a yellow knit hat.

4. The last boy is wearing a brown top hat.

5. The girl next to the boy with the red hat is wearing a blue straw hat.

Classifying: Mr. Lincoln's Hat

Abraham Lincoln wore a tall hat. He liked to keep things in his hat so he would not lose them.

Directions: Cut out the pictures of things Mr. Lincoln could have kept in his hat. Glue those pictures on the hat.

letters

candle

penny

one dollar

bowl

cat

watch

paper

Page is blank for cutting exercise on previous page.

Comprehension: Boats

Directions: Read about boats. Then answer the questions.

See the boats! They float on water. Some boats have sails. The wind moves the sails. It makes the boats go. Many people name their sailboats. They paint the name on the side of the boat.

1. What makes sailboats move?

- -

2. Where do sailboats float?

- -

3. What would you name a sailboat?

- -

Same and Different: Color the Boats

Directions: Find the three boats that are alike. Color them all the same. One boat is different. Color it differently.

Name: _____

Comprehension: A Boat Ride

Directions: Write a sentence under each picture to tell what is happening. Read the story you wrote.

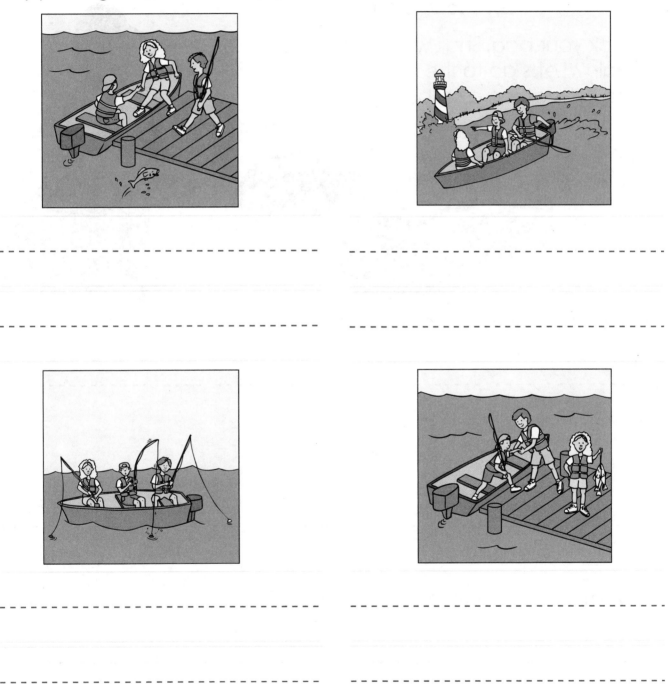

Comprehension: Travel

Directions: Read the story. Then answer the questions.

Let's Take a Trip!

Pack your bag. Shall we go by car, plane or train? Let's go to the sea. When we get there, let's go on a sailboat.

1. What are three ways to travel?

_____

2. Where will we go?

_____

3. What will we do when we get there?

_____

Predicting: Words and Pictures

Directions: Complete each story by choosing the correct picture. Draw a line from the story to the picture.

1. Shawnda got her books. She went

   to the bus stop. Shawnda got

   on the bus.

2. Marco planted a seed. He watered it.

   He pulled the weeds around it.

3. Abraham's dog was barking.

   Abraham got out the dog food.

   He put it in the dog bowl.

Predicting: Story Ending

Directions: Read the story. Draw a picture in the last box to complete the story.

That's my ball.

I got it first.

It's mine!

Predicting: Story Ending

Directions: Read the story. Draw a picture in the last box to complete the story.

Marco likes to paint.   He likes to help his dad.

He is tired when he's finished.

Predicting: Story Ending

Directions: Read each story. Circle the sentence that tells how the story will end.

Ann was riding her bike. She saw a dog in the park. She stopped to pet it. Ann left to go home.

The dog went swimming.

The dog followed Ann.

The dog went home with a cat.

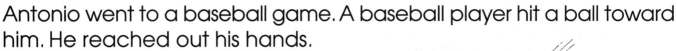

Antonio went to a baseball game. A baseball player hit a ball toward him. He reached out his hands.

The player caught the ball.

The ball bounced on a car.

Antonio caught the ball.

Making Inferences: Baseball

Traci likes baseball. She likes to win. Traci's team does not win.

Directions: Circle the correct answers.

1. Traci likes

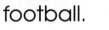 football.   soccer.   baseball.

2. Traci likes to

 win.   lose.

3. Traci uses a bat.

   Yes   No

4. Traci is   happy.   sad.

Grade 1 - Comprehensive Curriculum

Making Inferences: The Stars

Lynn looks at the stars. She sings a song about them. She makes a wish on them. The stars help Lynn sleep.

Directions: Circle the correct answers.

1. Lynn likes the

moon.   sun.   stars.

2. What song do you think she sings?

Row, Row, Row Your Boat

Twinkle, Twinkle Little Star

Happy Birthday to You

3. What does Lynn "make" on the stars?

a wish   a spaceship   lunch

Making Inferences: Feelings

Directions: Read each story. Choose a word from the box to show how each person feels.

happy	excited	sad	mad

1. Andy and Sam were best friends. Sam and his family moved far away. How does Sam feel?

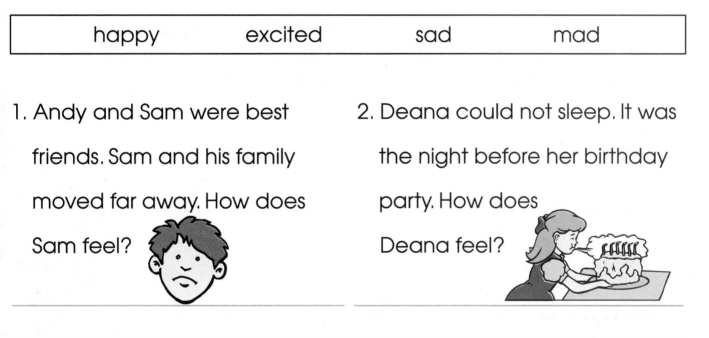

2. Deana could not sleep. It was the night before her birthday party. How does Deana feel?

_____

_____

3. Jacob let his baby brother play with his teddy bear. His brother lost the bear. How does Jacob feel?

4. Kia picked flowers for her mom. Her mom smiled when she got them. How does Kia feel?

_____

_____

Name: _____

Comprehension: Eating Ice Cream

Directions: Read the story. Write two things Sam could have done so he could have enjoyed eating his ice-cream cone.

It was a hot day. Sam went to the store and got an ice-cream cone. He sat at a table in the sun. Sam watched some friends play ball. Suddenly, his ice cream fell on the sidewalk.

1. -

   -

2. -

   -

Review

Directions: Write a sentence to complete this story.

1. Evan's dog runs away.

2. Evan chases it.

3. The dog runs into a store.

4. _____

_____

_____

_____

Directions: Read this story. Answer the questions.

Lea plays games with her little sister. Sometimes Lea hides from her sister. Her sister calls her name over and over. Lea does not answer. Lea thinks it is funny.

1. Is Lea being nice or mean to her sister? _____

2. Do you think her sister likes Lea to hide? _____

3. What would you do if you were Lea's sister?

_____

_____

Books

Directions: What do you know about books? Use the words in the box below to help fill in the lines.

title	book	author
illustrator	pages	left to right
fun	library	glossary

The name of the book is the _____.

_____ is the direction we read.

The person who wrote the words is the _____.

Reading is _____!

There are many books in the _____.

The person who draws the pictures is the _____.

The _____ is a kind of dictionary in the book to help you find the meanings of words.

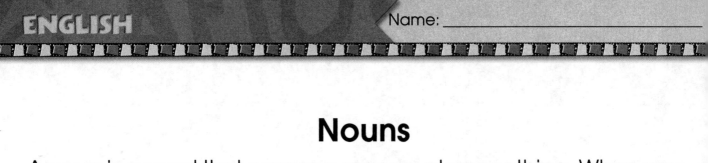

ENGLISH

Name: _____

Nouns

A noun is a word that names a person, place or thing. When you read a sentence, the noun is what the sentence is about.

Directions: Complete each sentence with a noun.

- -

The _____ is fat.

- -

My _____ is blue.

- -

The _____ has apples.

- -

The _____ is hot.

Name: _____

Nouns

Directions: Write these naming words in the correct box.

| store | zoo | child | baby | teacher | table |
| cat | park | gym | woman | sock | horse |

Person

_____   _____

_____   _____

Place

_____   _____

_____   _____

Thing

_____   _____

_____   _____

Grade 1 - Comprehensive Curriculum

Name: _____

Things That Go Together

Some nouns name things that go together.

Directions: Draw a line to match the nouns on the left with the things they go with on the right.

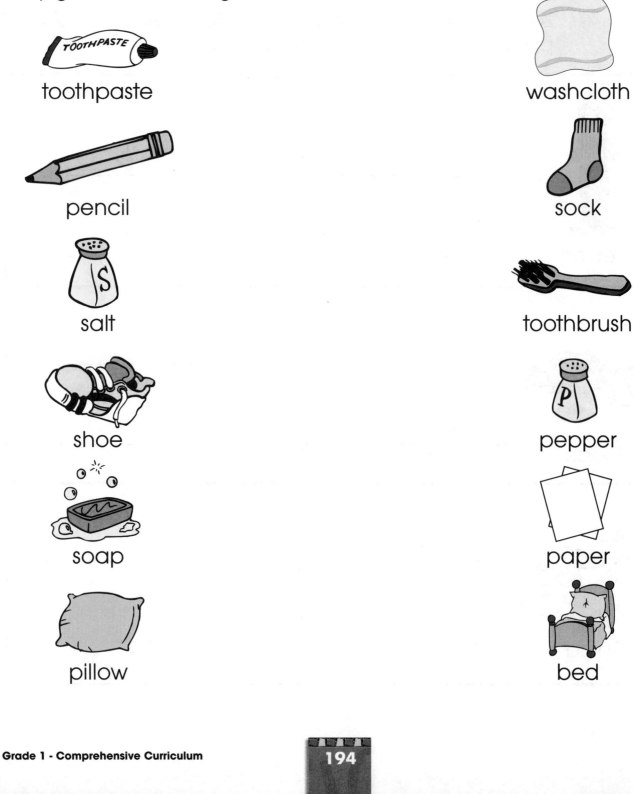

toothpaste

pencil

salt

shoe

soap

pillow

washcloth

sock

toothbrush

pepper

paper

bed

Things That Go Together

Directions: Draw a line to connect the objects that go together.

Grade 1 - Comprehensive Curriculum

Verbs

Verbs are words that tell what a person or a thing can do.

Example: The girl pats the dog.
The word **pats** is the verb. It shows action.

Directions: Draw a line between the verbs and the pictures that show the action.

eat

run

sleep

swim

sing

hop

Name: _____

Verbs

Directions:
Look at the picture and read the words. Write an action word in each sentence below.

1. The two boys like to _____ together.

2. The children _____ the soccer ball.

3. Some children like to _____ on the swing.

4. The girl can _____ very fast.

5. The teacher _____ the bell.

Grade 1 - Comprehensive Curriculum

Name: _____

Nouns and Verbs

A noun is a person or thing a sentence tells about. A verb tells what the person or thing does.

Directions: Circle the noun in each sentence. Underline the verb.

Example: The (cat) <u>sleeps</u>.

1. Jill plays a game on the computer.

2. Children swim in the pool.

3. The car raced around the track.

4. Mike throws the ball to his friend.

5. Monkeys swing in the trees.

6. Terry laughed at the clown.

Review

Directions: Cut out the words below. Glue naming words in the **Nouns** box. Glue action words in the **Verbs** box.

Nouns	Verbs

cut ✂ –

boy

jump

cat

sit

throw

house

swim

fork

Page is blank for cutting exercise on previous page.

Name: _____

Review

Directions: Read the sentences below. Draw a **red** circle around the nouns. Draw a **blue** line under the verbs.

1. The boy runs fast.

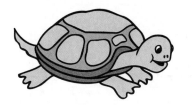

2. The turtle eats leaves.

3. The fish swim in the tank.

4. The girl hits the ball.

Words That Describe

Describing words tell us more about a person, place or thing.

Directions: Read the words in the box. Choose the word that describes the picture. Write it next to the picture.

happy	round	sick	cold	long

- -

- -

- -

- -

- -

Words That Describe

Directions: Read the words in the box. Choose the word that describes the picture. Write it next to the picture.

wet	round	funny	soft	sad	tall

Name: _____

Words That Describe

Directions: Circle the describing word in each sentence. Draw a line from the sentence to the picture.

1. The hungry dog is eating.

2. The tiny bird is flying.

3. Horses have long legs.

4. She is a fast runner.

5. The little boy was lost.

Name: _____

Words That Describe: Colors and Numbers

Colors and numbers can describe nouns.

Directions: Underline the describing word in each sentence. Draw a picture to go with each sentence.

A yellow moon was in the sky.

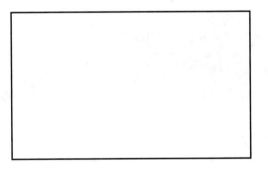

Two worms are on the road.

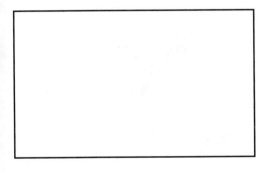

The tree had red apples.

The girl wore a blue dress.

Grade 1 - Comprehensive Curriculum

Sequencing: Comparative Adjectives

Directions: Look at each group of pictures. Write 1, 2 or 3 under the picture to show where it should be.

Example:

tallest ___3___   tall ___1___   taller ___2___

small _____   smallest _____   smaller _____

biggest _____   big _____   bigger _____

wider _____   wide _____   widest _____

Name: _____

Sequencing: Comparative Adjectives

Directions: Look at the pictures in each row. Write 1, 2 or 3 under the picture to show where it should be.

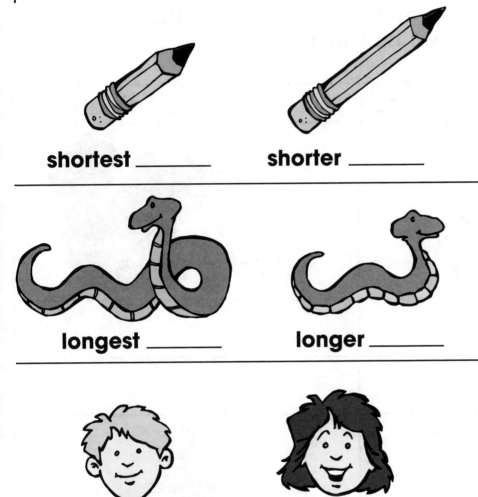

shortest _____   **shorter** _____   **short** _____

longest _____   **longer** _____   **long** _____

happy _____   **happier** _____   **happiest** _____

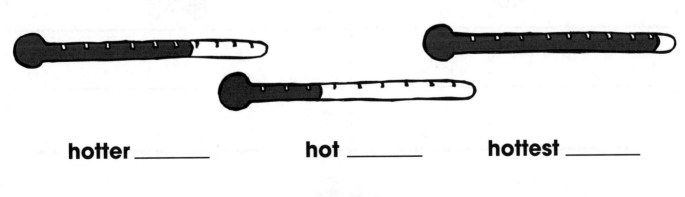

hotter _____   **hot** _____   **hottest** _____

Grade 1 - Comprehensive Curriculum

Synonyms

Synonyms are words that mean almost the same thing. **Start** and **begin** are synonyms.

Directions: Find the synonyms that describe each picture. Write the words in the boxes below the picture.

small   funny   large   sad   silly   little   big   unhappy

Synonyms

Synonyms are words that mean almost the same thing.

Directions: Read the word in the center of each flower. Find a synonym for each word on a bee at the bottom of the page. Cut out and glue each bee on its matching flower.

Grade 1 - Comprehensive Curriculum

Page is blank for cutting exercise on previous page.

Name: _____

Similarities: Synonyms

Directions: Circle the word in each row that is most like the first word in the row.

Example:

grin   (smile)   frown   mad

bag   jar   sack   box

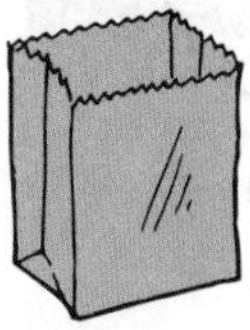

cat   fruit   animal   flower

apple   rot   cookie   fruit

around   circle   square   dot

brown   tan   black   red

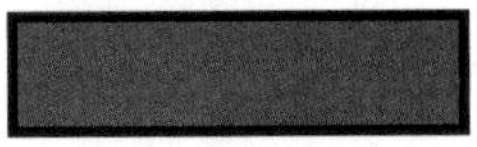

bird   dog   cat   duck

bee   fish   ant   snake

Grade 1 - Comprehensive Curriculum

Name: _____

Synonyms

Synonyms are words that have the same meaning.

Directions: Read each sentence and look at the underlined word. Circle the word that means the same thing. Write the new words.

1. The <u>little</u> dog ran.	tall	funny	small
2. The <u>happy</u> girl smiled.	glad	sad	good
3. The bird is in the <u>big</u> tree.	green	pretty	tall
4. He was <u>nice</u> to me.	kind	mad	bad
5. The baby is <u>tired.</u>	sleepy	sad	little

Name: _____

Synonyms

Directions: Read each sentence and look at the underlined word. Circle the word that means the same thing. Write the new words.

1. The boy was <u>mad</u>.   happy   angry   pup

2. The <u>dog</u> is brown.   pup   cat   rat

3. I like to <u>scream</u>.   soar   mad   shout

4. The bird can <u>fly</u>.   soar   jog   warm

5. The girl can <u>run</u>.   sleep   jog   shout

6. I am <u>hot</u>.   warm   cold   soar

- -

- -

Grade 1 - Comprehensive Curriculum

Name: _____

Similarities: Synonyms

Directions: Read each sentence. Read the word after the sentence. Find the word that is most like it in the sentence and circle it.

1. The flowers grew very tall.

 plants

2. Jan picked the apple from the tree.

applesauce

3. Juan's van is dirty.

truck

4. A dog makes a sound different from a cat.

 wolf

5. Dad put up a fence in the yard.

 gate

Similarities: Synonyms

Directions: Read the story. Write a word on the line that means almost the same as the word under the line.

Dan went to the _____ .
<u>store</u>

He wanted to buy _____ .
<u>food</u>

He walked very _____ .
<u>quickly</u>

The store had what he wanted. _____

He bought it using _____ .
<u>dimes</u>

Instead of walking home, Dan _____ .
<u>jogged</u>

Grade 1 - Comprehensive Curriculum

Name: _____

Antonyms

Antonyms are words that are opposites. **Hot** and **cold** are antonyms.
Directions: Draw a line between the antonyms.

closed

below

full

empty

above

old

new

open

Name: _____

Opposites

Directions: Draw lines to connect the words that are opposites.

up	wet
over	down
dry	dirty
clean	under

Grade 1 - Comprehensive Curriculum

Name: _____

Opposites

Opposites are things that are different in every way.

Directions: Draw a line between the opposites.

day

happy

big

open

front

little

closed

night

back

sad

Name: _____

Antonyms

Directions: Find the two words that are opposites. Cut out the balloon basket and glue it on the proper balloon.

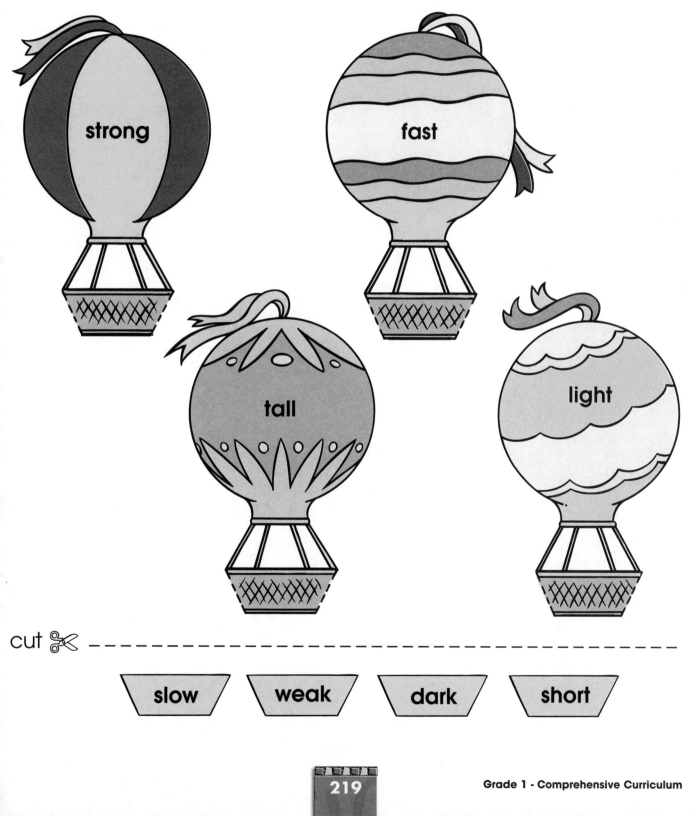

strong

fast

tall

light

cut ✂ --

slow   weak   dark   short

Grade 1 - Comprehensive Curriculum

Page is blank for cutting exercise on previous page.

Name: _____

Opposites

Directions: Circle the picture in each row that is the opposite of the first picture.

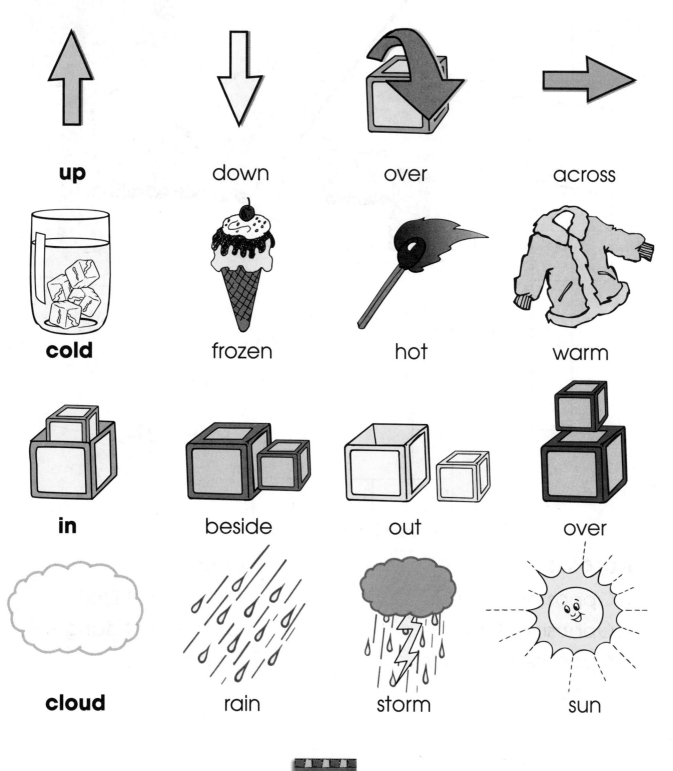

| up | down | over | across |

| **cold** | frozen | hot | warm |

| **in** | beside | out | over |

| **cloud** | rain | storm | sun |

Grade 1 - Comprehensive Curriculum

Name: _____

Opposites

Directions: Read each clue. Write the answers in the puzzle.

high   yes   left
heavy   tight
safe   full

Across:

1. Opposite of low
2. Opposite of no
4. Opposite of empty
6. Opposite of loose

Down:

1. Opposite of light
3. Opposite of dangerous
5. Opposite of right

Name: _____

Opposites

Directions: Cut out the pieces. Read the words. Find the pair of words that are opposites and put the pieces together. On the blank pieces, write your own pair of opposites.

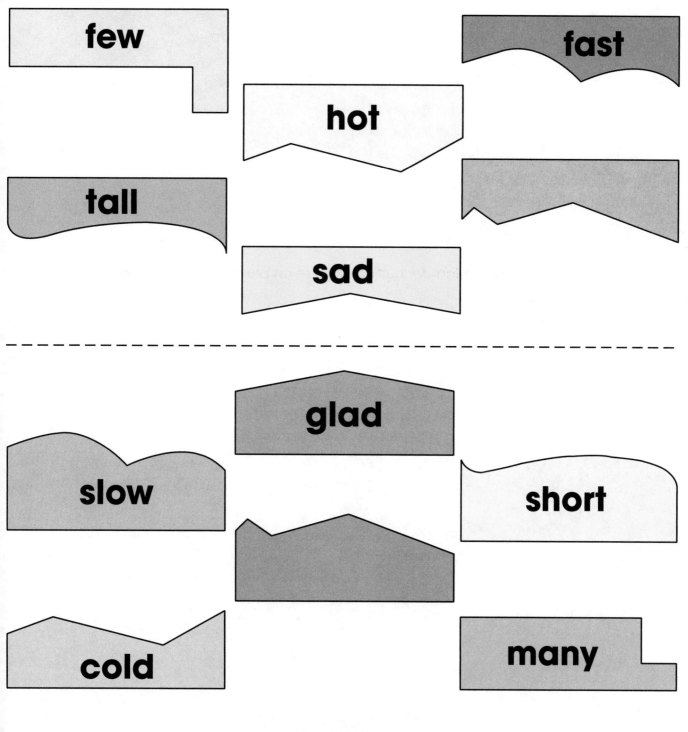

few

fast

hot

tall

sad

glad

slow

short

cold

many

Grade 1 - Comprehensive Curriculum

Page is blank for cutting exercise on previous page.

Opposites

Directions: Circle the two words in each sentence that are opposites.

1. Cold ice cream is good on a hot day.

2. Sam took off his wet socks and put on dry ones.

3. Do you like to run fast or slow?

4. The dog is black and the cat is white.

5. The elephant looked really big next to the small mouse.

6. The tiny seed grew into a large plant.

Name _____

Homophones

Homophones are words that **sound** the same but are spelled differently and mean something different. **Blew** and **blue** are homophones.

Directions: Look at the word pairs. Choose the word that describes the picture. Write the word on the line next to the picture.

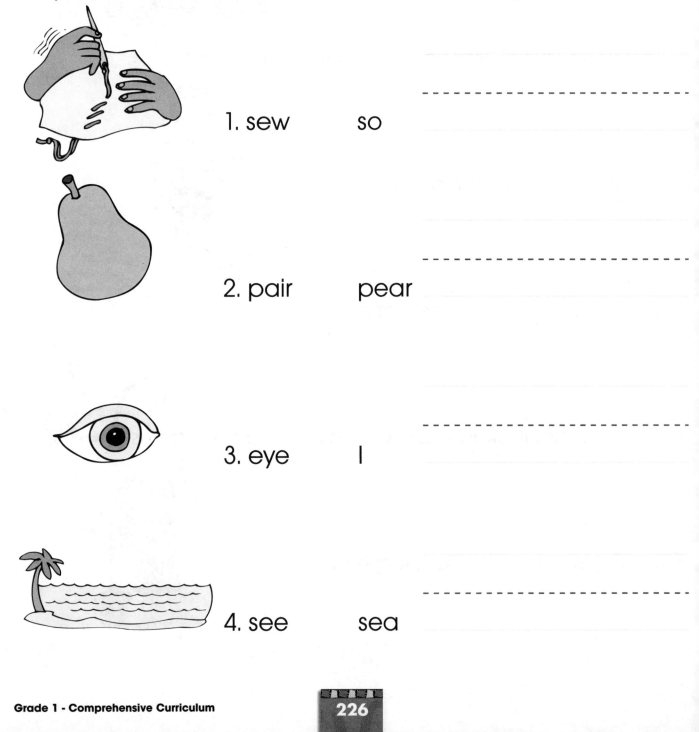

1. sew   so

- -

2. pair   pear

- -

3. eye   I

- -

4. see   sea

- -

Name: _____

Homophones

Directions: Read each sentence. Underline the two words that sound the same but are spelled differently and mean something different.

1. Tom ate eight grapes.

2. Becky read *Little Red Riding Hood*.

3. I went to buy two dolls.

4. Five blue feathers blew in the wind.

5. Would you get wood for the fire?

Name: _____

Following Directions: Days of the Week

Calendars show the days of the week in order. Sunday comes first. Saturday comes last. There are five days in between. An **abbreviation** is a short way of writing words. The abbreviations for the days of the week are usually the first three or four letters of the word followed by a period.

Example: Sunday — Sun.

Directions: Write the days of the week in order on the calendar. Use the abbreviations.

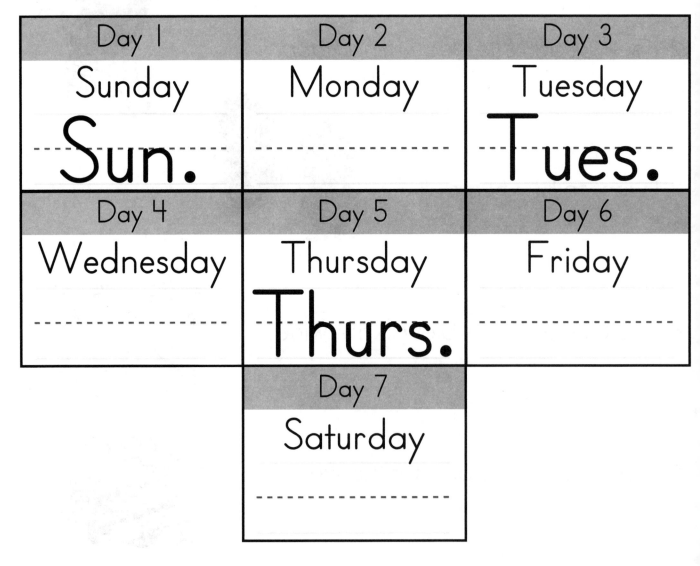

Day 1	Day 2	Day 3
Sunday	Monday	Tuesday
Sun.	- - - - - - -	Tues.

Day 4	Day 5	Day 6
Wednesday	Thursday	Friday
- - - - - - -	Thurs.	- - - - - - -

Day 7
Saturday
- - - - - - - - - -

Name: _____

Sentences

Sentences begin with capital letters.

Directions: Read the sentences and write them below. Begin each sentence with a capital letter.

Example: the cat is fat.

my dog is big.

- -

the boy is sad.

- -

bikes are fun!

- -

dad can bake.

- -

Grade 1 - Comprehensive Curriculum

Word Order

If you change the order of the words in a sentence, you can change the meaning of the sentence.

Directions: Read the sentences. Draw a circle around the sentence that describes the picture.

Example:

(The fox jumped over the dogs.)
The dogs jumped over the fox.

1. The cat watched the bird.
   The bird watched the cat.

2. The girl looked at the boy.
   The boy looked at the girl.

3. The turtle ran past the rabbit.
   The rabbit ran past the turtle.

Name: _____

Word Order

Word order is the order of words in a sentence which makes sense.

Directions: Cut out the words and put them in the correct order. Glue each sentence on another sheet of paper.

| I | like | bike. | to | ride | my |

| hot. | It | is | and | sunny |

| drink | I | can | water. |

| My | me. | with | plays | mom |

| tricks. | do | can | The | dog |

| you | go | store? | to | the | Can |

Page is blank for cutting exercise on previous page.

Name: _____

Word Order

Directions: Look at the picture. Put the words in order. Write the sentences on the lines below.

1. We made lemonade. some
2. good. It was
3. We the sold lemonade.
4. cost It five cents.
5. fun. We had

1. _____

2. _____

3. _____

4. _____

5. _____

Grade 1 - Comprehensive Curriculum

Name: _____

Word Order

Directions: Look at the picture. Put the words in the right order. Write the sentences on the lines below.

1. a Jan starfish. has
2. and Bill to Peg swim. like
3. The shining. sun is
4. sand. the in Jack plays
5. cold. water The is

1. _____

2. _____

3. _____

4. _____

5. _____

Name: _____

Review

Directions: Put the words in the right order to make a sentence. Write the sentences on the lines below.

1. a gerbil. has Ann
2. is The Mike. named gerbil
3. likes eat. Mike to
4. play. to Mike likes
5. happy a is gerbil. Mike

1. _____

2. _____

3. _____

4. _____

5. _____

Name: _____

Telling Sentences

Directions: Read the sentences and write them below. Begin each sentence with a capital letter. End each sentence with a period.

1. most children like pets
2. some children like dogs
3. some children like cats
4. some children like snakes
5. some children like all animals

1. _____

2. _____

3. _____

4. _____

5. _____

Name: _____

Telling Sentences

Directions: Read the sentences and write them below.
Begin each sentence with a capital letter.
End each sentence with a period.

1. i like to go to the store with Mom
2. we go on Friday
3. i get to push the cart
4. i get to buy the cookies
5. i like to help Mom

1. -

2. -

3. -

4. -

5. -

Asking Sentences

Directions: Write the first word of each asking sentence. Be sure to begin each question with a capital letter. End each question with a question mark.

1. _____ you like the zoo   **do**

2. _____ much does it cost   **how**

3. _____ you feed the ducks   **can**

4. _____ you see the monkeys   **will**

5. _____ time will you eat lunch   **what**

Asking Sentences

Directions: Read the asking sentences. Write the sentences below. Begin each sentence with a capital letter. End each sentence with a question mark.

1. what game will we play
2. do you like to read
3. how old are you
4. who is your best friend
5. can you tie your shoes

1.

2.

3.

4.

5.

Name: _____

Periods and Question Marks

Directions: Put a period or a question mark at the end of each sentence below.

1. Do you like parades

2. The clowns lead the parade

3. Can you hear the band

4. The balloons are big

5. Can you see the horses

Review

Directions: Look at the picture. In the space below, write one telling sentence about the picture. Then write one asking sentence about the picture.

Telling sentence:

- -

Asking sentence:

- -

Name: _____

Is and Are

We use **is** in sentences about one person or one thing. We use **are** in sentences about more than one person or thing.

Example: The dog **is** barking.
The dogs **are** barking.

Directions: Write **is** or **are** in the sentences below.

1. Jim _____ playing baseball.

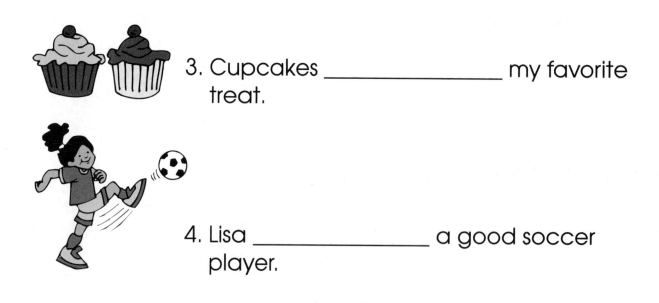

2. Fred and Sam _____ good friends.

3. Cupcakes _____ my favorite treat.

4. Lisa _____ a good soccer player.

Name: _____

Is and Are

Directions: Write **is** or **are** in the sentences below.
Example: Lisa __is__ sleeping.

1. Cats and dogs _____ good pets.

2. Bill _____ my best friend.

3. Apples _____ good to eat.

4. We _____ going to the zoo.

5. Pedro _____ coming to my house.

6. When _____ you all going to the zoo?

Vocabulary

Directions: Read the words. Trace and write them on the lines. Circle the word which completes each sentence. Write the word on the lines.

you and me _you and me_

_____

I will play with _____ .   you   me

You can go with _____ .   you   me

Can you run with _____ ?   you   me

Name: _____

Vocabulary

Directions: Read the words. Trace and write them on the lines. Then circle the word which completes each sentence. Write it on the line.

over

over

under

under

The kite is ------------------------ the tree.

over   under

The kite is ------------------------ the tree.

over   under

Grade 1 - Comprehensive Curriculum

Vocabulary

Directions: Read the words. Trace and write them on the lines. Then circle the word which completes each sentence. Write it on the line.

above   above

below   below

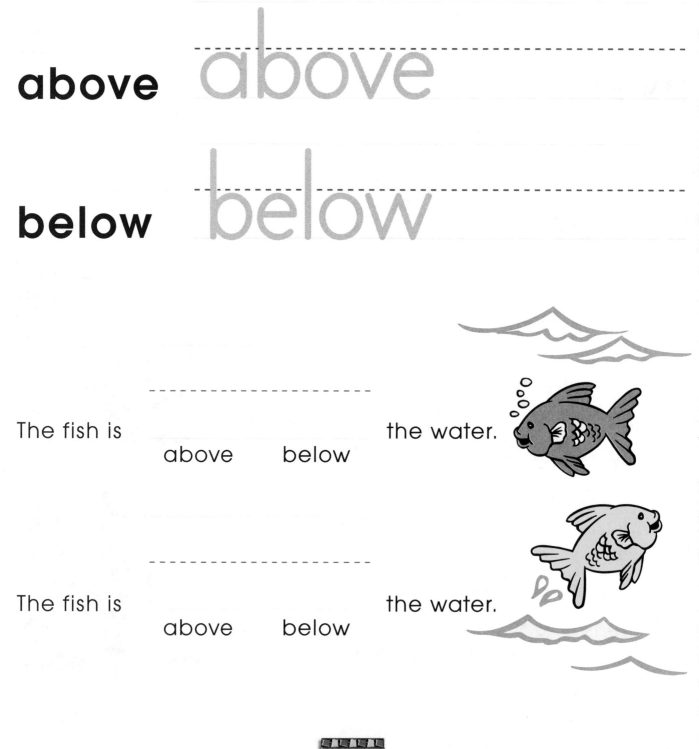

The fish is _____ the water.

          above   below

The fish is _____ the water.

          above   below

Name: _____

Vocabulary

Directions: Read and trace the words. Then circle the word which completes each sentence. Write it on the line.

inside

inside

outside

outside

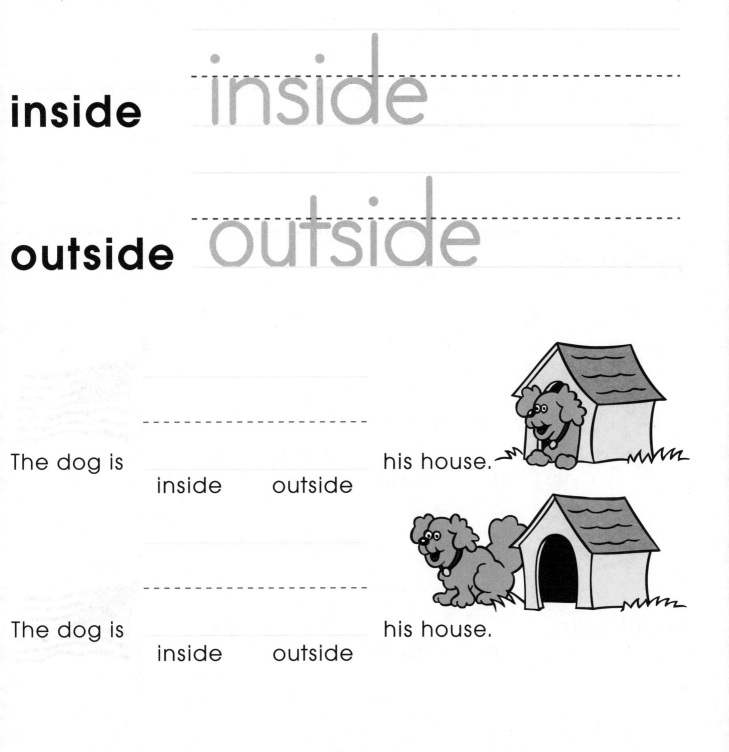

The dog is _____ his house.

inside   outside

The dog is _____ his house.

inside   outside

Name: _____

Vocabulary

Directions: Read the words. Trace and write them on the lines. Then circle the word which completes each sentence. Write it on the line.

up

down

The flag is _____ the pole.

        up   down

The flag is _____ the pole.

        up   down

Color Names

Directions: Trace the letters to write the name of each color. Then write the name again by yourself.

Example:

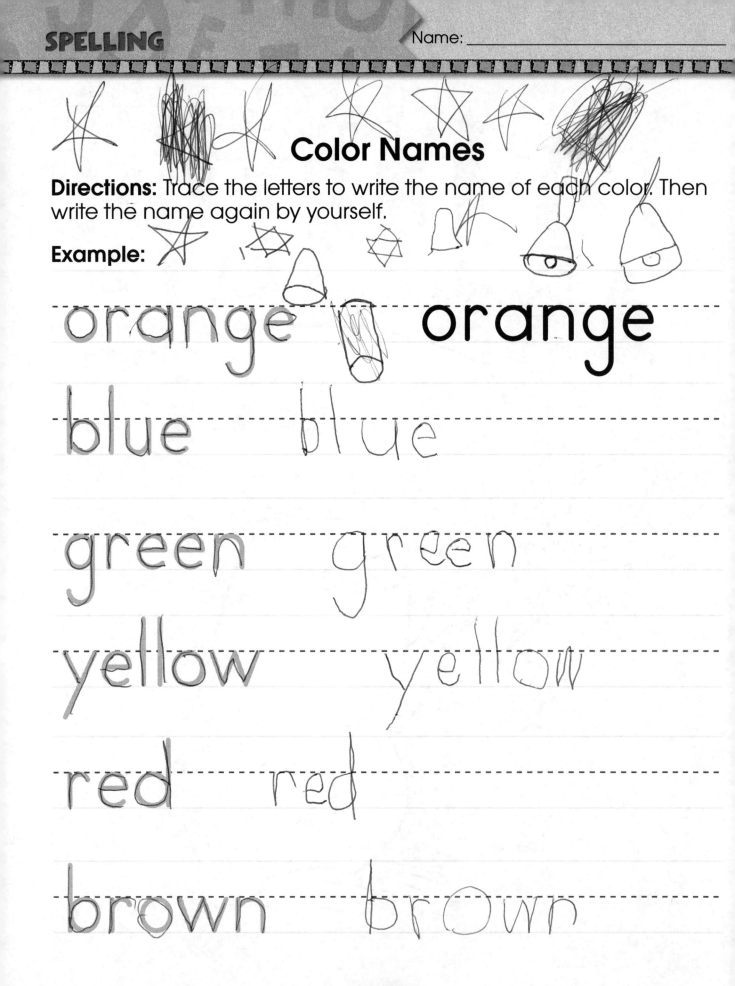

orange   orange

blue   blue

green   green

yellow   yellow

red   red

brown   brown

Name: _____

Color Names: Sentences

Directions: Use the color words to complete these sentences. Then put a period at the end.

Example: My new are orange.

green tree   blue bike   yellow chick   red ball

1. The baby 🐤 is - ☐

2. This 🌳 is - ☐

3. My 🔴 is big and - - - - - - - - - - - - - - - - - - ☐

4. My sister's 🚲 is - - - - - - - - - - - - - - - - - - - ☐

Color Names: Sentences

Directions: Some of these sentences tell a whole idea. Others have something missing. If something is missing, draw a line to the word that completes the sentence. Put a period at the end of each sentence.

He is holding up his

book

1. Ken has a new puppy.

2. I can read a

hand .

3. We like to play games.

tree

4. Pat wants to eat some

5. I will color the

cake

6. This is my birthday.

Color Names: Capital Letters

A sentence begins with a capital letter.

Directions: The words by each picture are mixed up. Write them to make a sentence that tells about the picture. Begin each sentence with a capital letter and end it with a period.

Example:  coat she has a red

She has a red coat.

1. box sees he a blue

_____

2. her is yellow flower

_____

3. red draws he a door

_____

Name: _____

Color Names: Crossword Puzzle

Directions: Complete each color name. Some words go down and some go across. Try to spell each word by yourself.

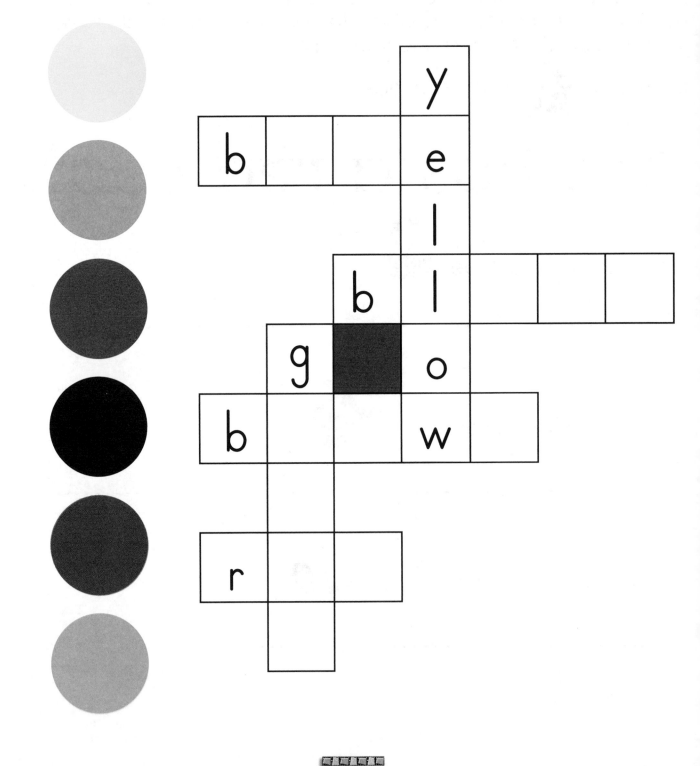

Color the Eggs

Directions: Read the words. Color the picture with the correct colors.

Grade 1 - Comprehensive Curriculum

Finish the Pictures

Directions: Read the words. Finish the pictures.

a red ball

a black hat

a yellow sun

a pink kite

an orange balloon

a blue umbrella

Name: _____

Animal Names

Directions: Fill in the missing letters for each word.

Example:

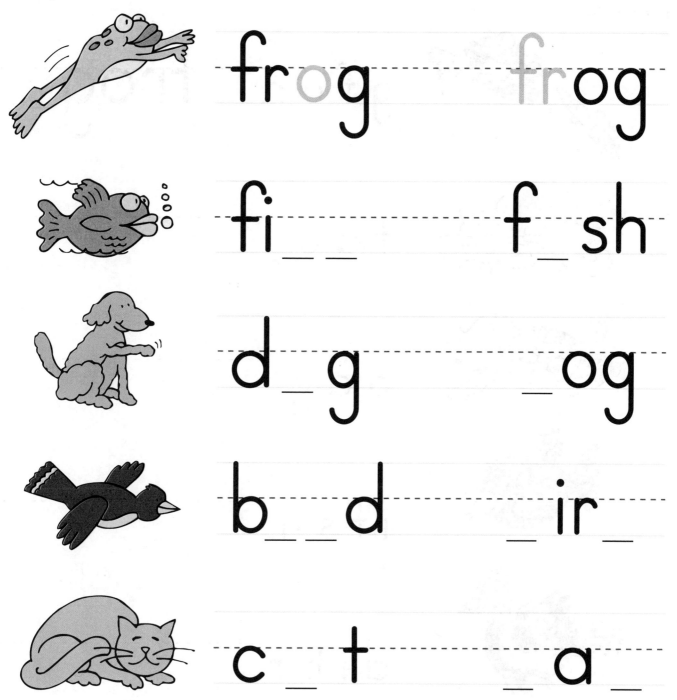

frog   fr o g

fi _ _   f _ sh

d _ g   _ og

b _ d   _ ir _

c _ t   _ a _

Grade 1 - Comprehensive Curriculum

Animal Names

Directions: The letters in the name of each animal are mixed up.
Write each word correctly.

Example:

g f o r ------ frog

t a c ----------

o d g ----------

i f s h ----------

d i b r ----------

Animal Names: Beginning Sounds

Directions: Say the name of each animal. Write the beginning sound under its name. Find two pictures in each row that begin with the same sound as the animal. Write the same first letter under them.

Example:

frog
f   f   _____   f   _____

cat
_____   _____   _____   _____   _____

fish
_____   _____   _____   _____   _____

dog
_____   _____   _____   _____   _____

bird
_____   _____   _____   _____   _____

Animal Names: Sentences

A **sentence** tells about something.

Directions: These sentences tell about animals. Write the word that completes each sentence.

Example:

My   frog   jumps high.

1. I take my   _ _ _ _ _ _ _ _ _ _ _ _ _ _ _ _   for a walk.

2. My   _ _ _ _ _ _ _ _ _ _ _ _ _ _ _ _   lives in water.

3. My   _ _ _ _ _ _ _ _ _ _ _ _ _ _ _ _   can sing.

4. My   _ _ _ _ _ _ _ _ _ _ _ _ _ _ _ _   has a long tail.

Name: _____

Animal Names: Sentences

Directions: Finish writing the name of each animal on the line. Draw a line from the first part of the sentence to the part which completes it. Put a period at the end of each sentence.

Example:

A green frog jumps in the water [.]

1. Ken's c _____ barks a lot ☐

2. My friend's d _____ climbs trees ☐

3. Pat's f _____ sits on his finger ☐

4. My little b _____ swims in the water ☐

Grade 1 - Comprehensive Curriculum

Name: _____

Review

Directions: Use the words in the pictures to write a sentence about each animal. Put a period at the end of each sentence.

Example: The 🐸 eats bugs.

The frog eats bugs.

The 🐱 drinks milk

- -

The 🐦 eats seeds

- -

The 🐭 jumps out

- -

The 🐟🐟 meet

- -

Name: _____

Things That Go

Directions: Trace the letters to write the name of each thing. Write each name again by yourself. Then color the pictures.

Example:

car   car

truck

train

bike

plane

Things That Go

Directions: Fill in the missing letters for each word.

Example:

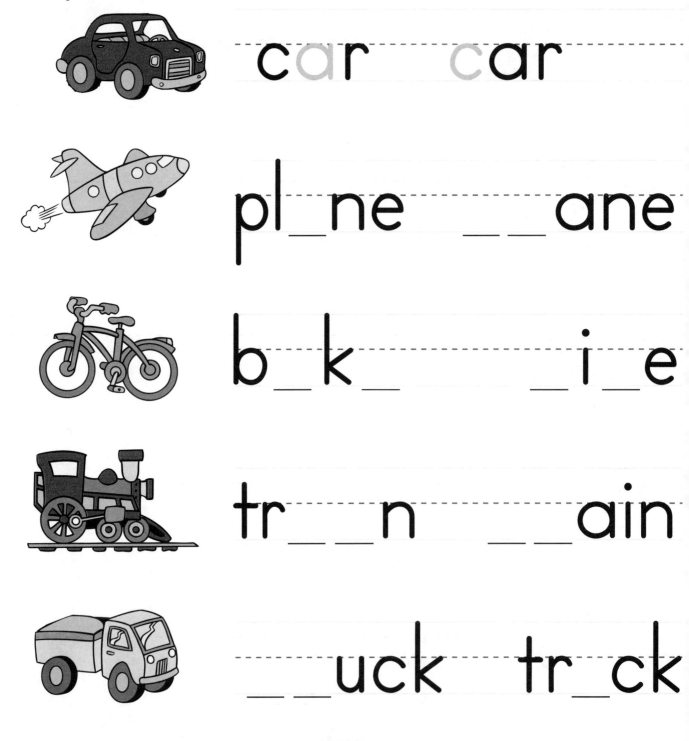

car   car

pl_ne   __ane

b_k_   _i_e

tr__n   __ain

__uck   tr_ck

Name: _____

Things That Go

Directions: The letters in the name of each thing are mixed up. Unscramble the letters and write each word correctly below.

Example:

r a c   **car**

a i t r n

e p l n a

k i b e

c k u t r

Grade 1 - Comprehensive Curriculum

Things That Go: Beginning Sounds

Directions: Say the name of each thing. Write the beginning sound under its name. Find two pictures in each row that begin with the same sound as the first picture. Write the same first letter under them.

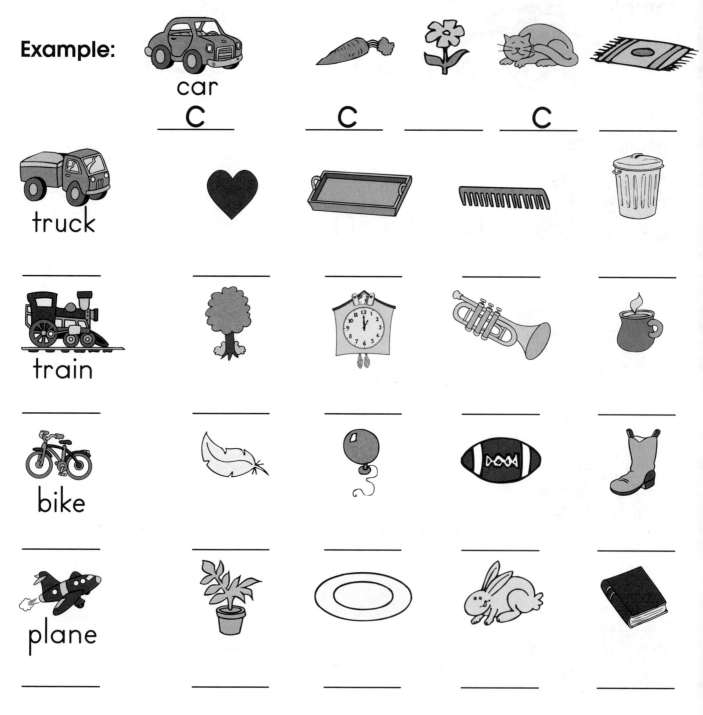

Example:

car
_C_   _C_   _____   _C_   _____

truck
_____   _____   _____   _____   _____

train
_____   _____   _____   _____   _____

bike
_____   _____   _____   _____   _____

plane
_____   _____   _____   _____   _____

Name: _____

Things That Go: Sentences

Directions: These sentences tell about things that go. Write the word that completes each sentence.

Example:

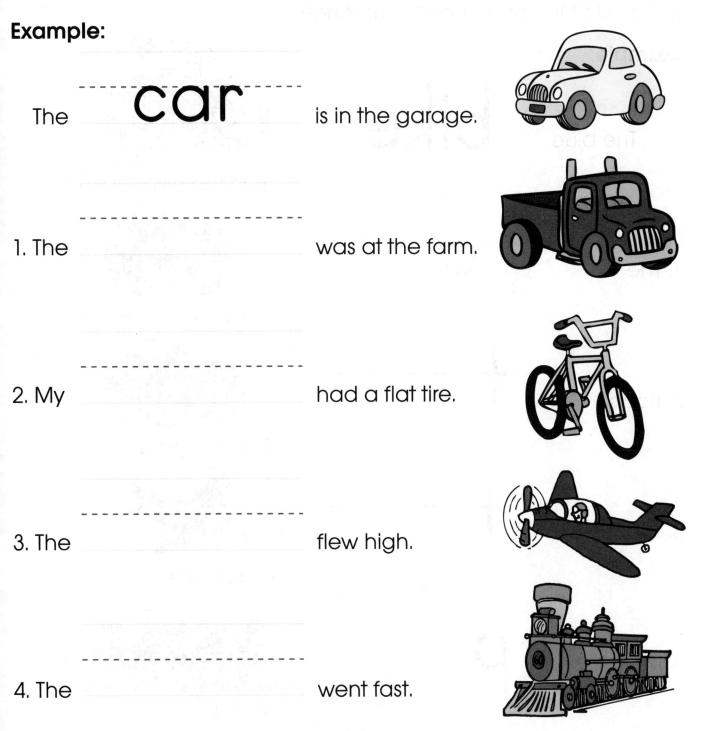

The __car__ is in the garage.

1. The _____ was at the farm.

2. My _____ had a flat tire.

3. The _____ flew high.

4. The _____ went fast.

Grade 1 - Comprehensive Curriculum

Name: _____

Things That Go: Sentences

Directions: Finish writing the names of the things that go. Draw a line from the first part of the sentence to the part which completes it. Put a period at the end of each sentence.

Example:

The blue   bike

is in the bike rack ⊡

1. The   c

climbed up the hill ☐

2. Bob's   t

is in the garage ☐

3. The   t

was in the field ☐

4. My dad's   p

is full ☐

Name: _____

Things That Go: Sentences

Directions: Draw a line from the first part of each sentence to the part which completes it. Put a period at the end of each sentence.

Example:

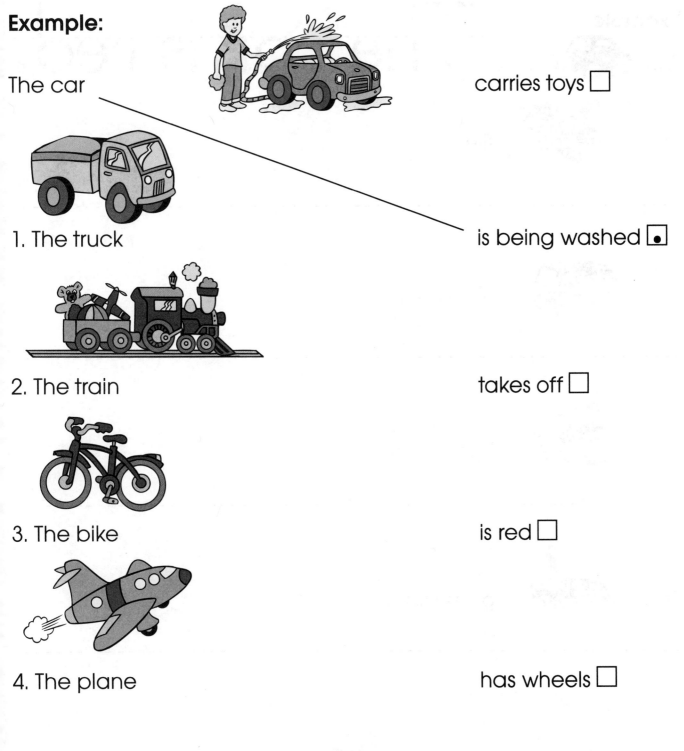

The car   carries toys ☐

1. The truck   is being washed ☒

2. The train   takes off ☐

3. The bike   is red ☐

4. The plane   has wheels ☐

Grade 1 - Comprehensive Curriculum

Name: _____

Review

Directions: Use the words in the pictures to write a sentence about each thing that goes. Put a period at the end of each sentence.

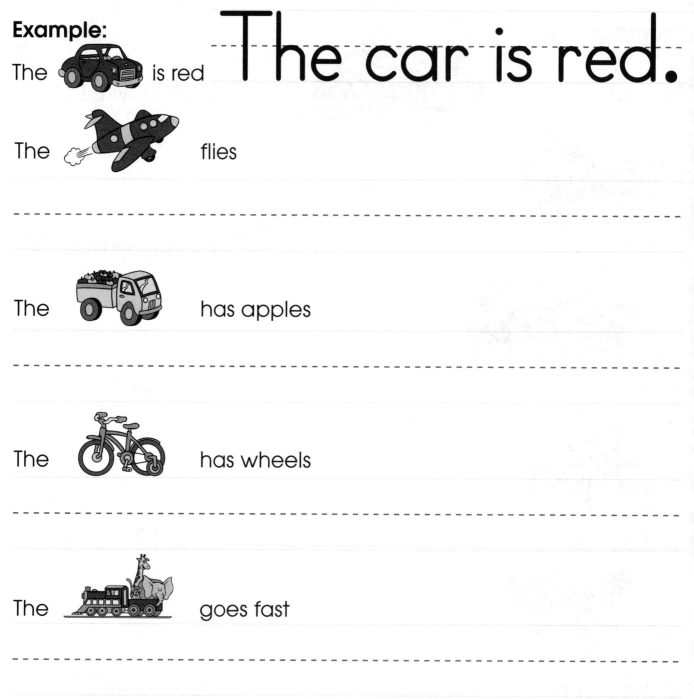

Example:

The is red

The car is red.

The [airplane] flies

_____

The [truck] has apples

_____

The [bicycle] has wheels

_____

The [train] goes fast

_____

Name: _____

Clothing Words

Directions: Trace the letters to write the name of each clothing word. Then write each name again by yourself.

Example:

shirt   shirt

pants

jacket

socks

shoes

dress

hat

Grade 1 - Comprehensive Curriculum

Clothing Words: Beginning Sounds

Directions: Circle the words that begin with the same sound.

shirt

pants

hat

Name: _____

Clothing Words: Sentences

Directions: Some of these sentences tell a whole idea. Others have something missing. If something is missing, draw a line to the word that completes the sentence. Put a period at the end of each sentence.

Example:

She is wearing a polka-dot

holes

1. The baseball player wore a

2. His pants were torn.

dress .

3. The socks had

4. The jacket had blue buttons.

hat

5. The shoes were brown.

Grade 1 - Comprehensive Curriculum

Clothing Words: Sentences

Directions: The words by each picture are mixed up. Write them to make a sentence that tells about the picture. Begin each sentence with a capital letter and end it with a period.

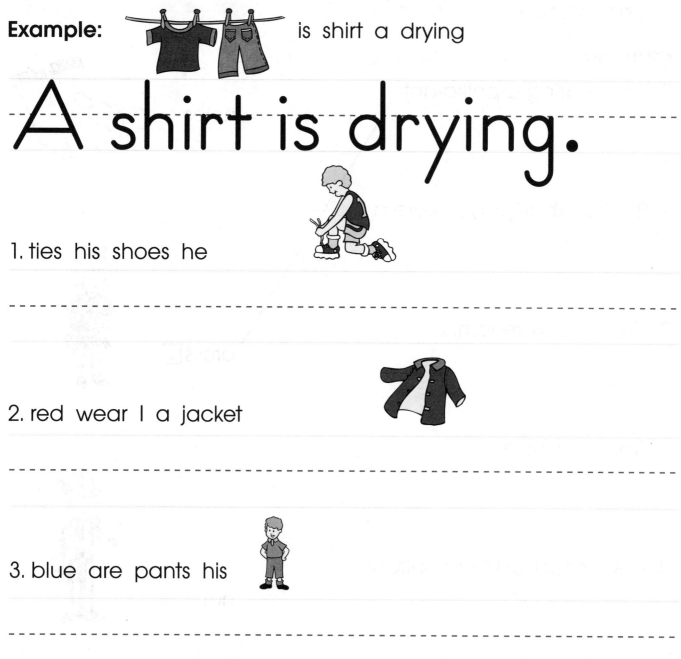

Example: is shirt a drying

A shirt is drying.

1. ties his shoes he

----

2. red wear I a jacket

----

3. blue are pants his

Name: _____

Clothing Words: Sentences

Directions: Use the clothing words to complete these sentences. Then put a period at the end.

Example:

Mike is wearing a **hat.**

1. Put on your socks before your _____ ☐

2. When it's cold, wear a _____ ☐

3. The little girl liked to wear a pink _____ ☐

4. He wore jeans with the _____ ☐

5. The man wore a suit coat and _____ ☐

6. The clown wore long, striped _____ ☐

Name: _____

Review

Directions: Write three sentences that tell about this picture. Begin each sentence with a capital letter and end it with a period.

1. _____

_____

2. _____

_____

3. _____

Name: _____

Food Names

Directions: Trace the letters to write the name of each food word. Write each name again by yourself. Then color the pictures.

Example:

bread **bread**

cookie

apple

cake

milk

egg

Grade 1 - Comprehensive Curriculum

Food Names: Beginning Sounds

Directions: Write the food names that answer the questions.

| egg   milk   ice cream   apple   cookie   cake |

1. Which food words start with the same sounds as the pictures?

_ _ _ _ _ _ _ _ _ _ _ _ _ _ _ _   _ _ _ _ _ _ _ _ _ _ _ _ _ _ _ _

_ _ _ _ _ _ _ _ _ _ _ _ _ _ _ _

2. Which food word ends with the same sound as the picture?

_ _

3. Which food words have two letters together that are the same?

_ _ _ _ _ _ _ _ _ _ _ _   _ _ _ _ _ _ _ _ _ _ _ _   _ _ _ _ _ _ _ _ _ _ _ _

Food Names: Asking Sentences

An **asking sentence** asks a question. Asking sentences end with a question mark.

Directions: Write each sentence on the line. Begin each sentence with a capital letter. Put a period at the end of the telling sentences and a question mark at the end of the asking sentences.

Example: do you like cake

Do you like cake?

1. the cow has spots

_____

2. is that cookie good

_____

3. she ate the apple

_____

Name: _____

Food Names: Asking Sentences

Directions: Change each telling sentence into an asking sentence by moving the words. Put a question mark at the end of each question.

Example: The girl is eating.

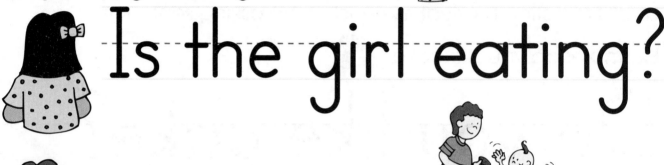

Is the girl eating?

1. He is sharing.

_____

2. He is drinking.

_____

3. She is baking.

_____

Name: _____

Food Names: Asking Sentences

Directions: Use the food names to answer each question.

1. Which one can you drink?

_____

2. Which one do you have to keep very cold?

_____

3. Which one grows on trees?

_____

4. Which one do you put birthday candles on?

_____

5. Which one do people sometimes eat in the morning?

_____

6. Which one do you like best?

_____

Grade 1 - Comprehensive Curriculum

Food Names: Sentences

Directions: In each sentence, write a word in the first blank to tell who is doing something. Write one of the food names in the second blank. Then draw a picture to go with each sentence.

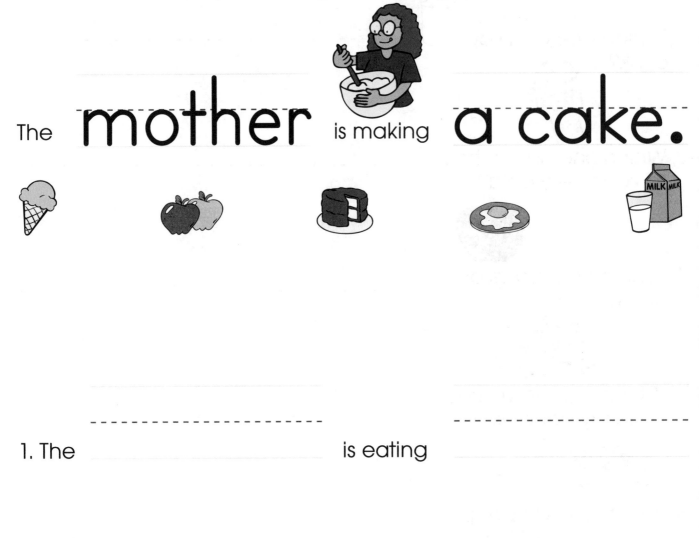

The **mother** is making **a cake.**

1. The _____ is eating _____

2. The _____ is buying _____

Name: _____

Food Names: Completing a Story

Directions: Write the food names in the story.

Kim got up in the morning.

"Do you want an _____ 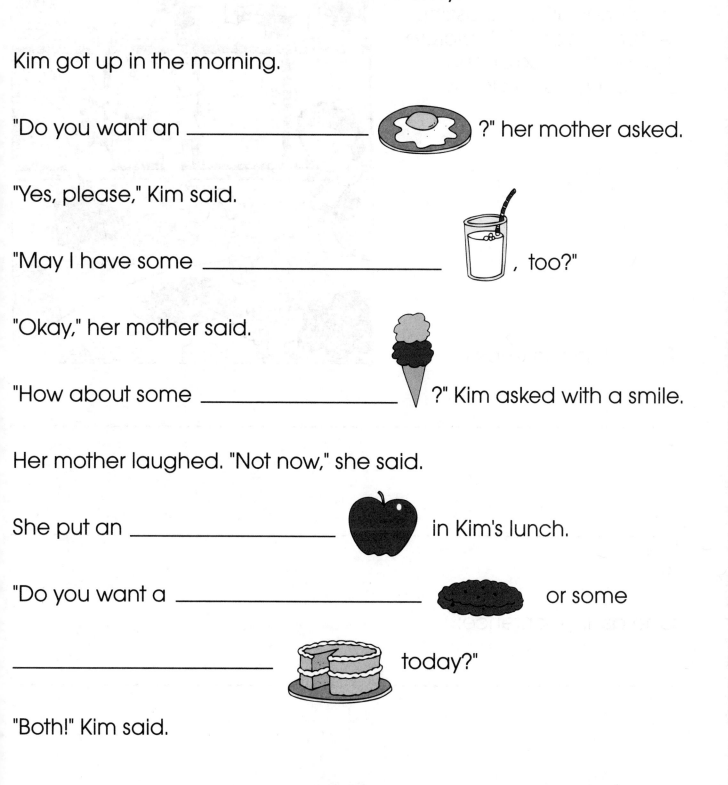 ?" her mother asked.

"Yes, please," Kim said.

"May I have some _____ , too?"

"Okay," her mother said.

"How about some _____ ?" Kim asked with a smile.

Her mother laughed. "Not now," she said.

She put an _____ in Kim's lunch.

"Do you want a _____ or some

_____ today?"

"Both!" Kim said.

Name: _____

Review

Directions: Write two telling sentences and one asking sentence about this picture. Use the food, color and animal words you know.

Two telling sentences:

1. --

2. --

One asking sentence:

Number Words

Directions: Trace the letters to write the name of each number. Write the numbers again by yourself. Then color the number pictures.

Example:

1 one   **one**

2 two

3 three

4 four

5 five

6 six

7 seven

8 eight

9 nine

10 ten

Number Words: Asking Sentences

Directions: Write each sentence on the line. Begin each sentence with a capital letter. Put a period at the end of the telling sentences and a question mark at the end of the asking sentences.

Example: may I eat two cookies

May I eat two cookies?

1. I see five flowers

- -

2. is one cat yellow

- -

3. are there six eggs

- -

Number Words: Asking Sentences

Directions: Use a number word to answer each question.

one	five	seven	three	eight

1. How many trees are there?

- -

2. How many flowers are there?

- -

3. How many presents are there?

- -

4. How many clocks are there?

- -

5. How many forks are there?

- -

Number Words: Asking Sentences

Directions: Use the number words to answer each question.

1. How many eyes do you have?

---

2. How many mouths do you have?

3. How many fingers do you have?

4. How many wheels are on a car?

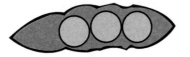

5. How many peas are in the pod?

---

6. How many cups do you see?

Number Words: Asking Sentences

Directions: Change each telling sentence into an asking sentence by moving the words. Put a question mark at the end of each question.

Example: He ate one cookie.

Is he eating one cookie?

1. She has two dogs.

- -

2. Three balls can bounce.

- -

3. One balloon is red.

- -

Review

Directions: Write two telling sentences and one asking sentence about this picture. Use the number words you know.

Two telling sentences:

1. _____

2. _____

One asking sentence:

_____

Name: _____

Action Words

Action words tell things we can do.

Directions: Trace the letters to write each action word. Then write the action word again by yourself.

Example:

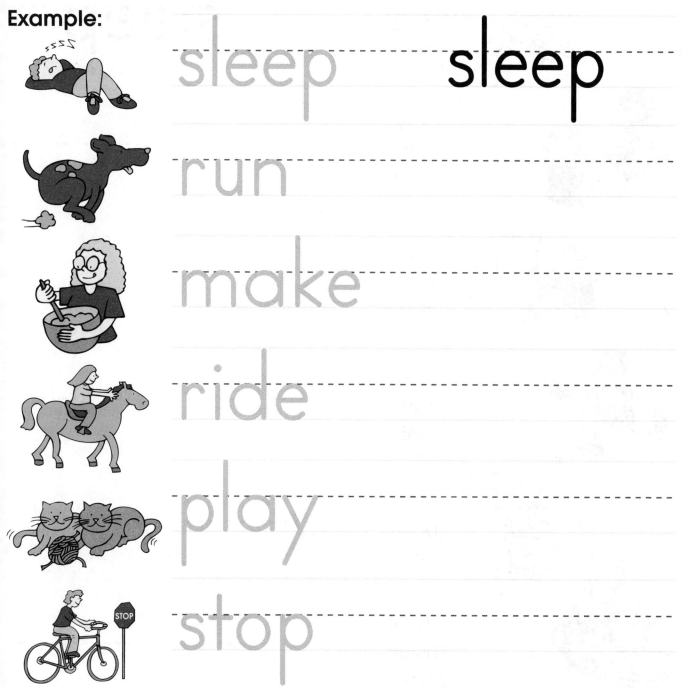

sleep   sleep

run

make

ride

play

stop

Grade 1 - Comprehensive Curriculum

Action Words

Directions: Circle the word that is spelled correctly. Then write the correct spelling in the blank.

Example:

seep
(sleep)
slep

sleep

paly
pay
play

seee
cee
see

rum
run
runn

jump
jumb
junp

mack
maek
make

Name: _____

Action Words

Directions: Read each sentence and write the correct words in the blanks.

Example:

go
sleep   I will ____go____ to bed and ____sleep____ all night.

1.
see
jump   The girls _____ the frogs _____.

2.
sit
run   After the boys _____, they _____ and rest.

3.
stop
play   They _____ at the park so they can _____.

4.
ride
make   They will _____ a car to _____ in.

Name: _____

Action Words: Beginning and Ending Sounds

Directions: Write the action words that answer the questions.

sit	run	make	see	jump	stop	play	ride

1. Which words begin with the same sound as 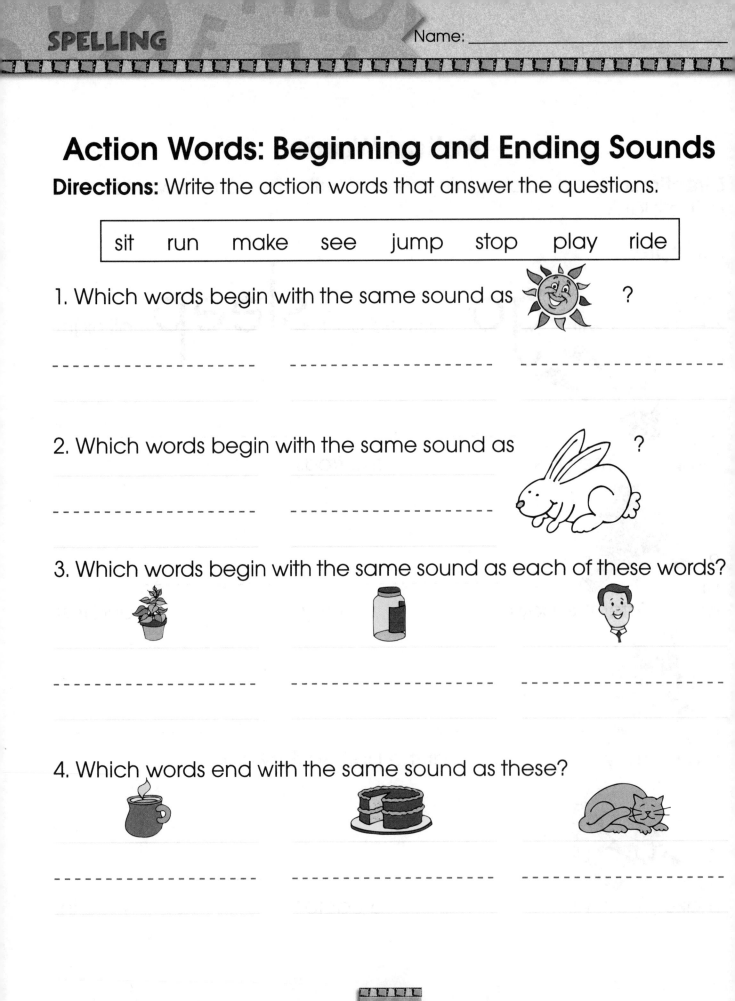 ?

------------------   ------------------   ------------------

2. Which words begin with the same sound as   ?

------------------   ------------------

3. Which words begin with the same sound as each of these words?

------------------   ------------------   ------------------

4. Which words end with the same sound as these?

------------------   ------------------   ------------------

Action Words: More Than One

To show more than one of something, add **s** to the end of the word.

Example: one cat two cats

Directions: In each sentence, add **s** to show more than one. Then write the action word that completes each sentence.

sit	jump	stop	ride

Example:

The frog **s** **sleep** in the sun.

1. The boy _____ _____ on the fence.

2. The car _____ _____ at the sign.

3. The girl _____ _____ in the water.

4. The dog _____ _____ in the wagon.

Action Words: Asking Sentences

Directions: Write an asking sentence about each picture. Begin each sentence with **can**. Add an action word. Begin each asking sentence with a capital letter and end it with a question mark.

Example:

I with you can

Can I sit with you?

she can

_____

with you can I

_____

can she fast

_____

Name: _____

Review

Directions: Write three telling sentences and one asking sentence about this picture. Put an action word in each sentence.

Three telling sentences:

1. _____

_____

2. _____

_____

3. _____

One asking sentence:

_____

Name: _____

Sense Words

Directions: Circle the word that is spelled correctly. Then write the correct spelling in the blank.

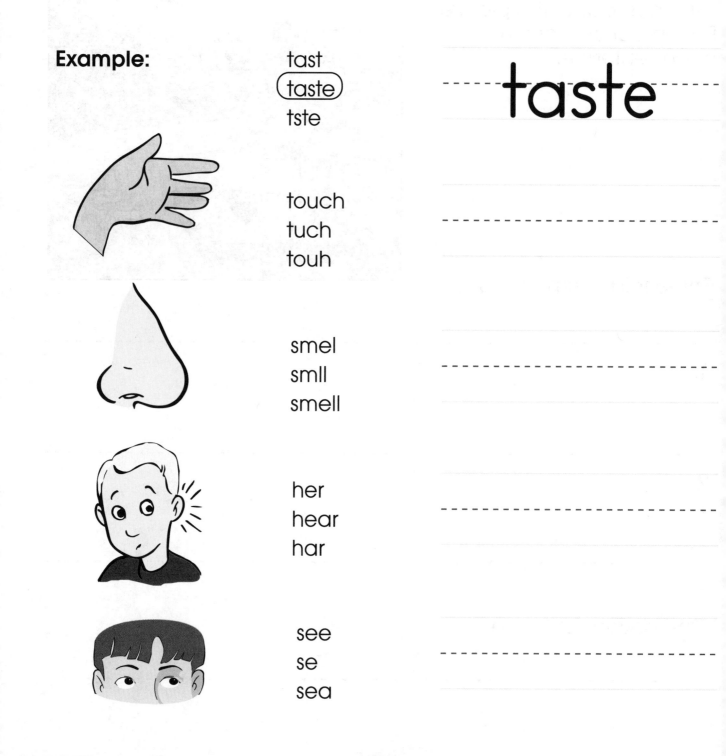

Example:

tast

(taste)

tste

taste

touch
tuch
touh

smel
smll
smell

her
hear
har

see
se
sea

Sense Words: Sentences

Directions: Read each sentence and write the correct words in the blanks.

Example:

taste
mouth
I can **taste** things with my **mouth**.

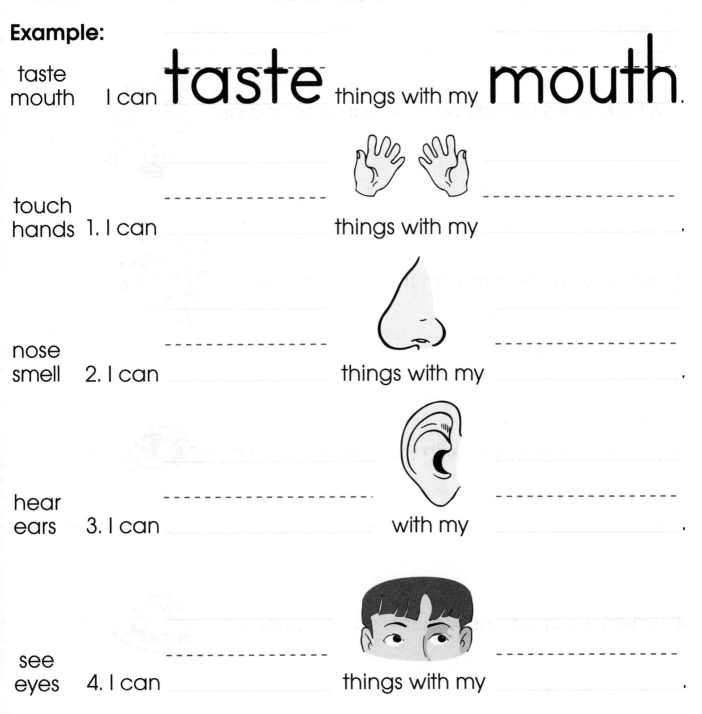

touch
hands
1. I can _____ things with my _____ .

nose
smell
2. I can _____ things with my _____ .

hear
ears
3. I can _____ with my _____ .

see
eyes
4. I can _____ things with my _____ .

Name: _____

Sense Words: Beginning Sounds

Directions: Use the sense words in the box to answer each question.

smell	see	taste	hear	touch

1. Which word begins with the same sound as [image] ?

- -

2. Which word begins with the same sound as [image] ?

- -

3. Which words begin with the same sound as [image] ?

-          -

4. Which word begins with the same sound as [image] ?

- -

Sense Words: More Than One

Directions: In each sentence, add **s** to show more than one. Then write the sense word that completes each sentence.

Example: The dog **s**   taste   the food.

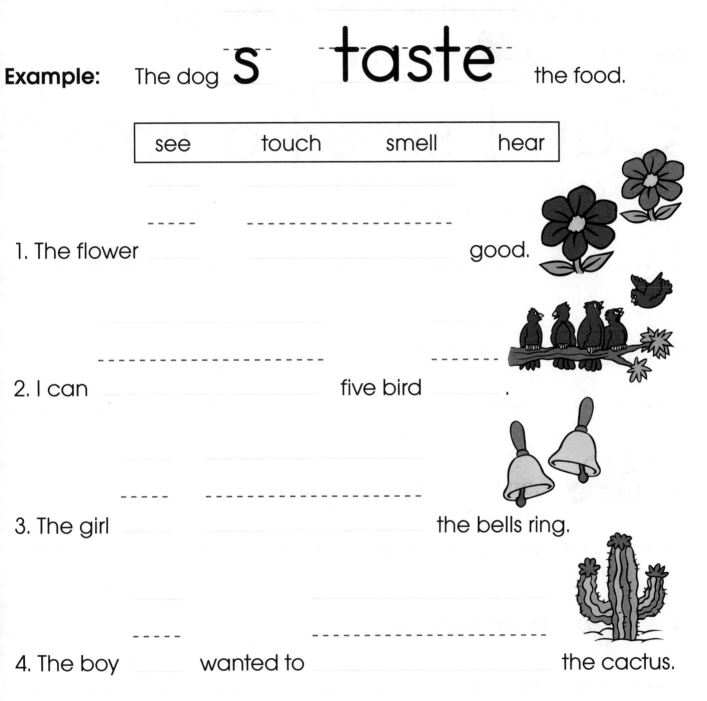

see	touch	smell	hear

1. The flower _____ _____ good.

2. I can _____ five bird _____ .

3. The girl _____ _____ the bells ring.

4. The boy _____ wanted to _____ the cactus.

Sense Words: Asking Sentences

Directions: Write an asking sentence about each picture. Begin each sentence with **can**. Add a sense word. Begin each asking sentence with a capital letter and end it with a question mark.

Example: 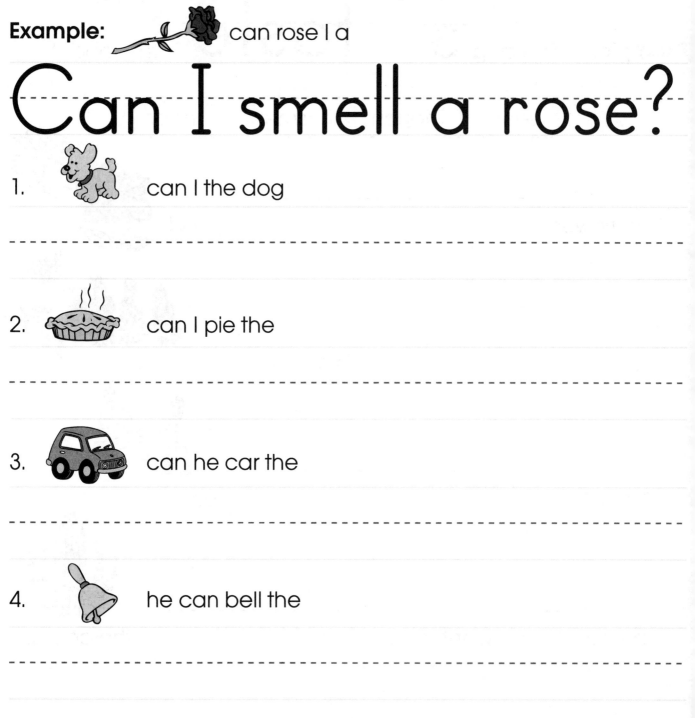 can rose I a

Can I smell a rose?

1. can I the dog

_ _

2. can I pie the

_ _

3. can he car the

_ _

4. he can bell the

_ _

Name: _____

Review

Directions: Write three telling sentences and one asking sentence about this picture. Use a sense word in each sentence.

Three telling sentences:

1. _____

2. _____

3. _____

One asking sentence:

_____

Name: _____

Weather Words: Beginning Sounds

Directions: Say the sound of the letter at the beginning of each row. Find the pictures in each row that begin with the same letter. Write the letter under the pictures.

Example:

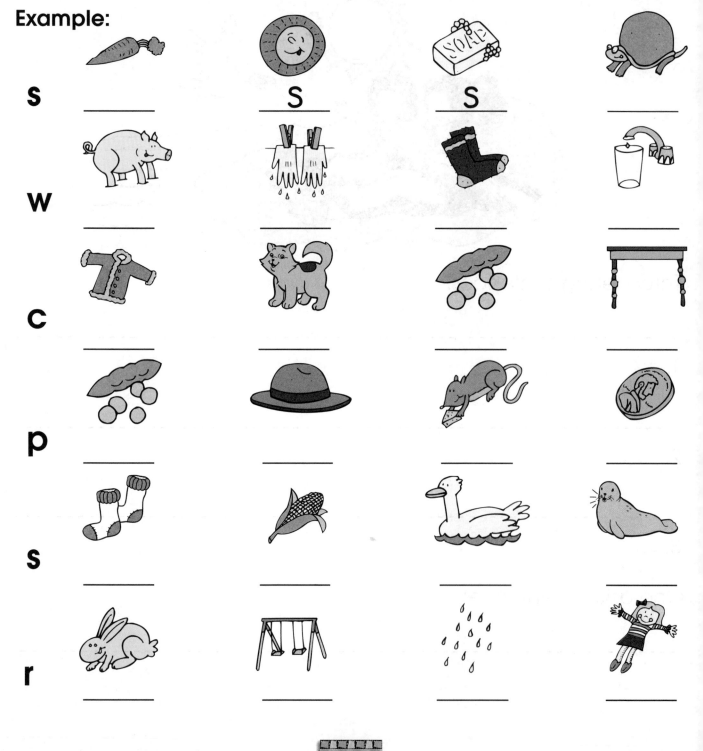

s   ____   S   S   ____

w

c

p

s

r

Name: _____

Weather Words: Sentences

Directions: Write the weather word that completes each sentence. Put a period at the end of the telling sentences and a question mark at the end of the asking sentences.

Example:

Do flowers grow in the _____ sun _____ ?

| rain | water | wet | hot |

1. The sun makes me _____ ☐

2. When it rains, the grass gets _____ ☐

3. Do you think it will _____ on our picnic ☐

4. Should you drink the _____ from the rain ☐

Weather Words: Sentences

Directions: Read the sentence parts below. Draw a line from the first part of the sentence to the second part that completes it.

Example: When I'm cold,——— I put on my coat.

I take off my shoes.

1. When it rains,

we ride our bikes to the park.

we play games inside.

2. I like snow

because I can eat lunch.

because I can make a snowman.

3. When the sun comes out,

the grass grows fast.

the grass gets wet.

4. At night, the rain

makes ice on my windows.

helps me go to sleep.

Name: _____

Weather Words: Completing a Story

Directions: Write the missing words to complete the story. The first letter of each word is written for you.

"Please may I go outside?" I asked.

"It's too C_____ ," my father told

me. "Maybe later the sun will come

out." Later, the sun did come out. Then it began to r_____

again. "May I go out now?" I asked again. Dad looked out the

window. "You will get W_____ ," he said. "But I want to

see if the r_____ helped our flowers grow," I said. "You

mean you want to play in the W_____ ," Dad said with

a smile. How did Dad know that?

Weather Words: Sentences

Directions: Read the two sentences on each line and draw a line between them. Then write each sentence again on the lines below. Begin each sentence with a capital letter and end each one with a period or a question mark.

Example: will it rain|the sky is dark

Will it rain?
The sky is dark.

1. she fell in the pond she got wet

----

2. do you like my hat it is red

Review

Directions: Write a telling sentence about each of these pictures. Then write an asking sentence about one of the pictures. Use the weather words and other words you know.

Telling sentences:

1.

2.

Asking sentence:

Name: _____

My World

Directions: Fill in the missing letters for each word.

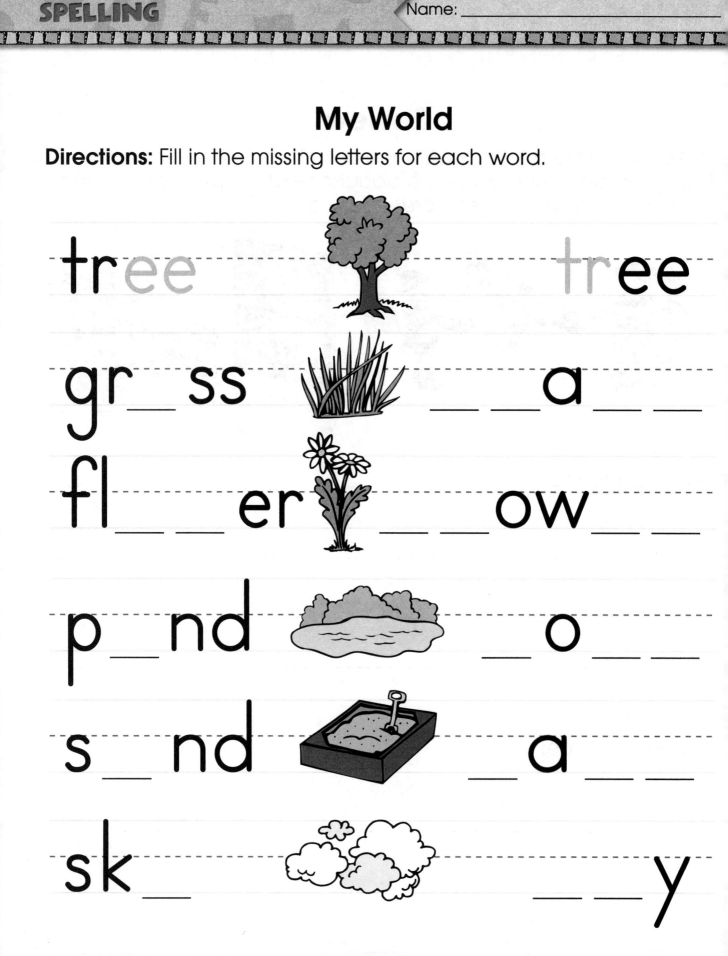

tree   tree

gr_ss   _ _ a _ _

fl_ _ _er   _ _ _ow_ _ _

p_nd   _ o _ _

s_nd   _ a _ _ _

sk_ _   _ _ y

Name: _____

My World

Directions: The letters in the words below are mixed up. Unscramble the letters and write each word correctly.

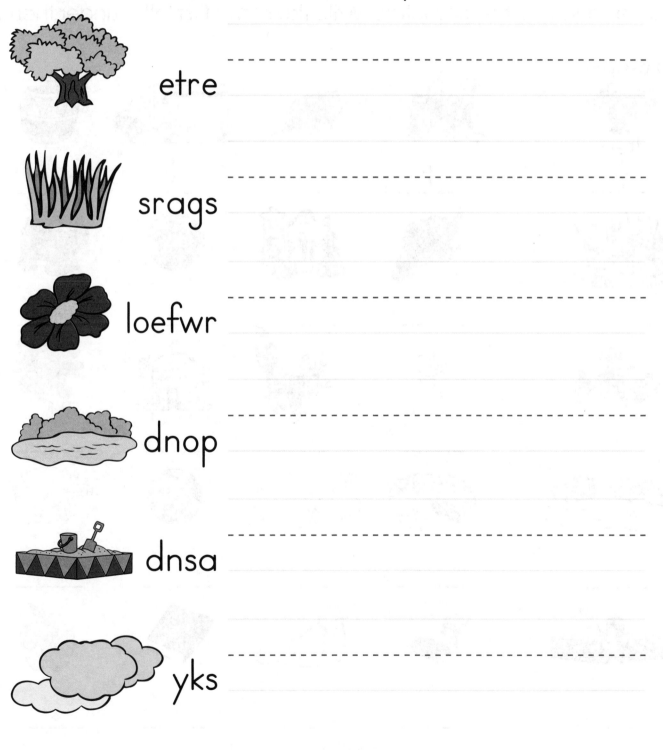

etre

----

srags

----

loefwr

----

dnop

----

dnsa

----

yks

Grade 1 - Comprehensive Curriculum

My World: Beginning Sounds

Directions: Say the name of each picture. Write the beginning sound under its name. Find two pictures in each row that begin with the same sound as the first picture. Write the same first letter under them.

Example:

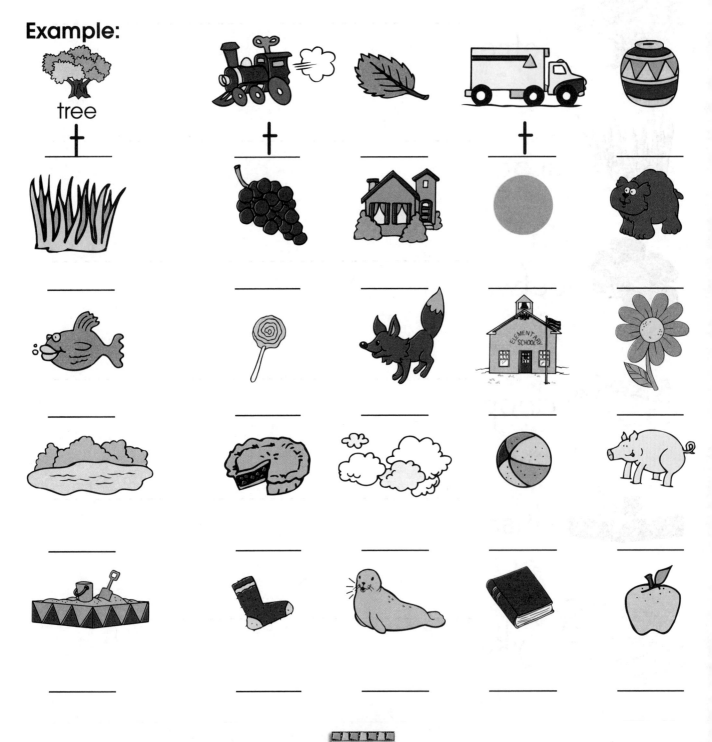

tree
†

†

†

Name: _____

My World: Sentences

Directions: Write the word that completes each sentence. Put a period at the end of the telling sentences and a question mark at the end of the asking sentences.

Example: Does the sun shine on the flowers ?

tree	grass	pond	sand	sky

1. The _____ was full of dark clouds☐

2. Can you climb the _____ ☐

3. Did you see the duck in the _____ ☐

4. Is the child playing in the _____ ☐

5. The _____ in the yard was tall☐

Name: _____

My World: Sentences

Directions: Read the two sentences on each line and draw a line between them. Then write each sentence again on the lines below. Begin each sentence with a capital letter, and end each one with a period or a question mark.

Example: the tree has leaves|can we rake some

The tree has leaves.
Can we rake some?

1. the lake is fun we swim in it

_____

_____

_____

2. the sky is so blue isn't it pretty

_____

_____

_____

Review

Directions: Write three telling sentences about the picture. Then write an asking sentence about the picture. Use the words that tell about your world and other words you know.

Telling sentences:

1. _____

2. _____

3. _____

Asking sentence:

_____

Name: _____

The Parts of My Body: Sentences

Directions: Write the word that completes each sentence. Put a period at the end of the telling sentences and a question mark at the end of the asking sentences.

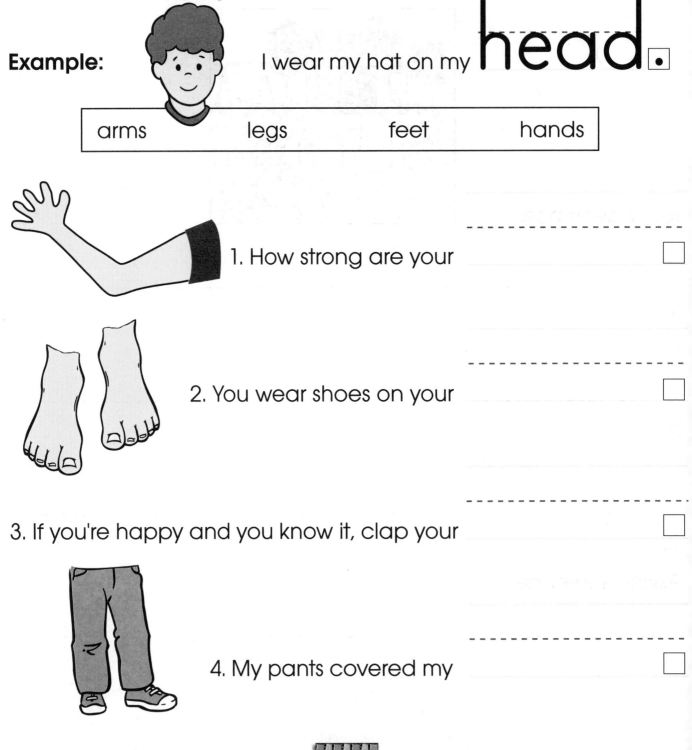

Example: I wear my hat on my **head** ∎

| arms | legs | feet | hands |

1. How strong are your

2. You wear shoes on your

3. If you're happy and you know it, clap your

4. My pants covered my

The Parts of My Body: Beginning Sounds

Directions: Say the sound of the letter at the beginning of each row. Find the pictures in each row that begin with the same letter. Write the letter under the pictures.

Example:

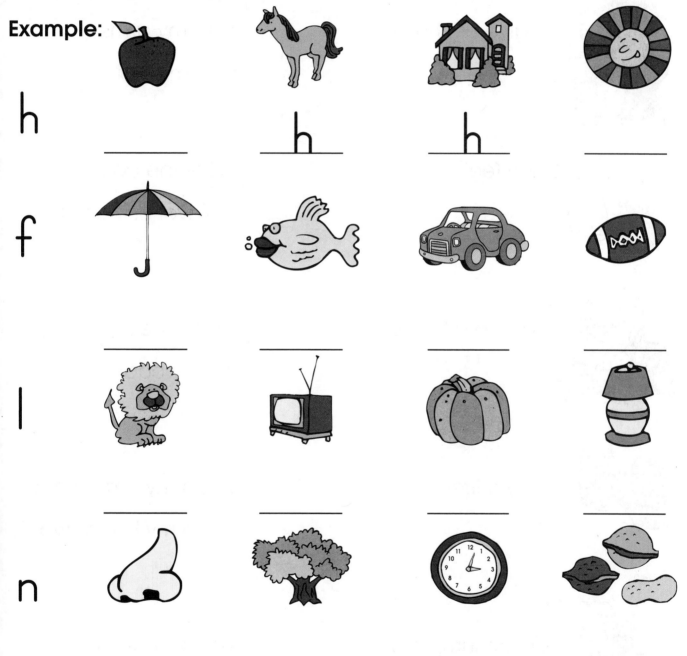

h   _____   h   h   _____

f

l

n

Name: _____

The Parts of My Body: Sentences

Directions: Read the sentence parts below. Draw a line from the first part of the sentence to the second part that completes it.

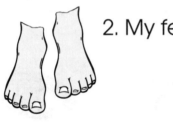

1. I give big hugs

with my arms.

with my car.

2. My feet

drive the car.

got wet in the rain.

3. I have a bump

on my head.

on my coat.

4. My mittens

keep my arms warm.

keep my hands warm.

5. I can jump high

using my legs.

using a spoon.

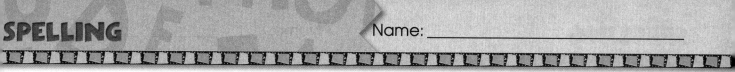
The Parts of My Body: Sentences

Directions: Read the two sentences on each line and draw a line between them. Then write each sentence again on the lines below. Begin each sentence with a capital letter, and end each one with a period or a question mark.

Example: wash your hands|they are dirty

Wash your hands.
They are dirty.

1. you have big arms are you very strong

----

2. I have two feet I can run fast

Name: _____

Review

Directions: Write a telling sentence about each of these pictures. Then write an asking sentence about one of the pictures. Use the words that name the parts of your body and other words you know.

Telling sentences:

1. _____

_____

2. _____

Asking sentence:

_____

Opposite Words

Some words are opposites. **Opposites** are things that are different in every way. **Dark** and **light** are opposites.

Directions: Trace the letters to write each word. Then write the word again by yourself.

Example:

new   new

old

big

little

lost

found

Name: _____

Opposite Words

Directions: Circle one word in each sentence that is not spelled correctly. Then write the word correctly.

dark	found	old	first	lost

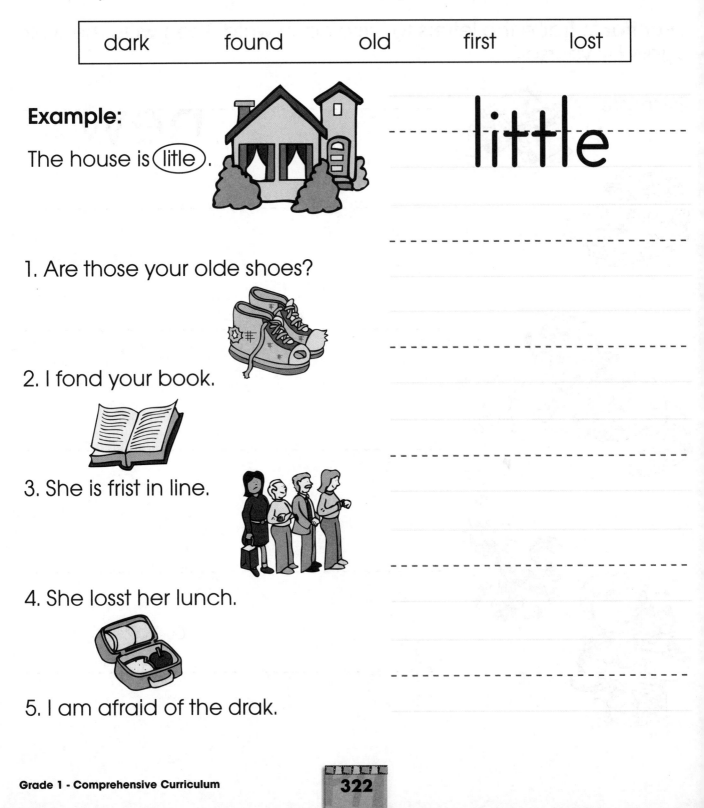

Example:

The house is (litle).

little

1. Are those your olde shoes?

2. I fond your book.

3. She is frist in line.

4. She losst her lunch.

5. I am afraid of the drak.

Name: _____

Opposite Words: Beginning and Ending Sounds

Directions: Write the opposite words that answer the questions.

dark	found	old	light	new	first	lost	last

1. Which words begin with the same sound as [ladder] ?

- -

2. Which words begin with the same sound as [feather] ?

- -

3. Which words begin with the same sound as each of these words?

[deer] - **9** -

4. Which two words end with the same sound as [roadrunner] ?

- -

Grade 1 - Comprehensive Curriculum

Opposite Words: Sentences

Directions: Read the sentence by the first picture. Then look at the next picture. Write a sentence that tells about it.

Example: The dog is little.

The dog is big.

found	new	first	lost	old	last

1. His book is lost.

- -

2. The dog eats first.

- -

3. I like my old shirt.

- -

Name: _____

Opposite Words: Sentences

Directions: Read the sentence about the first picture. Write another sentence about the picture beside it. Use the opposite words.

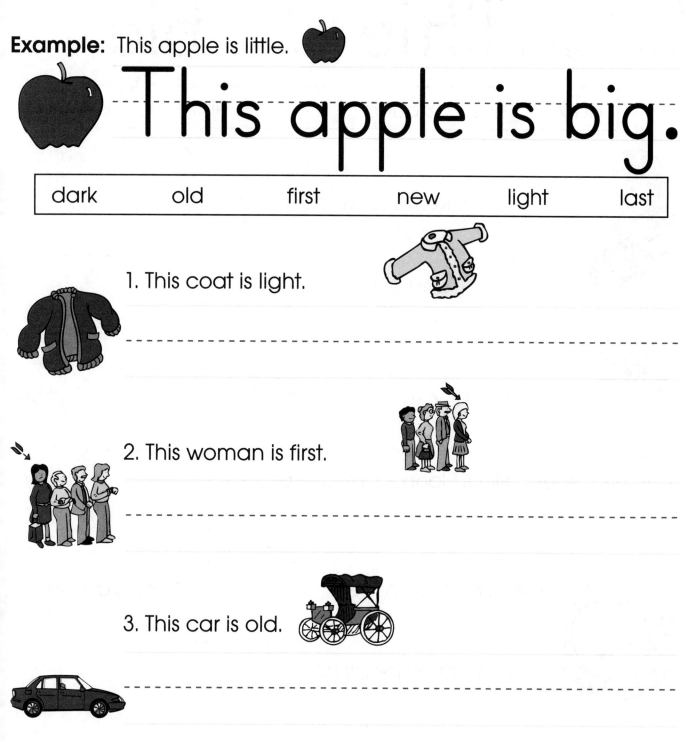

Example: This apple is little.

This apple is big.

| dark | old | first | new | light | last |

1. This coat is light.

_____

2. This woman is first.

_____

3. This car is old.

_____

Grade 1 - Comprehensive Curriculum

Name: _____

Opposite Words: Sentences

Directions: Write opposite words to complete these sentences.

Example:

The rain made my **little** flower grow **big** .

dark	first	found	last	light	lost

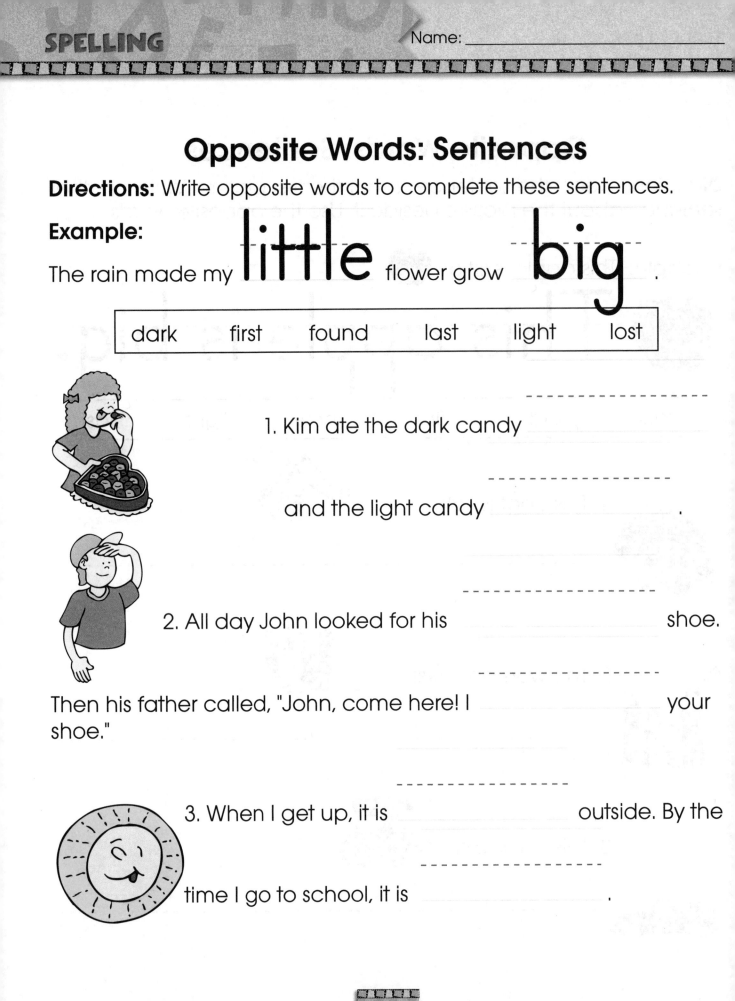

1. Kim ate the dark candy _____

and the light candy _____ .

2. All day John looked for his _____ shoe.

Then his father called, "John, come here! I _____ your shoe."

3. When I get up, it is _____ outside. By the

time I go to school, it is _____ .

Review

Directions: Look at the pictures in each row. Write one sentence about the last picture in each row. Begin each sentence with a capital letter and end it with a period.

- -

- -

Name: _____

More Action Words

Directions: Fill in the missing letters for each word.

Example:

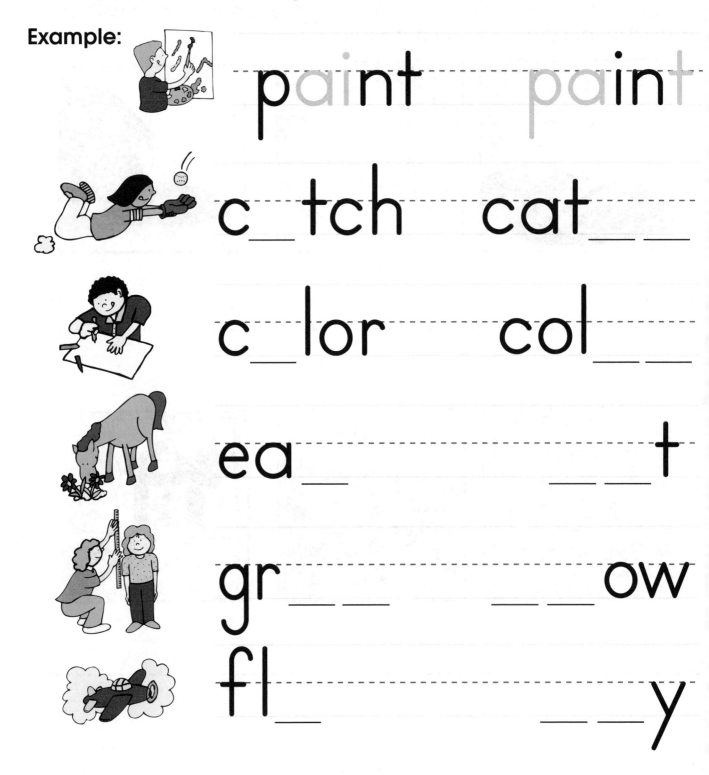

paint   paint

c_tch   cat____

c_lor   col___

ea____   ____t

gr____   ____ow

fl____   ____y

Name: _____

More Action Words:
Beginning and Ending Sounds

Words that **rhyme** have the same ending sound.

Directions: Write the words that answer the questions.

| catch | fly | eat | grow | buy | color |

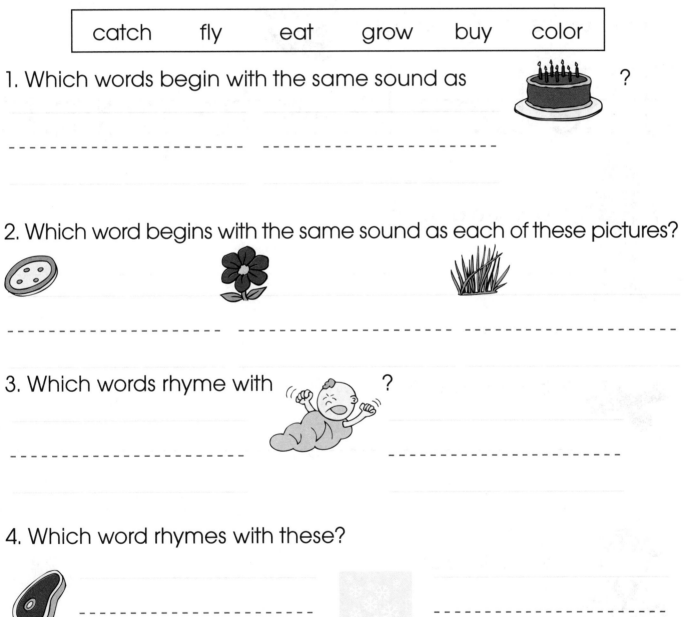

1. Which words begin with the same sound as ?

----------------------   ----------------------

2. Which word begins with the same sound as each of these pictures?

----------------------   ----------------------   ----------------------

3. Which words rhyme with   ?

----------------------   ----------------------

4. Which word rhymes with these?

----------------------   ----------------------

Grade 1 - Comprehensive Curriculum

Name: _____

More Action Words: Sentences

Directions: Write a sentence that tells about the picture. Use the words next to the picture. Remember to begin each sentence with a capital letter and end it with a period.

Example: likes boy to paint the

The boy likes to paint.

1. boy see grow the

----

2. bird the can fly

----

3. she will color

More Action Words: Sentences

Directions: Put the two sentences together to make one new sentence.

Example: The ball is red. The ball is blue.

The ball is red and blue.

1. I eat apples. I eat cookies.

_____

_____

2. We buy milk. We buy eggs.

_____

_____

Grade 1 - Comprehensive Curriculum

Review

Directions: Use the action words you know to write sentences that tell about these pictures. Write a question about the last picture.

Example:

The flowers grow.

- -

- -

Write a question about this picture.

- -

People Words

Directions: Trace the letters to write each word. Then write the word again by yourself.

girl

boy

man

woman

people

children

Grade 1 - Comprehensive Curriculum

People Words

Directions: Write a people word in each sentence to tell who is doing something.

1. The _____ was last in line at the toy store.

2. The _____ took a walk in the woods.

3. The _____ had to help her father.

4. The _____ had a surprise for the children.

5. Some _____ like to eat outside.

6. Something came out of the box when the _____ opened it.

Name: _____

People Words

Sometimes we use other words in place of people names. For **boy** or **man**, we can use the word **he**. For **girl** or **woman**, we can use the word **she**. For two or more people, we can use the word **they**.

Directions: Write the words **he**, **she** or **they** in these sentences.

Example: The boy likes cookies.   <u>He</u>   likes cookies.

1. The girl is running fast.   _____ is running fast.

2. The man reads the paper.   _____ reads the paper.

3. The woman has a cold.   _____ has a cold.

4. Two children came to school.   _____ came to school.

People Words: Sentences

Directions: Write the people word that completes each sentence.

people   man   girl   children   boy   woman

1. The _____ feeds the cat.

2. The _____ are buying dessert.

3. What is the _____ painting?

4. The _____ will grow corn.

5. The dog runs to the _____.

6. There are long lines of _____.

MATH

Number Recognition

Directions: Write the numbers 1-10. Color the bear.

Number Recognition 1, 2, 3, 4, 5

Directions: Use the color codes to color the parrot.

Color:
1's red
2's blue
3's yellow
4's green
5's orange

Grade 1 - Comprehensive Curriculum

Number Recognition 6, 7, 8, 9, 10

Directions: Use the code to color the carousel horse.

Color:
6 's purple
7 's yellow
8 's black
9 's pink
10 's brown

Name: _____

Number Recognition

Directions: Count the number of objects in each group. Draw a line to the correct number.

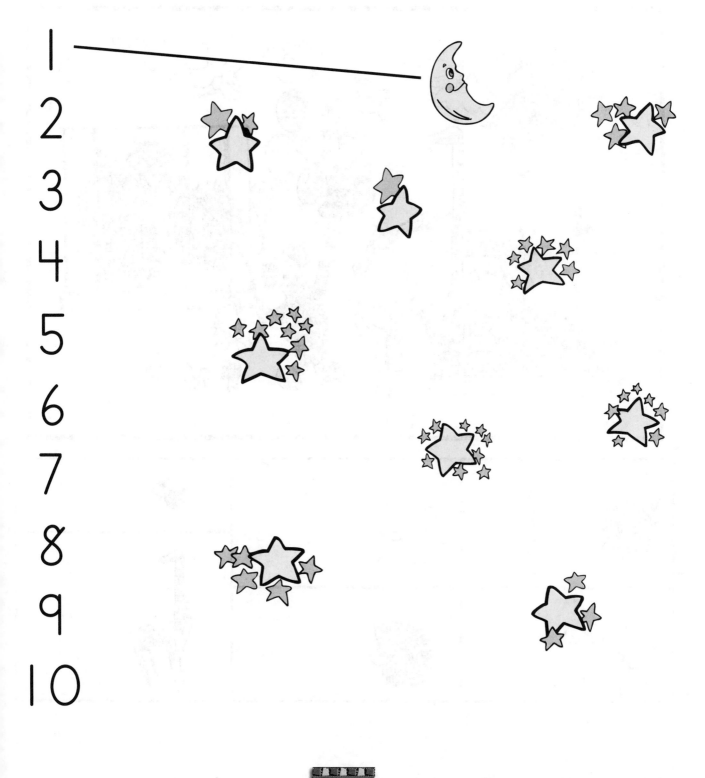

1
2
3
4
5
6
7
8
9
10

Grade 1 - Comprehensive Curriculum

Name: _____

Counting

Directions: How many are there of each shape? Write the answers in the boxes. The first one is done for you.

Name: _____

Counting

Directions: How many are there of each picture? Write the answers in the boxes. The first one is done for you.

Grade 1 - Comprehensive Curriculum

Name: _____

Review

Directions: Count the flowers and write the answers.

Directions: Fill in the missing numbers. Connect the dots to finish the picture.

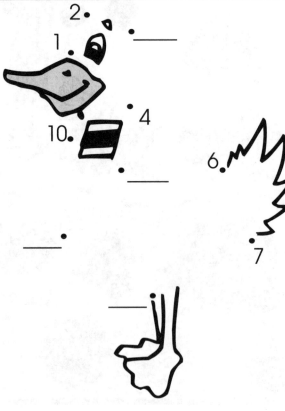

Name: _____

Number Recognition

Directions: Cut out the pieces. Mix them up and match the number with the picture.

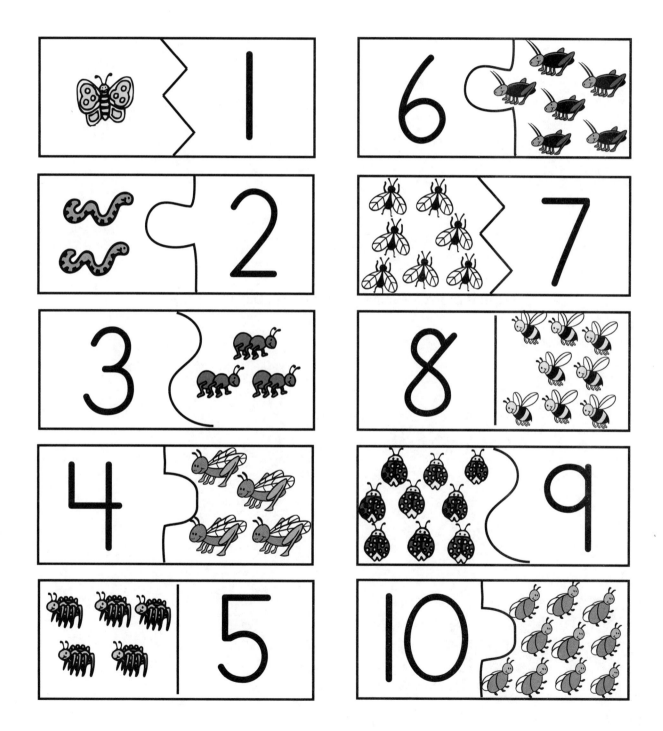

Grade 1 - Comprehensive Curriculum

Page is blank for cutting exercise on previous page.

Number Word Find

Directions: Find the number words 0 through 12 hidden in the box.

```
t  e  a  z  w  z  x  a  b  i  g  t  e  n
o  l  z  r  b  e  r  e  v  e  d  l  a  j
t  w  e  l  v  e  a  b  o  n  e  c  d  z
i  a  r  p  q  d  p  s  u  j  x  e  i  w
c  f  o  p  l  s  c  k  i  q  u  i  i  o
m  s  t  f  v  i  o  e  t  t  f  g  h  d
t  n  u  w  u  x  g  z  w  h  g  h  r  o
n  i  n  e  k  f  d  f  o  u  r  t  j  f
a  s  g  l  q  c  w  k  o  s  n  v  m  i
n  y  c  e  b  o  n  h  h  p  o  m  p  v
b  e  x  v  s  s  e  v  e  n  w  e  n  e
t  h  r  e  e  r  t  a  l  j  k  x  q  z
m  o  a  n  e  n  i  m  u  t  w  a  y  x
```

Words to find:

zero	four	eight	eleven
one	five	nine	twelve
two	six	ten	
three	seven		

Grade 1 - Comprehensive Curriculum

Number Words

Directions: Number the buildings from one to six.

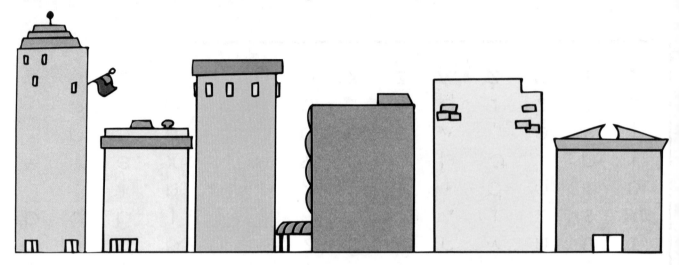

Directions: Draw a line from the word to the number.

two	1
five	3
six	5
four	6
one	2
three	4

Name: _____

Number Words

Directions: Number the buildings from five to ten.

Directions: Draw a line from the word to the number.

nine   8

seven   10

five   7

eight   5

six   9

ten   6

Number Recognition Review

Directions: Match the correct number of objects with the number. Then match the number with the word.

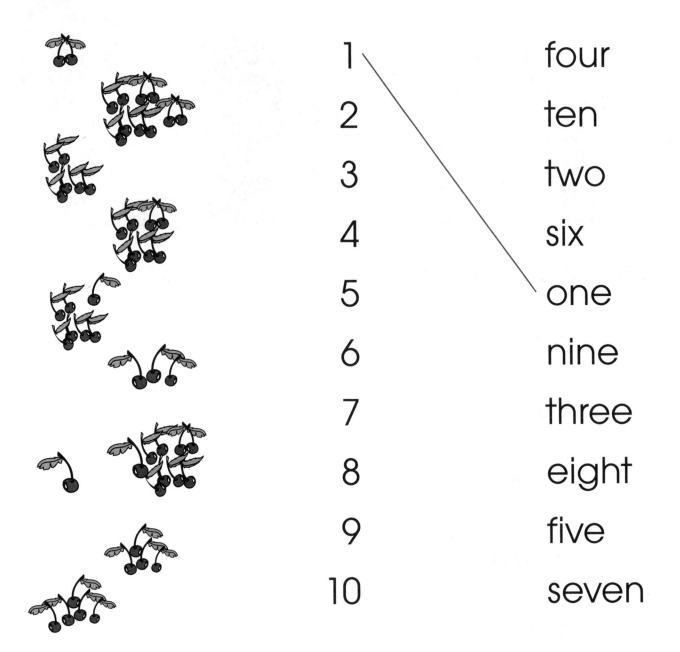

1		four
2		ten
3		two
4		six
5		one
6		nine
7		three
8		eight
9		five
10		seven

Number Match

Directions: Cut out the pictures and number words below. Mix them up and match them again.

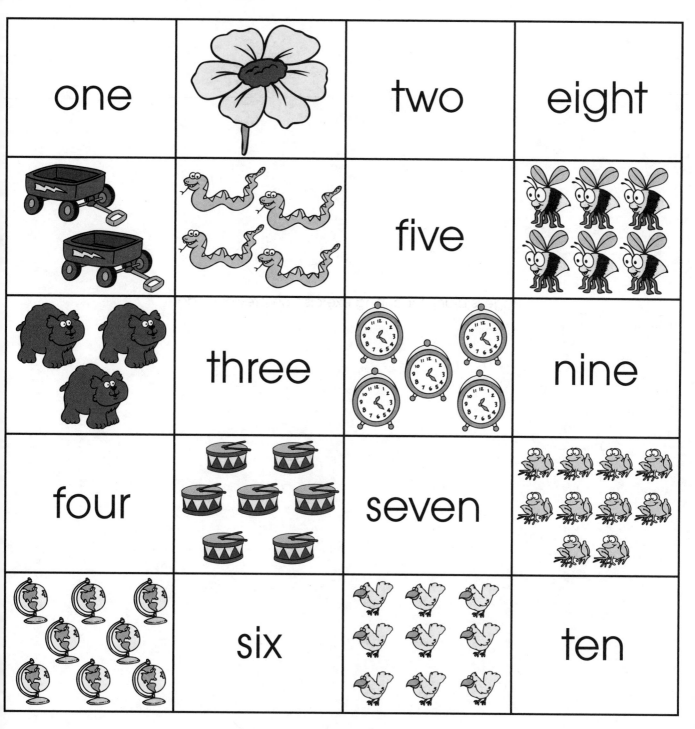

one		two	eight
		five	
	three		nine
four		seven	
	six		ten

Grade 1 - Comprehensive Curriculum

Page is blank for cutting exercise on previous page.

Name: _____

Sequencing Numbers

Sequencing is putting numbers in the correct order.

1, 2, 3, 4, 5, 6, 7, 8, 9, 10

Directions: Write the missing numbers.

Example: 4, ___5___ , 6

3, _____ , 5   7, _____ , 9   8, _____ , 10

6, _____ , 8   _____ , 3 , 4   _____ , 5 , 6

5, 6, _____   _____ , 6 , 7   _____ , 3 , 4

_____ , 4 , 5   _____ , 7 , 8   5, _____ , 7

2, 3, _____   1, 2, _____   7, 8, _____

2, _____ , 4   _____ , 2 , 3   4, _____ , 6

6, 7, _____   3, 4, _____   1, _____ , 3

7, 8, _____   _____ , 3 , 4   _____ , 9 , 10

353

Name: _____

Number Crossword Puzzle

Directions: Write the correct number word in the boxes provided.

Across
2. 4
3. 8
5. 2
7. 7
9. 10

Down
1. 0
2. 5
4. 3
6. 1
7. 6
8. 9

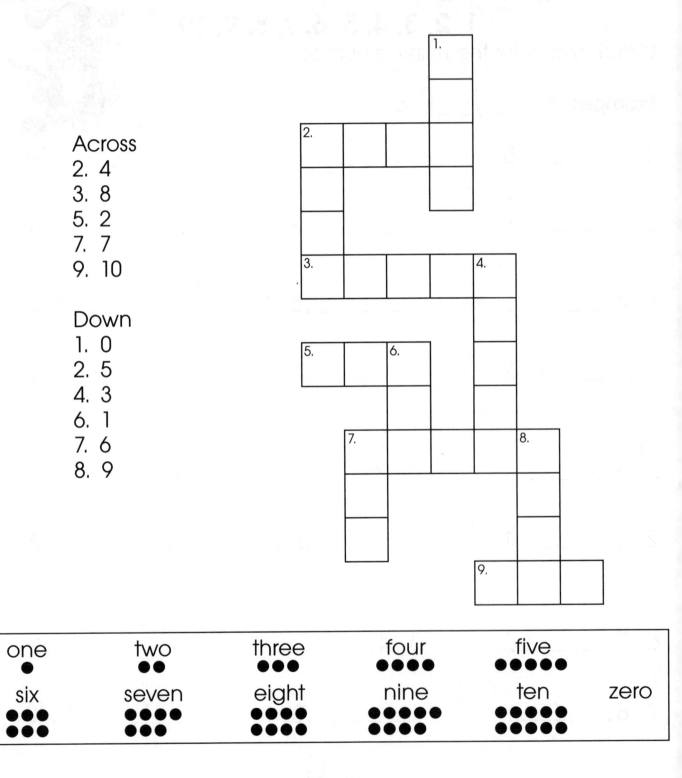

Review

Directions: Count the objects and write the number.

- - - - - - - - - -   - - - - - - - - - -   - - - - - - - - - -

Directions: Match the number to the word.

two	1
four	9
seven	2
three	3
one	4
nine	7

Ordinal Numbers

Ordinal numbers are used to indicate order in a series, such as **first**, **second** or **third**.

Directions: Draw a line to the picture that corresponds to the ordinal number in the left column.

eighth

third

sixth

ninth

seventh

second

fourth

first

fifth

tenth

Ordinal Numbers

Directions: Draw an **X** on the first vegetable, draw a circle around the second vegetable, and draw a square around the third vegetable.

Directions: Write the ordinal number below the picture.

✂ **Cut** the children apart. Mix them up. Then put them back in the correct order.

| first | second | third | fourth | fifth | sixth | seventh | eighth | ninth | tentt |

Page is blank for cutting exercise on previous page.

Name: _____

Sequencing: At the Movies

Directions: The children are watching a movie. Read the sentences. Cut out the pictures below. Glue them where they belong in the picture.

1. The first child is eating popcorn.
2. The third child is eating candy.
3. The fourth child has a cup of fruit punch.
4. The second child is eating a big pretzel.

Grade 1 - Comprehensive Curriculum

Page is blank for cutting exercise on previous page.

Sequencing: Standing in Line

Directions: These children are waiting to see a movie. Look at them and follow the instructions.

1. Color the person who is first in line yellow.

2. Color the person who is last in line brown.

3. Color the person who is second in line pink.

4. Circle the person who is at the end of the line.

Name: _____

Addition 1, 2

Addition means "putting together" or adding two or more numbers to find the sum. "+" is a plus sign. It means to add the 2 numbers. "=" is an equals sign. It tells how much they are together.

Directions: Count the cats and tell how many.

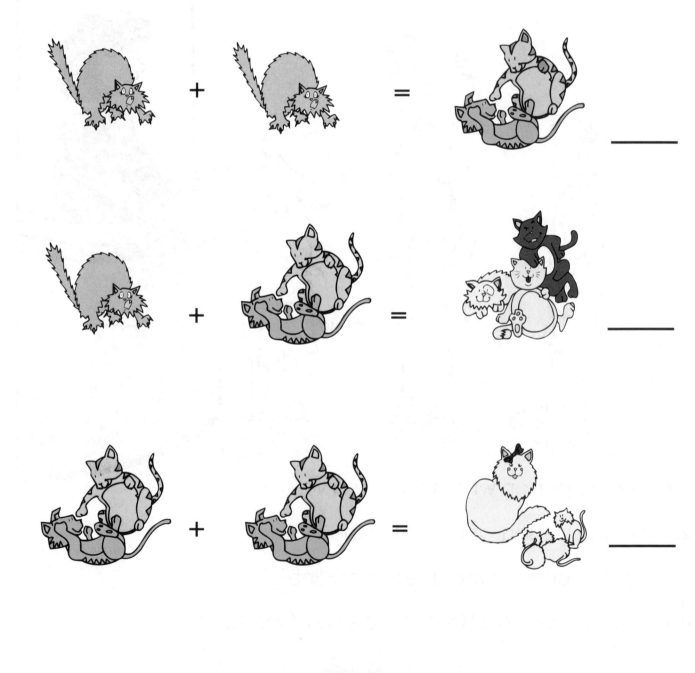

Addition

Directions: Count the shapes and write the numbers below to tell how many in all.

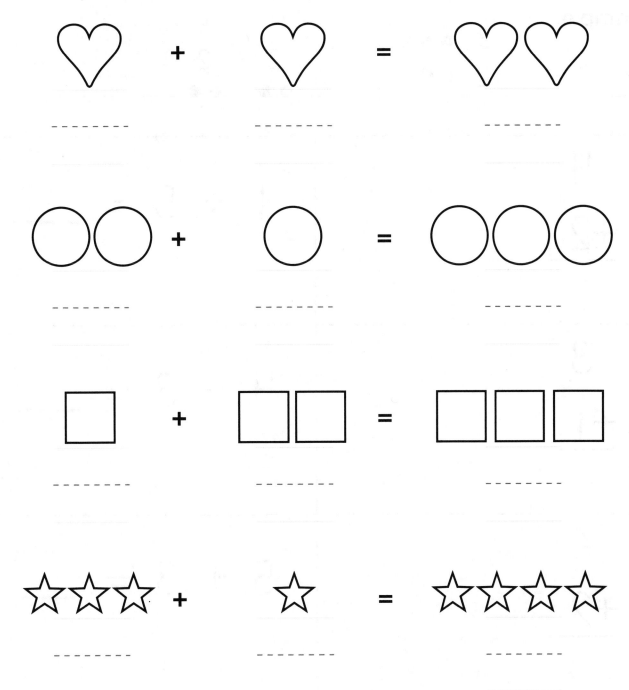

Grade 1 - Comprehensive Curriculum

Name: _____

Addition

Directions: Draw the correct number of dots next to the numbers in each problem. Add up the number of dots to find your answer.

Example:

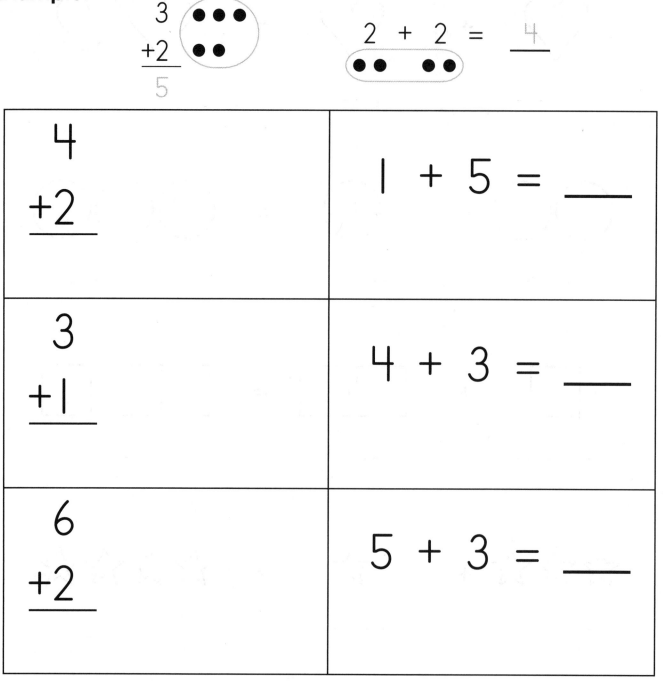

$$3 + 2 = 5$$

$$2 + 2 = \underline{4}$$

4 $+2$	$1 + 5 = \underline{}$
3 $+1$	$4 + 3 = \underline{}$
6 $+2$	$5 + 3 = \underline{}$

Grade 1 - Comprehensive Curriculum

Name: _____

Addition 3, 4, 5, 6

Directions: Practice writing the numbers and then add. Draw dots to help, if needed.

3 -

4 -

5 -

6 -

$$\begin{array}{r} 2 \\ +4 \\ \hline \end{array} \qquad \begin{array}{r} 1 \\ +4 \\ \hline \end{array}$$

$$\begin{array}{r} 3 \\ +2 \\ \hline \end{array} \qquad \begin{array}{r} 1 \\ +2 \\ \hline \end{array}$$

Addition 4, 5, 6, 7

Directions: Practice writing the numbers and then add. Draw dots to help, if needed.

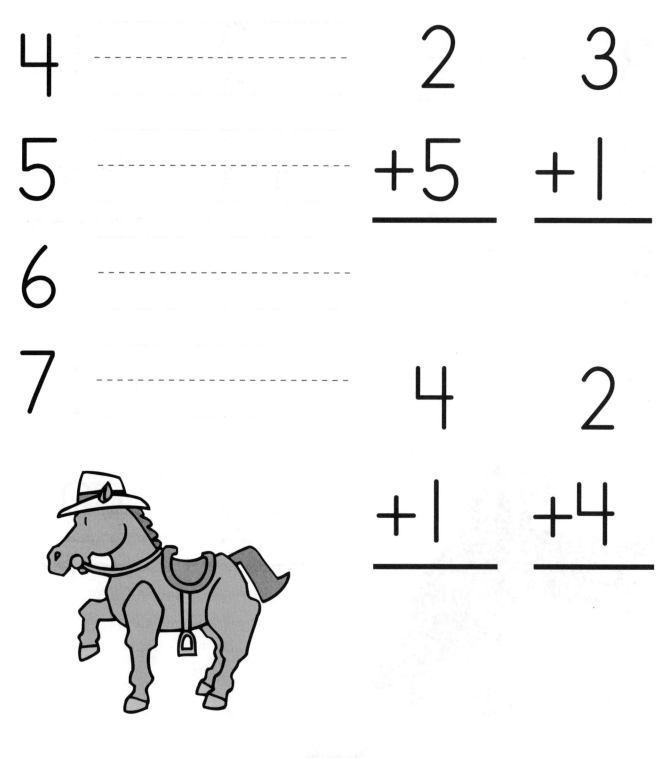

4 -

5 -

6 -

7 -

$$\begin{array}{r} 2 \\ +5 \\ \hline \end{array}$$

$$\begin{array}{r} 3 \\ +1 \\ \hline \end{array}$$

$$\begin{array}{r} 4 \\ +1 \\ \hline \end{array}$$

$$\begin{array}{r} 2 \\ +4 \\ \hline \end{array}$$

Addition 6, 7, 8

Directions: Practice writing the numbers and then add. Draw dots to help, if needed.

6 - - - - - - - - - - - - - - - - -

7 - - - - - - - - - - - - - - - - -

8 - - - - - - - - - - - - - - - - -

$$\begin{array}{r} 3 \\ +4 \\ \hline \end{array}$$
$$\begin{array}{r} 5 \\ +1 \\ \hline \end{array}$$

$$\begin{array}{r} 2 \\ +6 \\ \hline \end{array}$$
$$\begin{array}{r} 4 \\ +4 \\ \hline \end{array}$$

Addition 7, 8, 9

Directions: Practice writing the numbers and then add. Draw dots to help, if needed.

7 -

8 -

9 - - - - - - - - - - - - - - - -

$$\begin{array}{r} 8 \\ +1 \\ \hline \end{array}$$

$$\begin{array}{r} 3 \\ +5 \\ \hline \end{array}$$

$$\begin{array}{r} 2 \\ +7 \\ \hline \end{array}$$

$$\begin{array}{r} 6 \\ +1 \\ \hline \end{array}$$

Addition Table

Directions: Add across and down with a friend. Fill in the spaces.

+	0	1	2	3	4	5
0	0					
1	1	2				
2			4			
3	3			6		
4						
5						10

Do you notice any number patterns in the Addition Table?

Subtraction 1, 2, 3

Subtraction means "taking away" or subtracting one number from another. "−" is a minus sign. It means to subtract the second number from the first.

Directions: Practice writing the numbers and then subtract. Draw dots and cross them out, if needed.

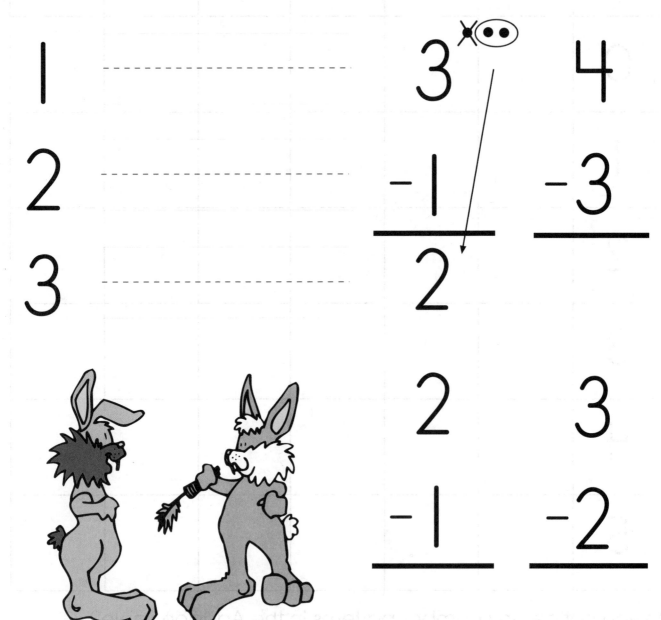

Name: _____

Subtraction 3, 4, 5, 6

Directions: Practice writing the numbers and then subtract.
Draw dots and cross them out, if needed.

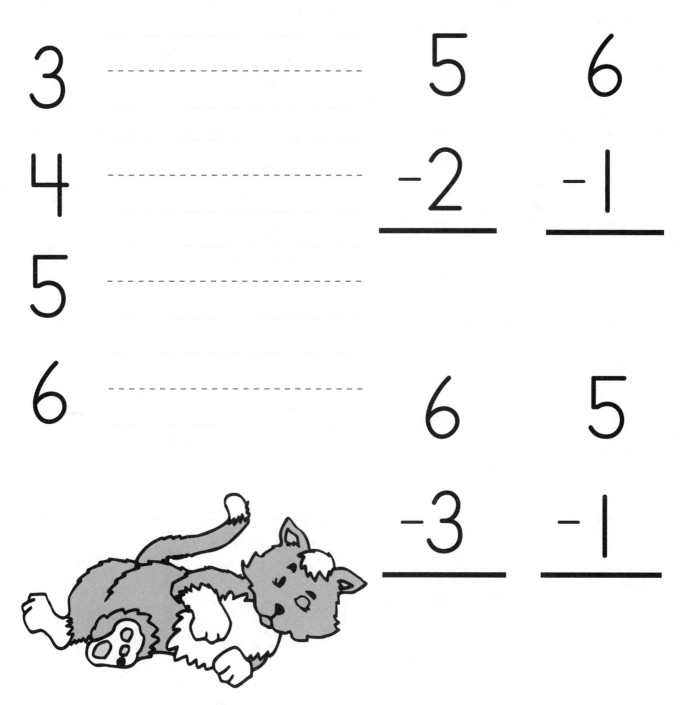

3 – – – – – – – – – – – – – – – – –

$$\begin{array}{r} 5 \\ -2 \\ \hline \end{array} \qquad \begin{array}{r} 6 \\ -1 \\ \hline \end{array}$$

4 – – – – – – – – – – – – – – – – –

5 – – – – – – – – – – – – – – – –

6 – – – – – – – – – – – – – – – – –

$$\begin{array}{r} 6 \\ -3 \\ \hline \end{array} \qquad \begin{array}{r} 5 \\ -1 \\ \hline \end{array}$$

Grade 1 - Comprehensive Curriculum

Name: _____

Subtraction

Directions: Draw the correct number of dots next to the numbers in each problem. Cross out the ones subtracted to find your answer.

Example:

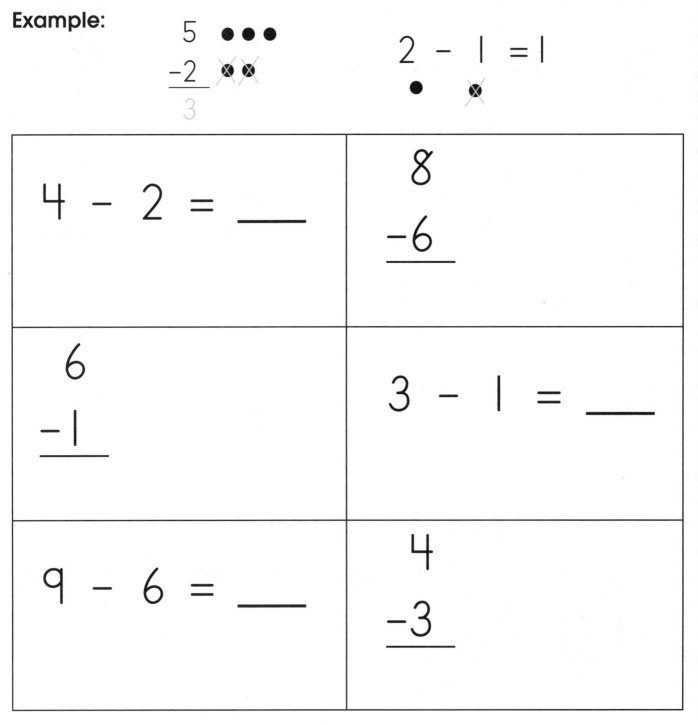

$$\begin{array}{r} 5 \\ -2 \\ \hline 3 \end{array} \quad \bullet\bullet\bullet \\ \text{✗✗}$$

$$2 - 1 = 1$$

$$4 - 2 = \underline{}$$

$$\begin{array}{r} 8 \\ -6 \\ \hline \end{array}$$

$$\begin{array}{r} 6 \\ -1 \\ \hline \end{array}$$

$$3 - 1 = \underline{}$$

$$9 - 6 = \underline{}$$

$$\begin{array}{r} 4 \\ -3 \\ \hline \end{array}$$

Name: _____

Review

Directions: Trace the numbers. Work the problems.

1 2 3 4 5 6 7 8 9 10

$$\begin{array}{r} 9 \\ -3 \\ \hline \end{array}$$

$$\begin{array}{r} 6 \\ +2 \\ \hline \end{array}$$

$$\begin{array}{r} 3 \\ +4 \\ \hline \end{array}$$

$$\begin{array}{r} 2 \\ -1 \\ \hline \end{array}$$

$$\begin{array}{r} 5 \\ +4 \\ \hline \end{array}$$

$$\begin{array}{r} 9 \\ -5 \\ \hline \end{array}$$

$$\begin{array}{r} 7 \\ +2 \\ \hline \end{array}$$

$$\begin{array}{r} 8 \\ -6 \\ \hline \end{array}$$

$$\begin{array}{r} 4 \\ -2 \\ \hline \end{array}$$

$$\begin{array}{r} 6 \\ +3 \\ \hline \end{array}$$

$$\begin{array}{r} 9 \\ -7 \\ \hline \end{array}$$

$$\begin{array}{r} 1 \\ +7 \\ \hline \end{array}$$

Grade 1 - Comprehensive Curriculum

Zero

Directions: Write the number.

Example:

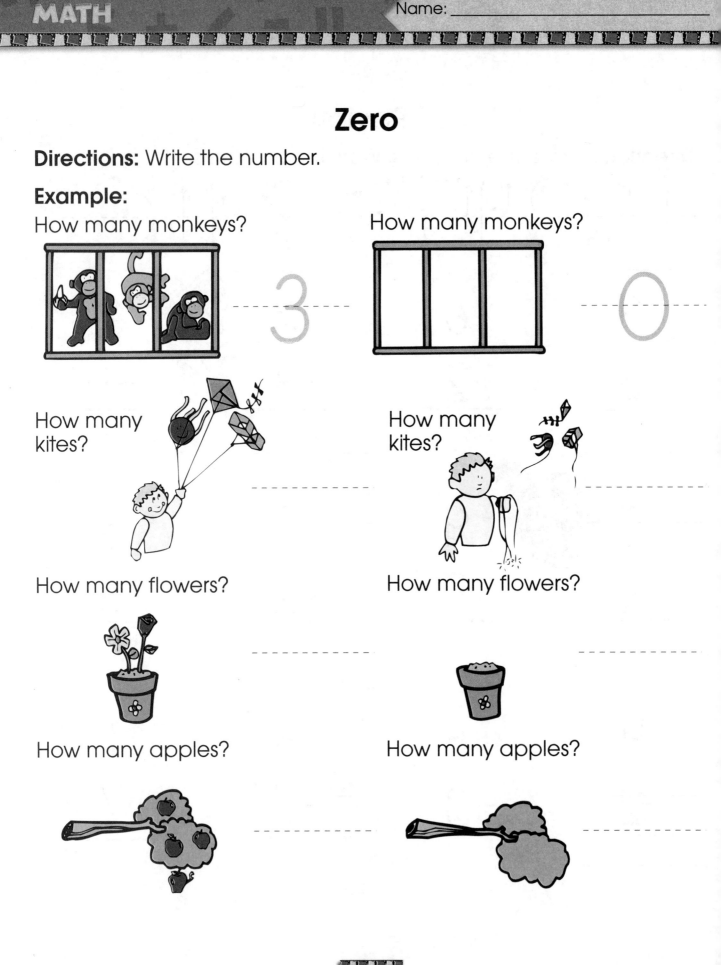

How many monkeys?

3

How many monkeys?

0

How many kites?

How many kites?

How many flowers?

How many flowers?

How many apples?

How many apples?

Name: _____

Zero

Directions: Write the number that tells how many.

How many sailboats?

 - - - - - - - - - - - - - - -

How many sailboats?

- - - - - - - - - - - - - - -

How many eggs?

 - - - - - - - - - - - - - - -

How many eggs?

 - - - - - - - - - - - - - - -

How many marshmallows?

 - - - - - - - - - - - - - - -

How many marshmallows?

 - - - - - - - - - - - - - - -

How many candles?

 - - - - - - - - - - - - - - -

How many candles?

 - - - - - - - - - - - - - - -

Grade 1 - Comprehensive Curriculum

Name: _____

Picture Problems: Addition

Directions: Solve the number problem under each picture.

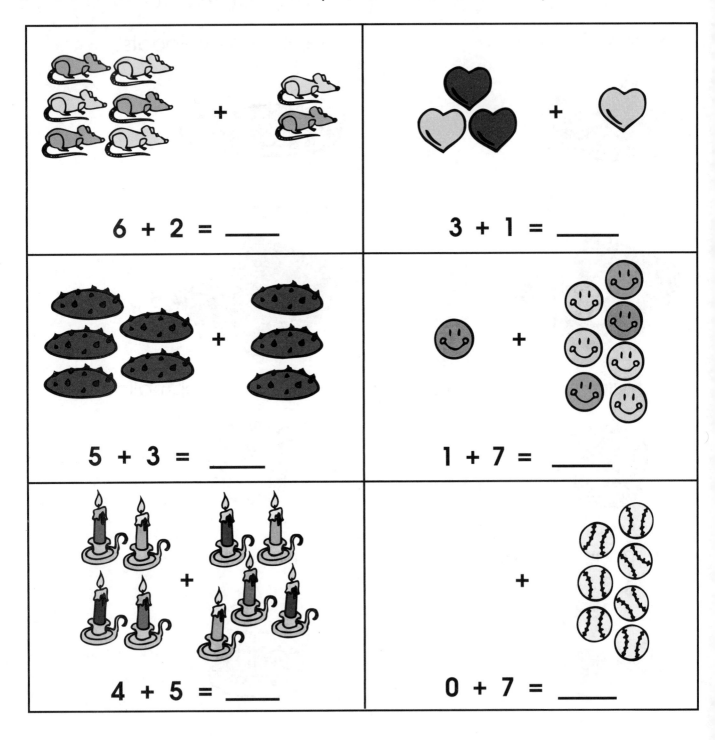

$6 + 2 = $ _____

$3 + 1 = $ _____

$5 + 3 = $ _____

$1 + 7 = $ _____

$4 + 5 = $ _____

$0 + 7 = $ _____

Name: _____

Picture Problems: Addition

Directions: Solve the number problem under each picture.

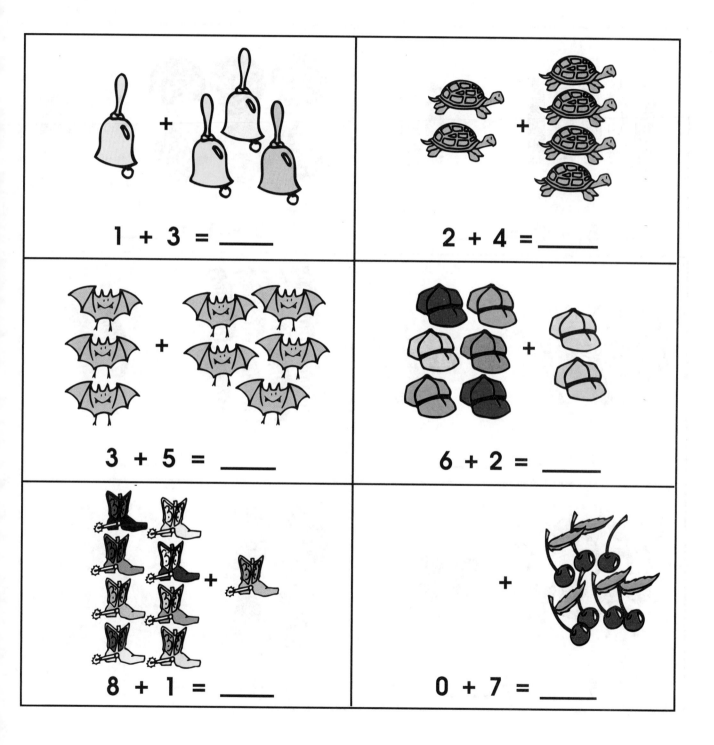

1 + 3 = _____

2 + 4 = _____

3 + 5 = _____

6 + 2 = _____

8 + 1 = _____

0 + 7 = _____

Grade 1 - Comprehensive Curriculum

Name: _____

Picture Problems: Subtraction

Directions: Solve the number problem under each picture.

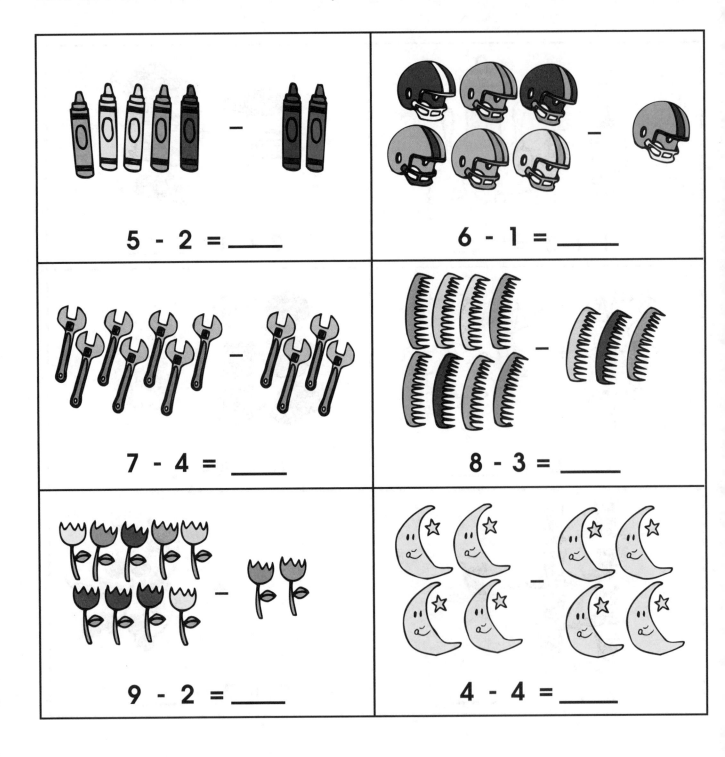

5 - 2 = _____

6 - 1 = _____

7 - 4 = _____

8 - 3 = _____

9 - 2 = _____

4 - 4 = _____

Name: _____

Picture Problems: Subtraction

Directions: Solve the number problem under each picture.

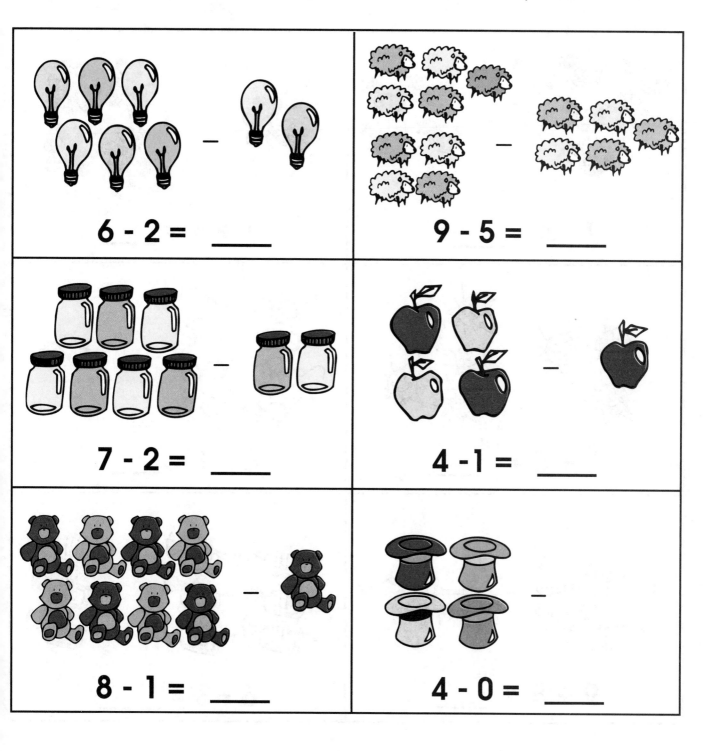

6 - 2 = ____

9 - 5 = ____

7 - 2 = ____

4 - 1 = ____

8 - 1 = ____

4 - 0 = ____

Grade 1 - Comprehensive Curriculum

Name: _____

Picture Problems: Addition and Subtraction

Directions: Solve the number problem under each picture.

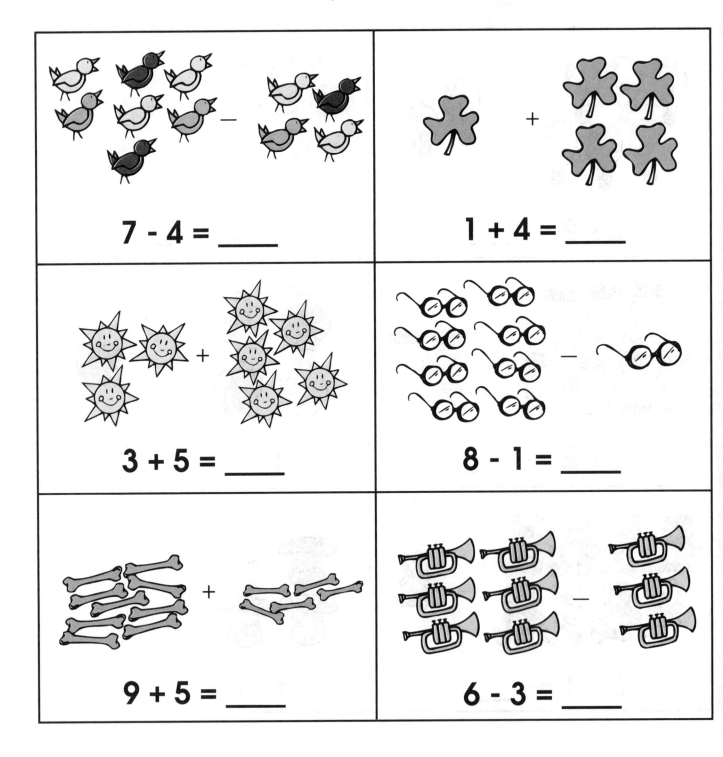

7 - 4 = ____

1 + 4 = ____

3 + 5 = ____

8 - 1 = ____

9 + 5 = ____

6 - 3 = ____

Name: _____

Picture Problems: Addition and Subtraction

Directions: Solve the number problem under each picture.
Write **+** or **−** to show if you should add or subtract.

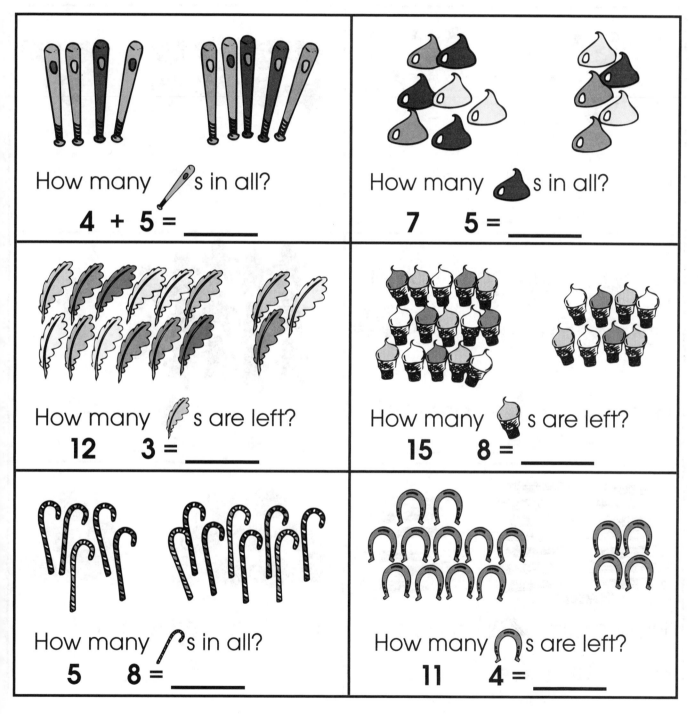

How many 🏏s in all?

4 + 5 = _____

How many 🍫s in all?

7   5 = _____

How many 🪶s are left?

12   3 = _____

How many 🍦s are left?

15   8 = _____

How many 🍬s in all?

5   8 = _____

How many ⊓s are left?

11   4 = _____

Grade 1 - Comprehensive Curriculum

Picture Problems: Addition and Subtraction

Directions: Solve the number problem under each picture.
Write **+** or **–** to show if you should add or subtract.

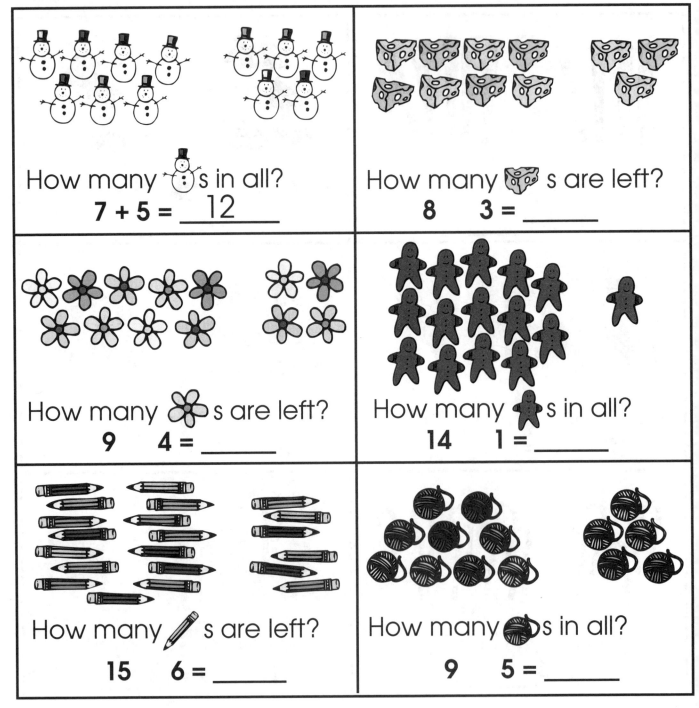

How many ⛄s in all?

7 + 5 = ___12___

How many 🧀s are left?

8   3 = _____

How many 🌼s are left?

9   4 = _____

How many 🍪s in all?

14   1 = _____

How many ✏️s are left?

15   6 = _____

How many 🧶s in all?

9   5 = _____

Name: _____

Review: Addition and Subtraction

Directions: Solve the number problem under each picture.
Write **+** or **–** to show if you should add or subtract.

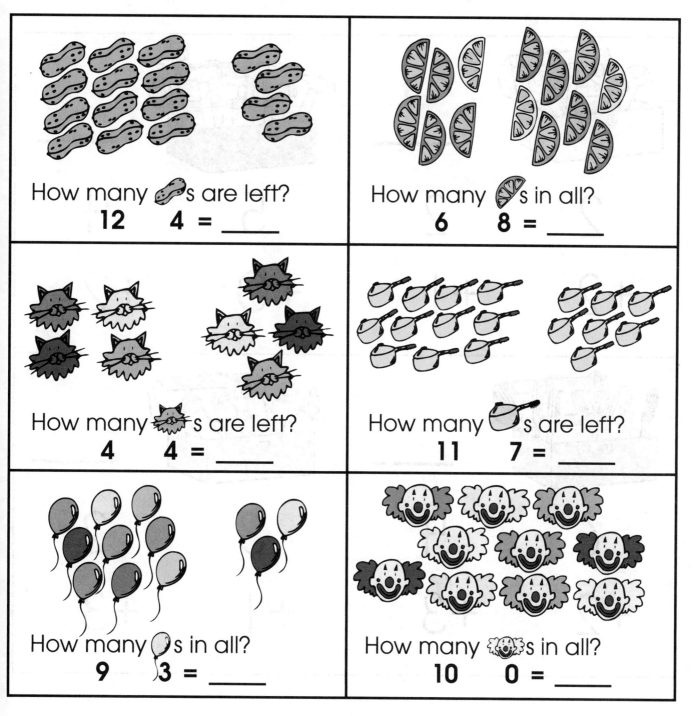

How many s are left?

12   4 = _____

How many s in all?

6   8 = _____

How many s are left?

4   4 = _____

How many s are left?

11   7 = _____

How many s in all?

9   3 = _____

How many s in all?

10   0 = _____

Addition 1-5

Directions: Count the tools in each tool box. Write your answers in the blanks. Circle the problem that matches your answer.

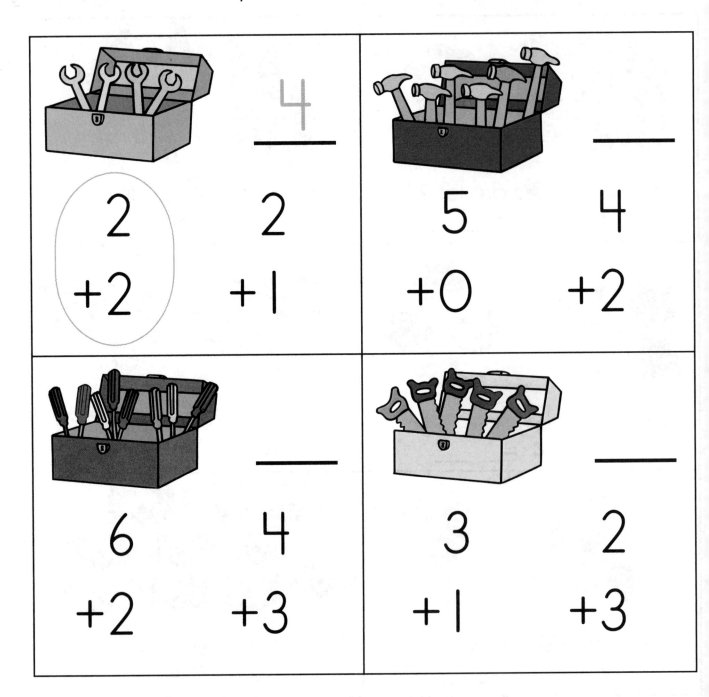

$$4$$

$$\begin{array}{r} 2 \\ +2 \end{array}$$ $$\begin{array}{r} 2 \\ +1 \end{array}$$

$$\underline{}$$

$$\begin{array}{r} 5 \\ +0 \end{array}$$ $$\begin{array}{r} 4 \\ +2 \end{array}$$

$$\underline{}$$

$$\begin{array}{r} 6 \\ +2 \end{array}$$ $$\begin{array}{r} 4 \\ +3 \end{array}$$

$$\underline{}$$

$$\begin{array}{r} 3 \\ +1 \end{array}$$ $$\begin{array}{r} 2 \\ +3 \end{array}$$

Name: _____

Addition 1-5

Directions: Look at the red numbers and draw that many more flowers in the pot. Count them to get your total.

Example: $3 + 2 = \underline{5}$

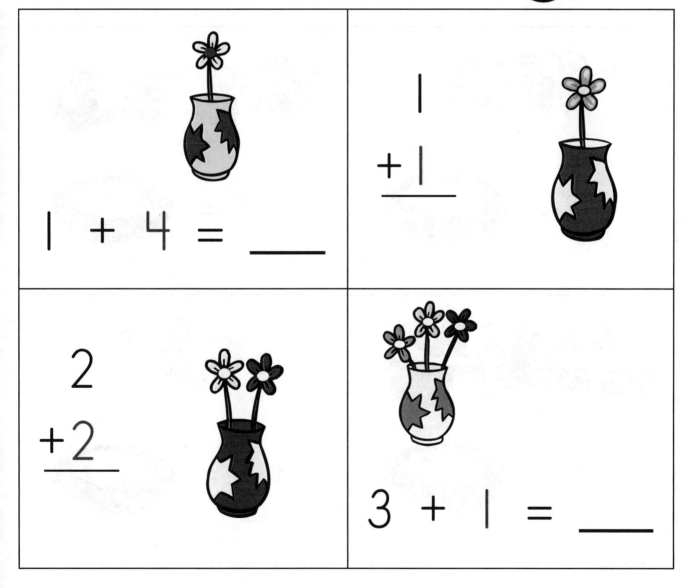

$1 + 4 = \underline{}$

$$\begin{array}{r} 1 \\ + 1 \\ \hline \end{array}$$

$$\begin{array}{r} 2 \\ + 2 \\ \hline \end{array}$$

$3 + 1 = \underline{}$

Grade 1 - Comprehensive Curriculum

Name: _____

Addition 1-5

Directions: Add the numbers. Put your answers in the nests.

Example: $2 + 3 =$ 5

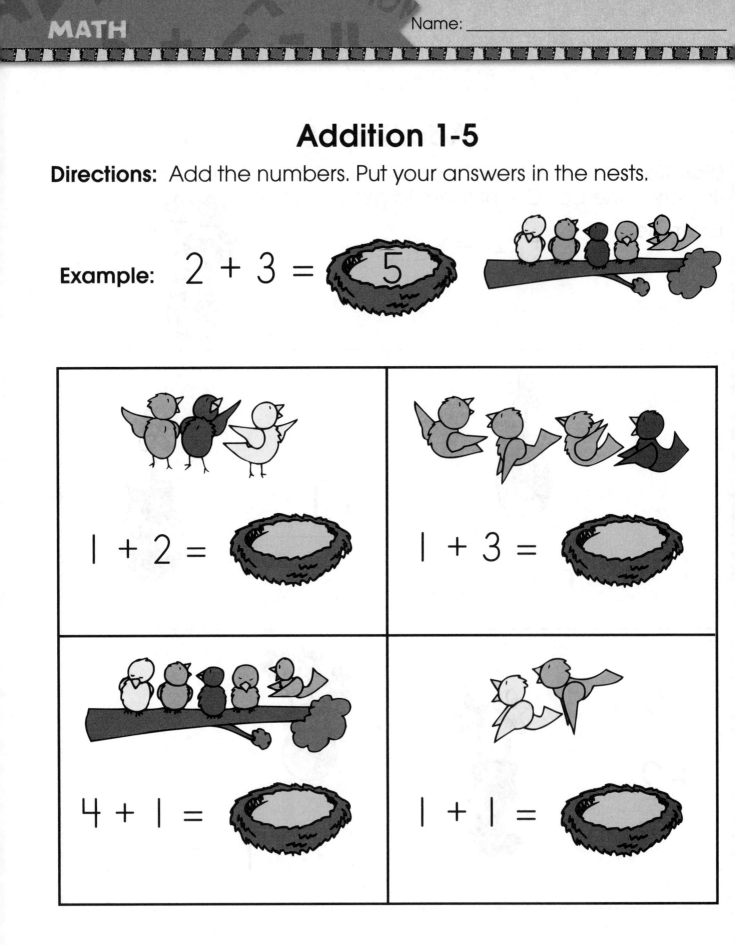

$1 + 2 =$

$1 + 3 =$

$4 + 1 =$

$1 + 1 =$

Name: _____

Addition 6-10

Directions: Add the numbers. Put your answers in the doghouses.

Example: 4 + 2 = 6

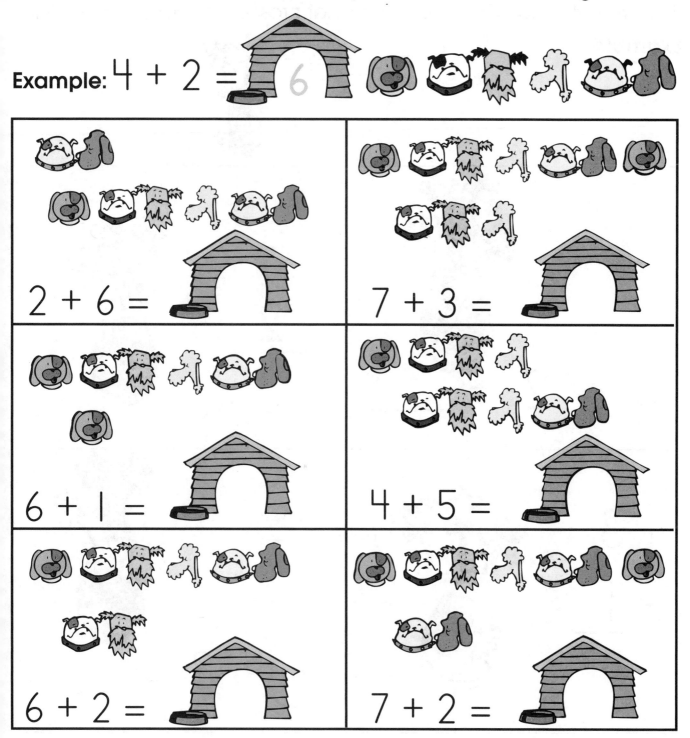

2 + 6 =

7 + 3 =

6 + 1 =

4 + 5 =

6 + 2 =

7 + 2 =

Grade 1 - Comprehensive Curriculum

Name: _____

Subtraction 1-5

Directions: Subtract the red numbers by crossing out that many flowers in the pot. Count the ones not crossed out to get the total.

Example: 2 – 1 = __1__

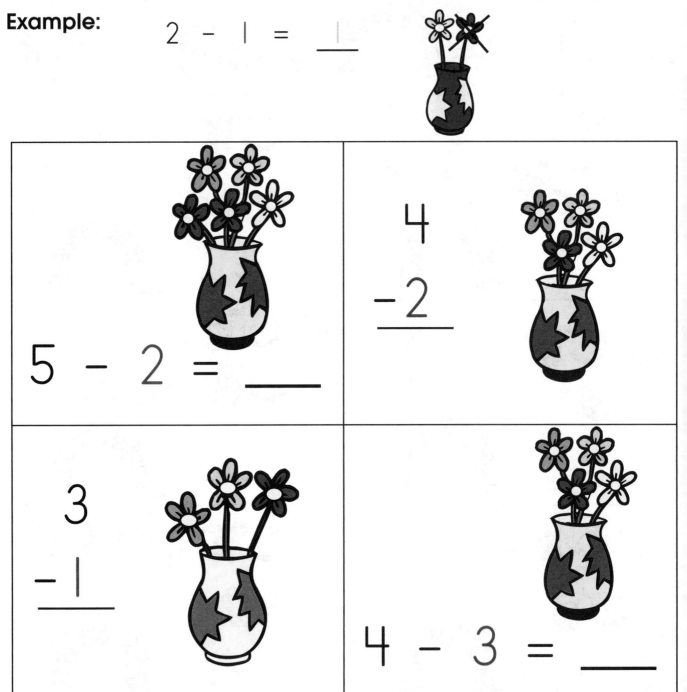

5 – 2 = ___

4
–2
___

3
–1
___

4 – 3 = ___

Name: _____

Subtraction 1-5

Directions: Count the fruit in each bowl. Write your answers on the blanks. Circle the problem that matches your answer.

Grade 1 - Comprehensive Curriculum

MATH

Name: _____

Subtraction 6-10

Directions: Count the flowers. Write your answer on the blank. Circle the problem that matches your answer.

Name: _____

Addition and Subtraction

Directions: Solve the problems. Remember, addition means "putting together" or adding two or more numbers to find the sum. Subtraction means "taking away" or subtracting one number from another.

1 + 3 = ____   4 – 3 = ____   4 + 5 = ____

6 + 1 = ____   7 – 2 = ____   8 – 4 = ____

                       9 – 1 = ____   10 – 3 = ____

                       5 – 2 = ____   6 + 3 = ____

                       8 + 2 = ____   5 + 5 = ____

Grade 1 - Comprehensive Curriculum

Name: _____

Addition and Subtraction

Remember, addition means "putting together" or adding two or more numbers to find the sum. Subtraction means "take away" or subtracting one number from another.

Directions: Solve the problems. From your answers, use the code to color the quilt.

Color:
- 6 = blue
- 7 = yellow
- 8 = green
- 9 = red
- 10 = orange

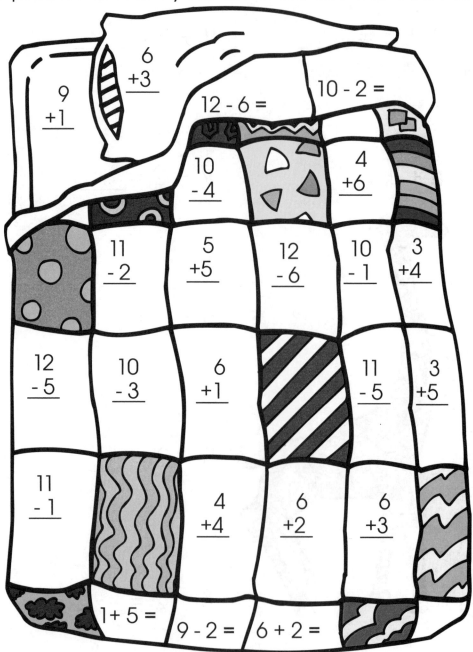

Name: _____

Place Value: Tens and Ones

The place value of a digit, or numeral, is shown by where it is in the number. For example, in the number **23**, **2** has the place value of **tens**, and **3** is ones.

Directions: Count the groups of ten crayons and write the number by the word **tens**. Count the other crayons and write the number by the word **ones**.

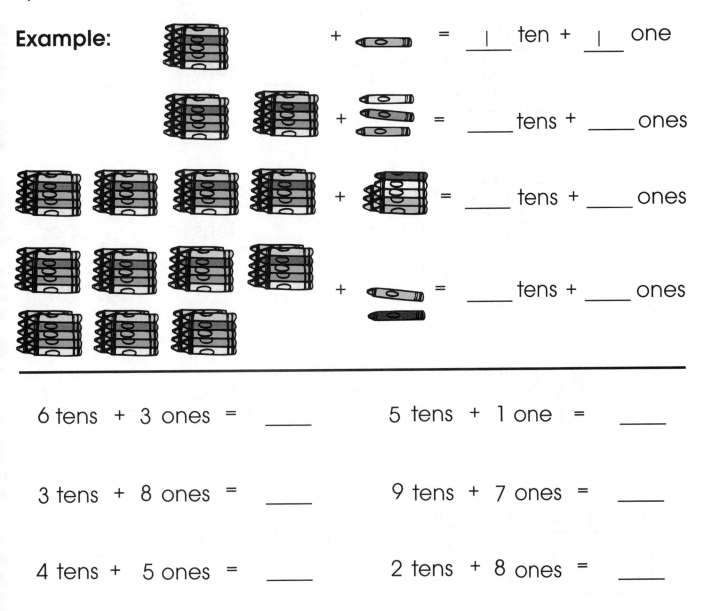

Example:

+ = __1__ ten + __1__ one

+ = ____ tens + ____ ones

+ = ____ tens + ____ ones

+ = ____ tens + ____ ones

---

6 tens + 3 ones = ____   5 tens + 1 one = ____

3 tens + 8 ones = ____   9 tens + 7 ones = ____

4 tens + 5 ones = ____   2 tens + 8 ones = ____

Grade 1 - Comprehensive Curriculum

Place Value: Tens and Ones

Directions: Count the groups of ten blocks and write the number by the word tens. Count the other blocks and write the number by the word ones.

Example:

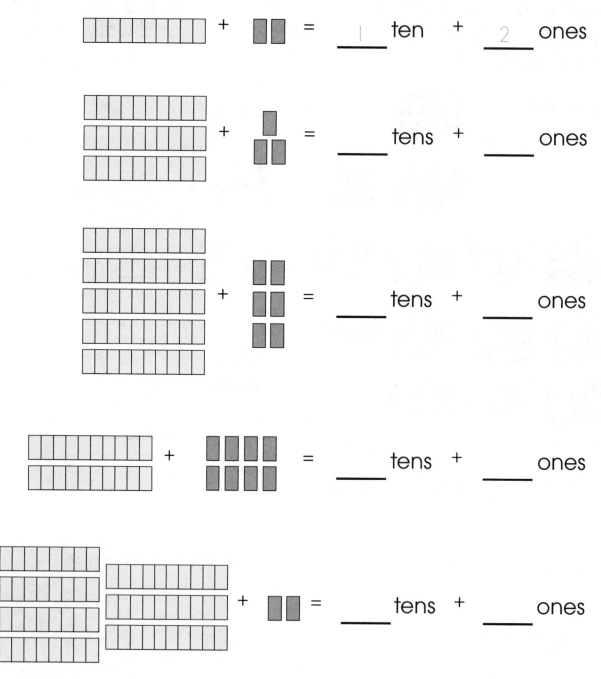

_____ 1 ten   +   2 ones

_____ tens   +   _____ ones

_____ tens   +   _____ ones

_____ tens   +   _____ ones

_____ tens   +   _____ ones

Name: _____

Place Value: Tens and Ones

Directions: Write the answers in the correct spaces.

		tens	ones		
3 tens, 2 ones		3	2	=	32
3 tens, 7 ones		___	___	=	___
9 tens, 1 one		___	___	=	___
5 tens, 6 ones		___	___	=	___
6 tens, 5 ones		___	___	=	___
6 tens, 8 ones		___	___	=	___
2 tens, 8 ones		___	___	=	___
4 tens, 9 ones		___	___	=	___
1 ten, 4 ones		___	___	=	___
8 tens, 2 ones		___	___	=	___
4 tens, 2 ones		___	___	=	___

28 = ___ tens, ___ ones

64 = ___ tens, ___ ones

56 = ___ tens, ___ ones

72 = ___ tens, ___ ones

38 = ___ tens, ___ ones

17 = ___ ten, ___ ones

63 = ___ tens, ___ ones

12 = ___ ten, ___ ones

Grade 1 - Comprehensive Curriculum

Review: Place Value

The place value of each digit, or numeral, is shown by where it is in the number. For example, in the number **123**, **1** has the place value of **hundreds**, **2** is **tens** and **3** is **ones**.

Directions: Count the groups of crayons and add.

Example:

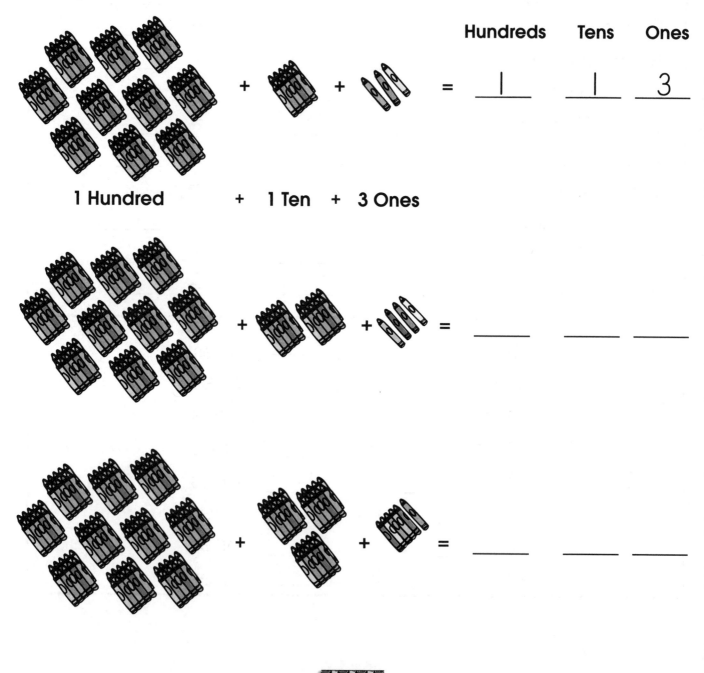

	Hundreds	Tens	Ones
	1	1	3

1 Hundred   +   1 Ten   +   3 Ones

Name: _____

Counting by Fives

Directions: Count by fives to draw the path to the playground.

Grade 1 - Comprehensive Curriculum

Counting by Fives

Directions: Use tally marks to count by fives. Write the number next to the tallies.

Example: A tally mark stands for one = I. Five tally marks look like this = IIII

卌 _____

卌 卌 _____

卌 卌 卌 _____

卌 卌 卌 _____

卌 卌 卌 卌 _____

卌 卌 卌 卌 卌 _____

卌 卌 卌 卌 卌 _____

卌 卌 卌 卌 卌 卌 _____

卌 卌 卌 卌 卌 卌 卌 _____

卌 卌 卌 卌 卌 卌 卌 卌 _____

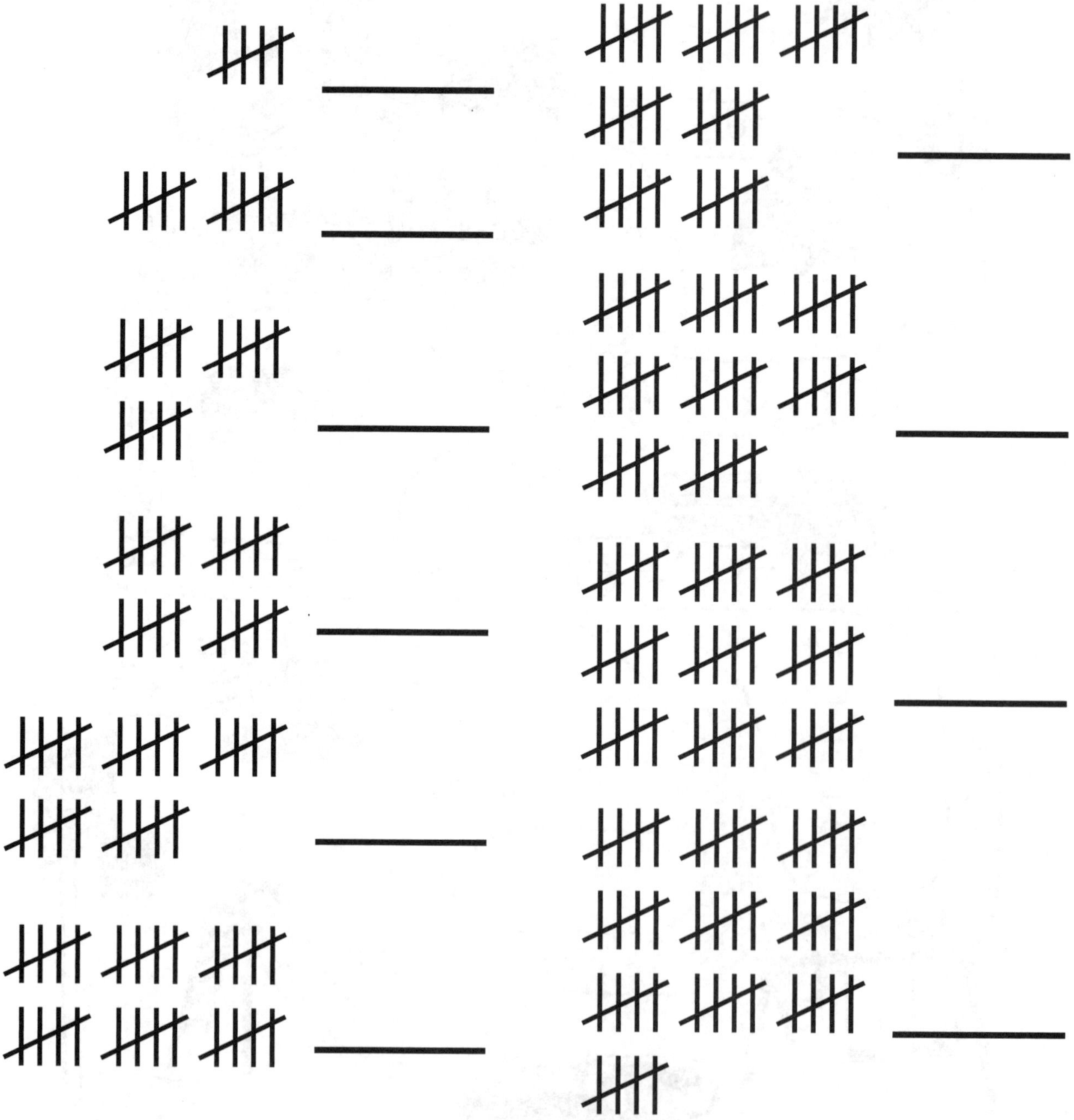

Name: _____

Counting by Tens

Directions: Count in order by tens to draw the path the boy takes to the store.

Grade 1 - Comprehensive Curriculum

Name: _____

Counting by Tens

Directions: Use the groups of 10's to count to 100.

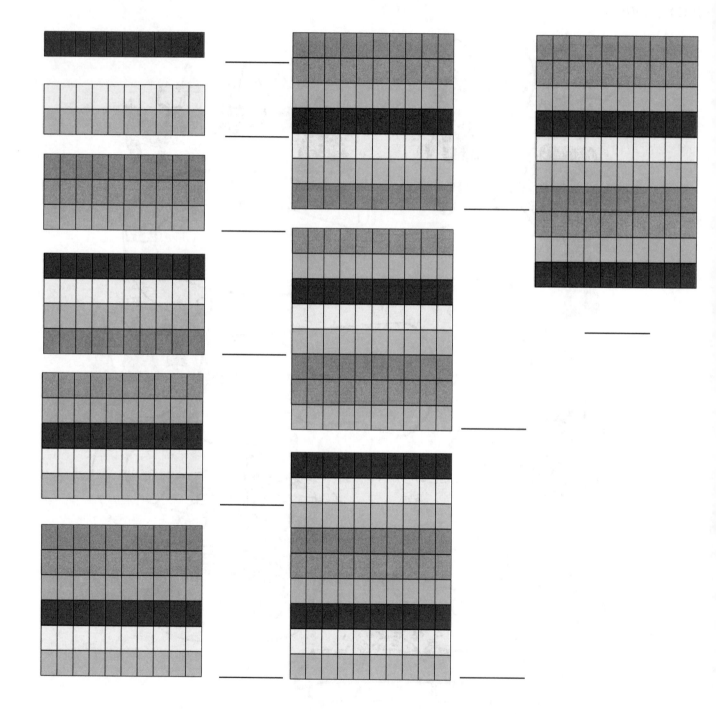

Addition: 10-15

Directions: Circle groups of ten crayons. Add the remaining ones to make the correct number.

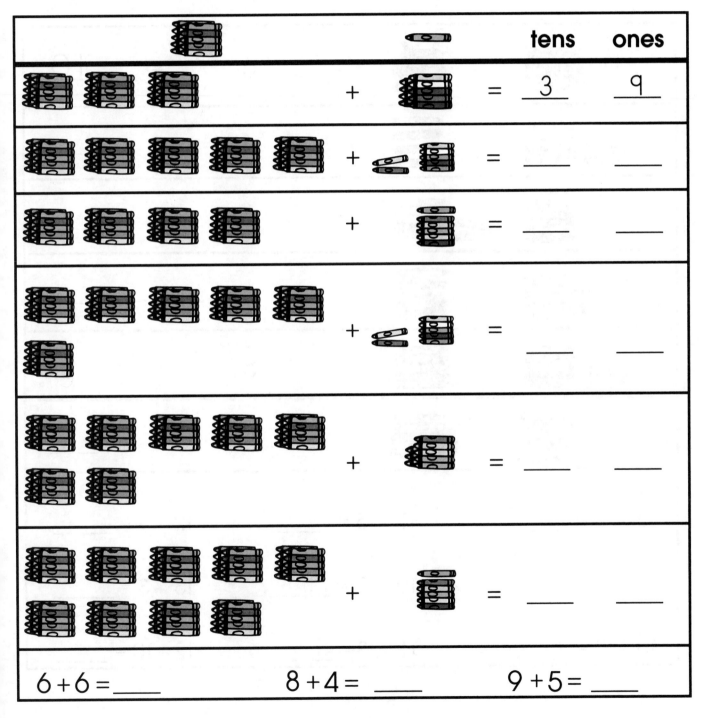

		tens	ones
(3 groups) + (1 group) =		3	9
(5 groups) + (2 + 1 group) =		___	___
(4 groups) + (1 group) =		___	___
(6 groups) + (1 + 1 group) =		___	___
(7 groups) + (1 group) =		___	___
(9 groups) + (1 group) =		___	___

$6 + 6 =$ ___ $8 + 4 =$ ___ $9 + 5 =$ ___

Grade 1 - Comprehensive Curriculum

Name: _____

Subtraction: 10-15

Directions: Count the crayons in each group. Put an **X** through the number of crayons being subtracted. How many are left?

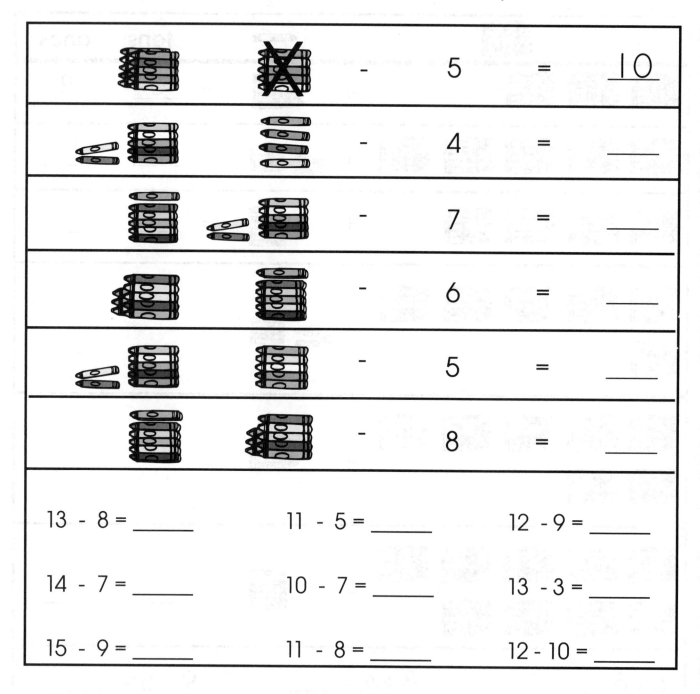

		- 5	=	10
		- 4	=	___
		- 7	=	___
		- 6	=	___
		- 5	=	___
		- 8	=	___

13 - 8 = _____   11 - 5 = _____   12 - 9 = _____

14 - 7 = _____   10 - 7 = _____   13 - 3 = _____

15 - 9 = _____   11 - 8 = _____   12 - 10 = _____

Name: _____

Shapes: Square

A square is a figure with four corners and four sides of the same length. This is a square ▢.

Directions: Find the squares and circle them.

Directions: Trace the word. Write the word.

- -

square

Shapes: Circle

A circle is a figure that is round. This is a circle ○.

Directions: Find the circles and put a square around them.

Directions: Trace the word. Write the word.

circle

- -

Shapes: Square and Circle

Directions: Practice drawing squares. Trace the samples and make four of your own.

Directions: Practice drawing circles. Trace the samples and make four of your own.

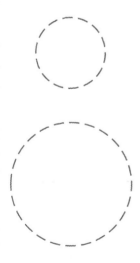

Shapes: Triangle

A triangle is a figure with three corners and three sides. This is a triangle △.

Directions: Find the triangles and put a circle around them.

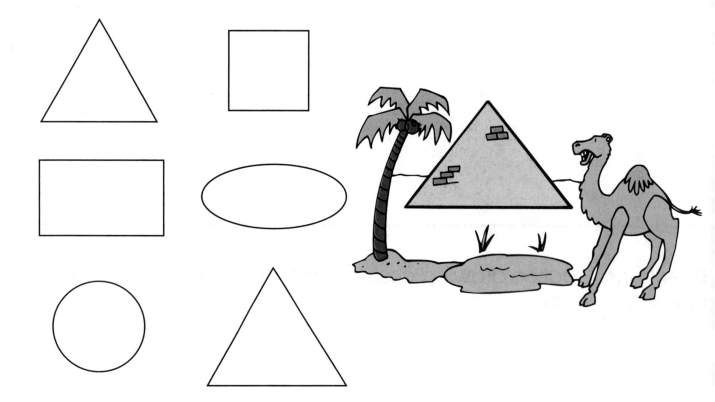

Directions: Trace the word. Write the word.

triangle --

Name: _____

Shapes: Rectangle

A rectangle is a figure with four corners and four sides. Sides opposite each other are the same length. This is a rectangle ▭ .

Directions: Find the rectangles and put a circle around them.

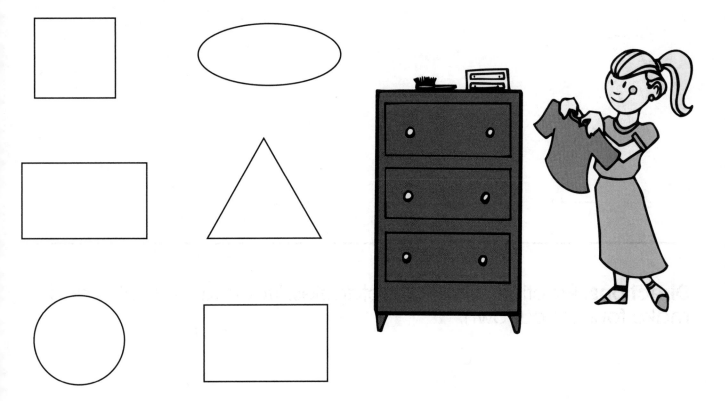

Directions: Trace the word. Write the word.

rectangle _____

Grade 1 - Comprehensive Curriculum

Name: _____

Shapes: Triangle and Rectangle

Directions: Practice drawing triangles. Trace the samples and make four of your own.

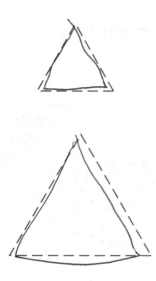

Directions: Practice drawing rectangles. Trace the samples and make four of your own.

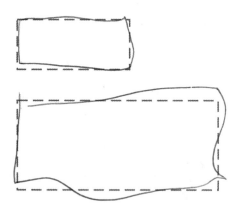

Patterns: Rectangles

Directions: In each picture, there is more than one rectangle. Trace each rectangle with a different color crayon. Under each picture, write how many rectangles you found.

_____ rectangles

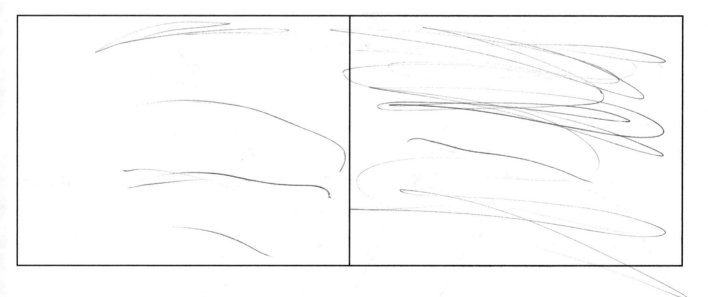

_____ rectangles

Patterns: Triangles

Directions: In each picture there is more than one triangle. Trace each triangle with a different color crayon. Under each picture, write how many triangles you found.

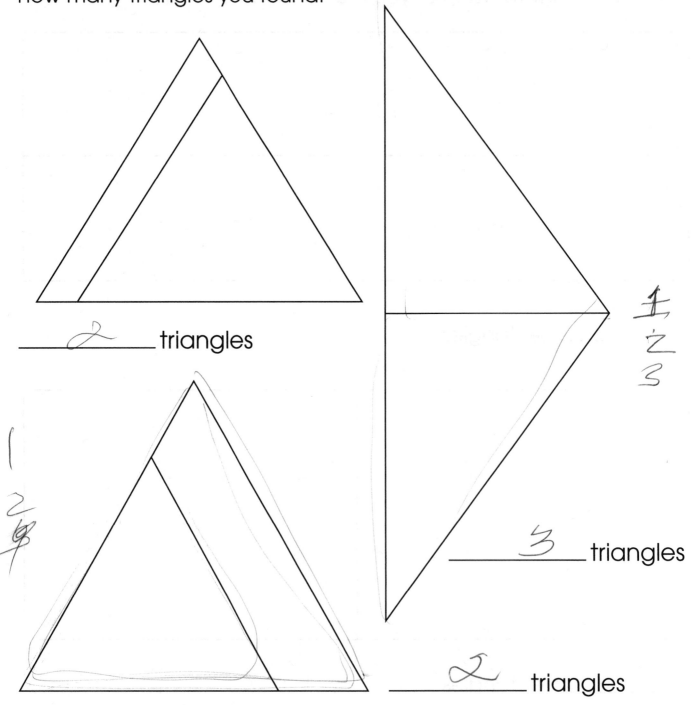

_____ triangles

1
2
3

1
2
4

_____ 3 _____ triangles

_____ 2 _____ triangles

Shapes: Oval and Diamond

An oval is an egg-shaped figure. A diamond is a figure with four sides of the same length. Its corners form points at the top, sides and bottom. This is an oval ⬭. This is a diamond ◇.

Directions: Color the ovals red. Color the diamonds blue.

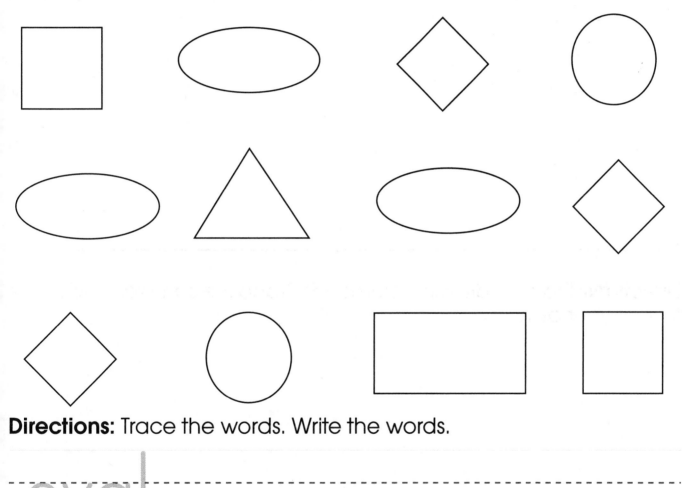

Directions: Trace the words. Write the words.

oval

diamond

Shapes: Oval and Diamond

Directions: Practice drawing ovals. Trace the samples and make four of your own.

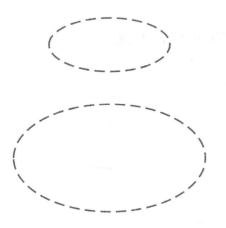

Directions: Practice drawing diamonds. Trace the samples and make four of your own.

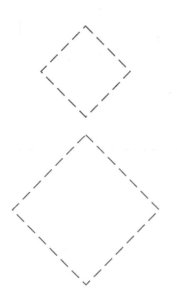

Name: _____

Following Directions: Shapes and Colors

Directions: Color the squares ☐ purple.

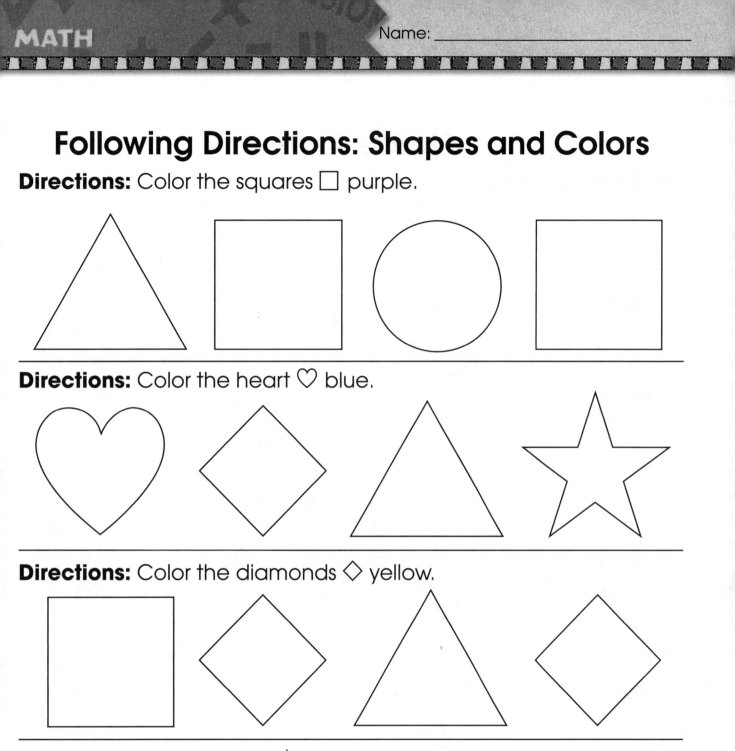

Directions: Color the heart ♡ blue.

Directions: Color the diamonds ◇ yellow.

Directions: Color the star ☆ red.

Grade 1 - Comprehensive Curriculum

Name: _____

Shape Review

Directions: Color the shapes in the picture as shown.

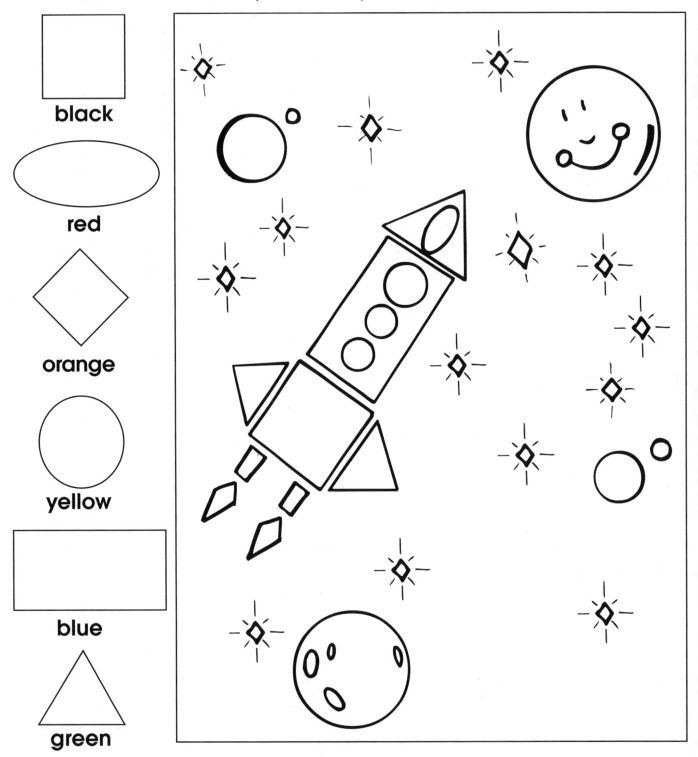

black

red

orange

yellow

blue

green

Shape Review

Directions: Trace the circles
Trace the squares
Trace the rectangles
Trace the triangles
Trace the ovals
Trace the diamonds

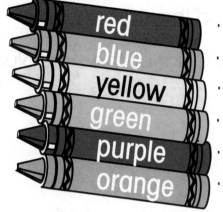

red .
blue .
yellow .
green .
purple .
orange .

Name: _____

Classifying: Stars

Help Bob find the stars.

Directions: Color all the stars blue.

How many stars did you and Bob find?_____

Classifying: Shapes

Mary and Rudy are taking a trip into space. Help them find the stars, moons, circles and diamonds.

Directions: Color the shapes.

Use yellow for ☆'s.   Use blue for ☾'s.

Use red for ◯'s.   Use purple for ◇'s.

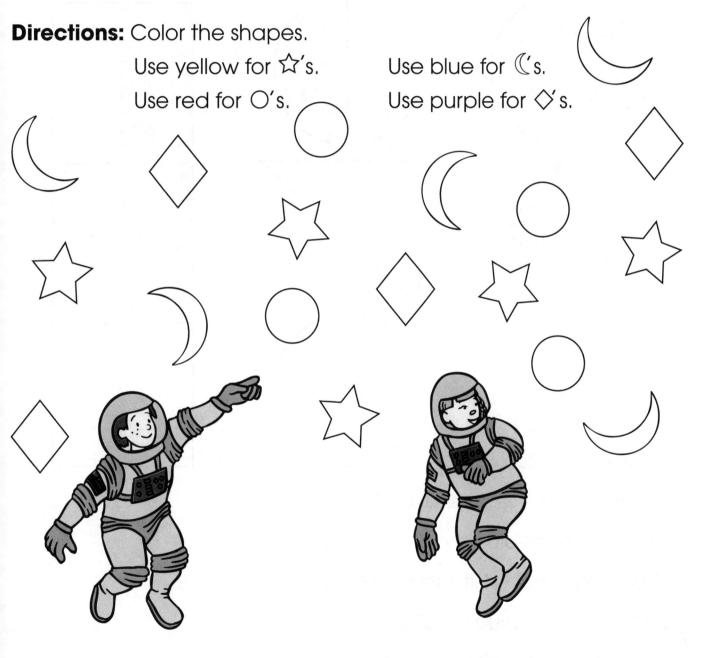

How many stars? _____   How many moons? _____

How many circles? _____   How many diamonds? _____

Classifying: Shapes

Directions: Look at the shapes. Answer the questions.

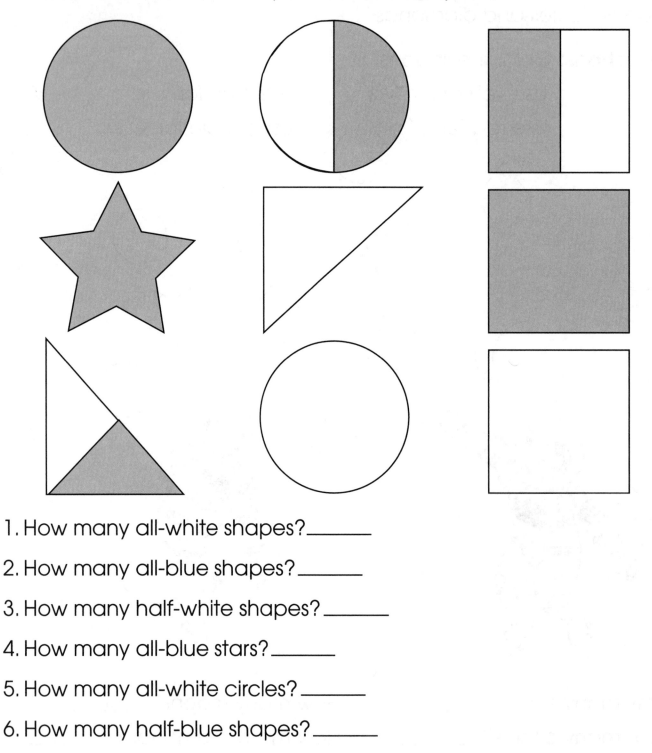

1. How many all-white shapes? _____

2. How many all-blue shapes? _____

3. How many half-white shapes? _____

4. How many all-blue stars? _____

5. How many all-white circles? _____

6. How many half-blue shapes? _____

Same and Different: Shapes

Directions: Color the shape that looks the same as the first shape in each row.

Grade 1 - Comprehensive Curriculum

Name: _____

Same and Different: Shapes

Directions: Draw an **X** on the shapes in each row that do not match the first shape.

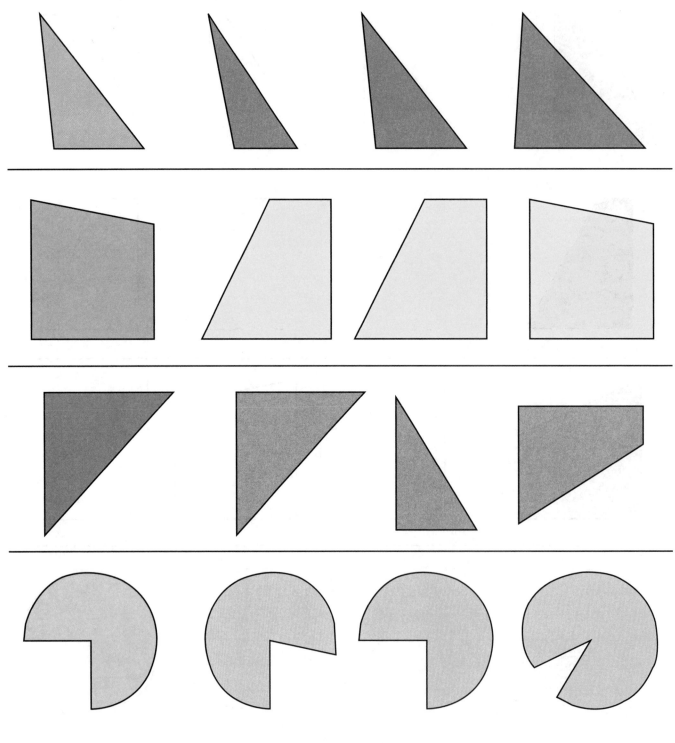

Name: _____

Copying: Shapes and Colors

Directions: Color your circle to look the same.

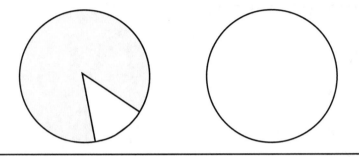

Directions: Color your square to look the same.

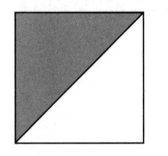

Directions: Trace the triangle. Color it to look the same.

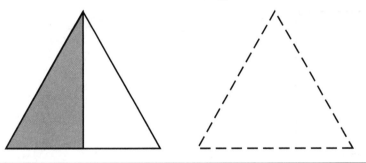

Directions: Trace the star. Color it to look the same.

Grade 1 - Comprehensive Curriculum

Copying: Shapes and Colors

Directions: Color the second shape the same as the first one. Then draw and color the shape two more times.

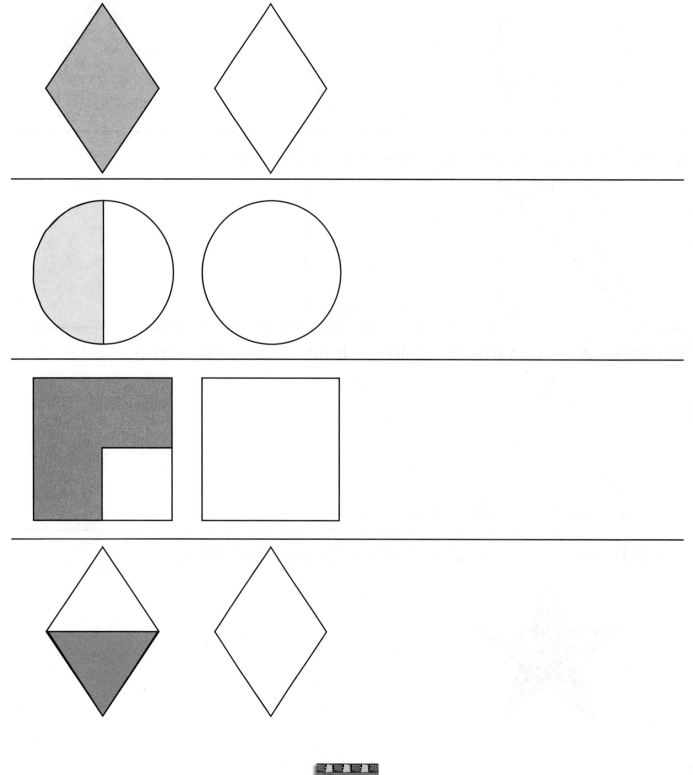

Name: _____

Patterns: Shapes

Directions: Draw a line from the box on the left to the box on the right with the same shape and color pattern.

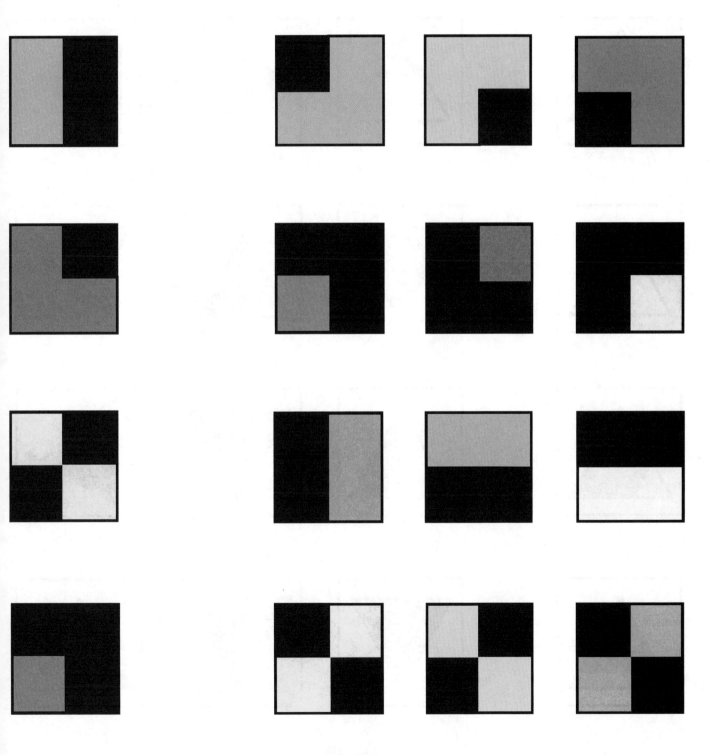

Grade 1 - Comprehensive Curriculum

Patterns: Shapes

Directions: Draw a line from the box on the left to the box on the right with the same shape and color pattern.

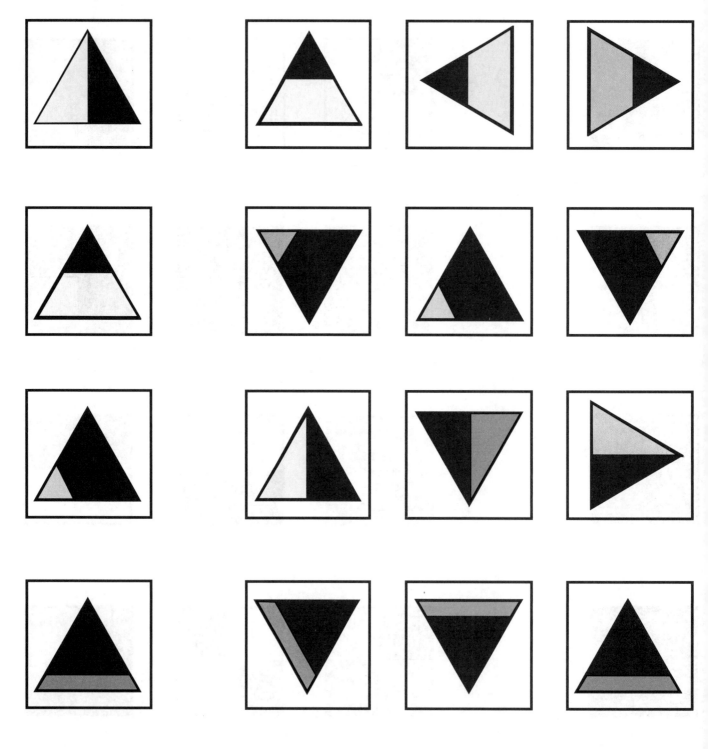

Name: _____

Patterns: Find and Copy

Directions: Circle the shape in the middle box that matches the one on the left. Draw another shape with the same pattern in the box on the right.

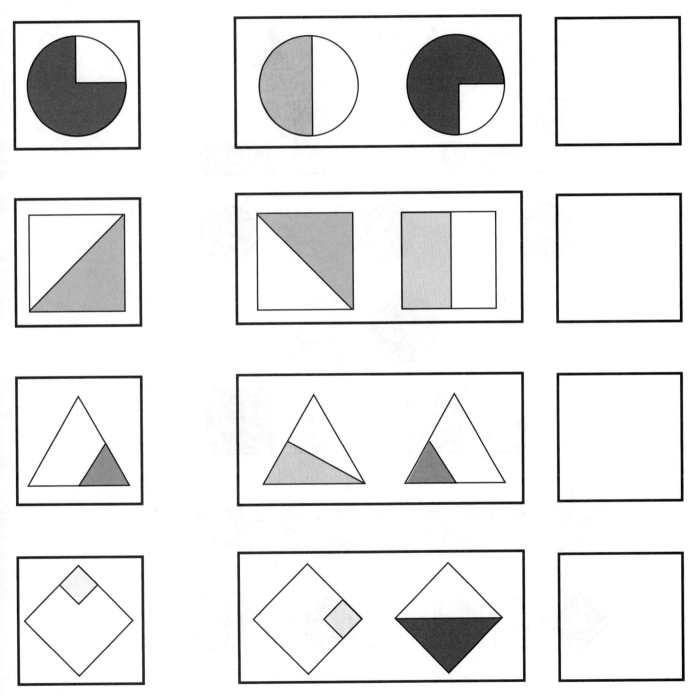

Grade 1 - Comprehensive Curriculum

Patterns

Directions: Draw what comes next in each pattern.

Example:

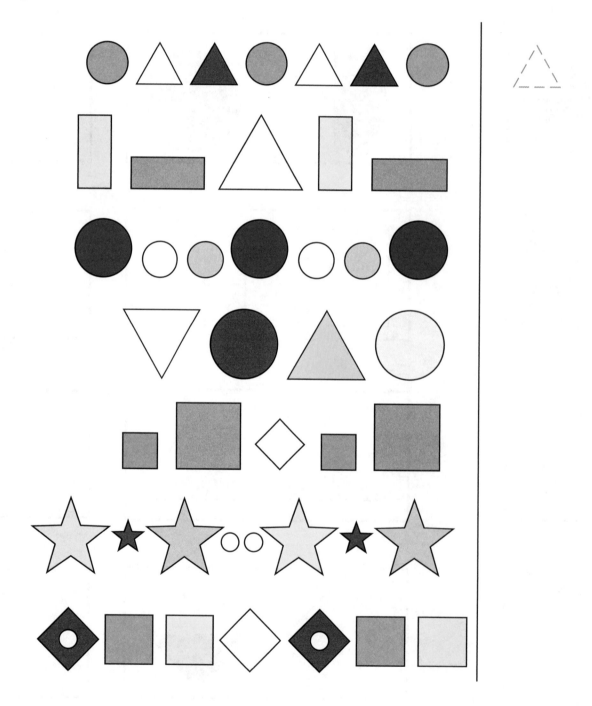

Patterns

Directions: Fill in the missing shape in each row. Then color it.

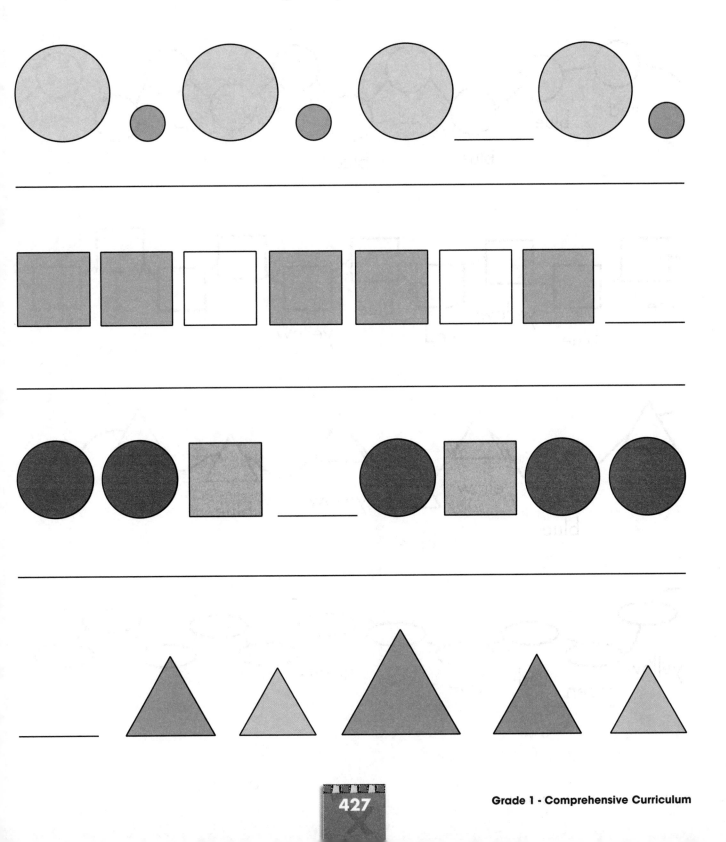

Grade 1 - Comprehensive Curriculum

Name: _____

Patterns

Directions: Color to complete the patterns.

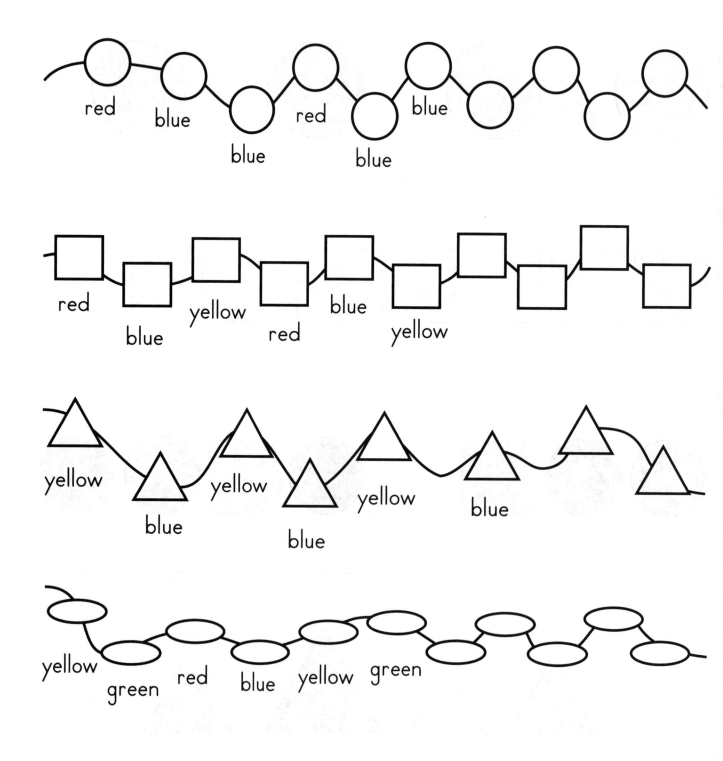

red   blue   blue   red   blue   blue

red   blue   yellow   red   blue   yellow

yellow   blue   yellow   blue   yellow   blue

yellow   green   red   blue   yellow   green

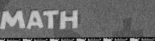
Fractions: Whole and Half

A fraction is a number that names part of a whole, such as $\frac{1}{2}$ or $\frac{3}{4}$.

Directions: Color half of each object.

Example:

Whole apple

Half an apple

$$\frac{1}{2}$$

Name: _____

Fractions: Halves $\frac{1}{2}$

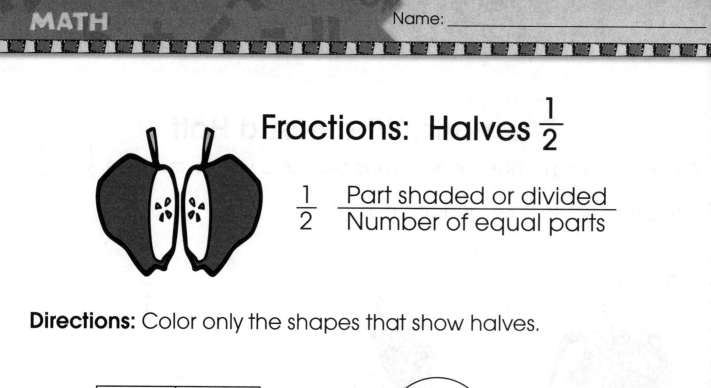

$\dfrac{1}{2}$ $\dfrac{\text{Part shaded or divided}}{\text{Number of equal parts}}$

Directions: Color only the shapes that show halves.

Name: _____

Fractions: Thirds $\frac{1}{3}$

Directions: Circle the objects that have 3 equal parts.

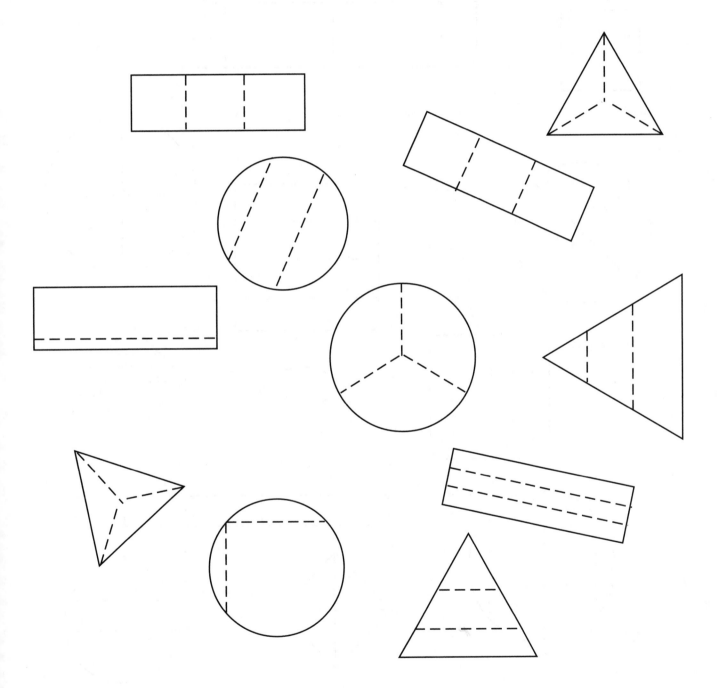

Grade 1 - Comprehensive Curriculum

Name: _____

Fractions: Fourths $\frac{1}{4}$

Directions: Circle the objects that have four equal parts.

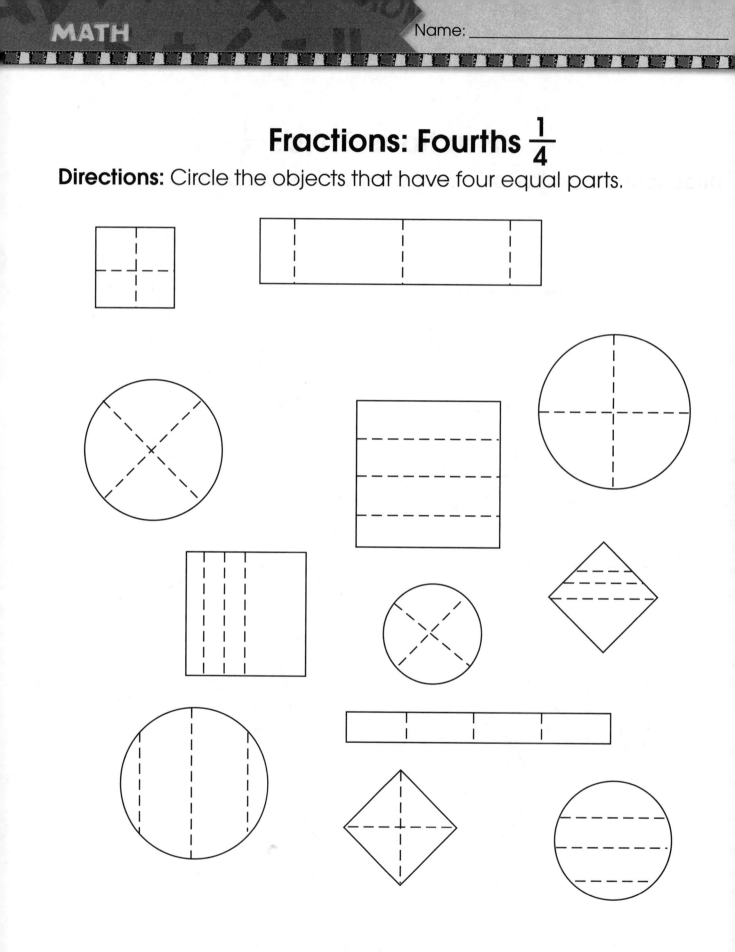

Name: _____

Fractions: Thirds and Fourths

Directions: Each object has 3 equal parts. Color one section.

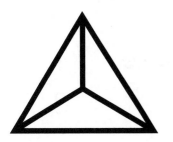  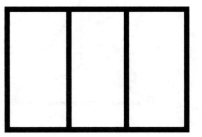

Directions: Each object has 4 equal parts. Color one section.

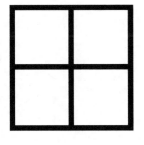 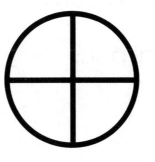 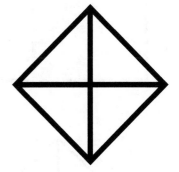

Grade 1 - Comprehensive Curriculum

Name: _____

Review: Fractions

Directions: Count the equal parts, then write the fraction.

Example:

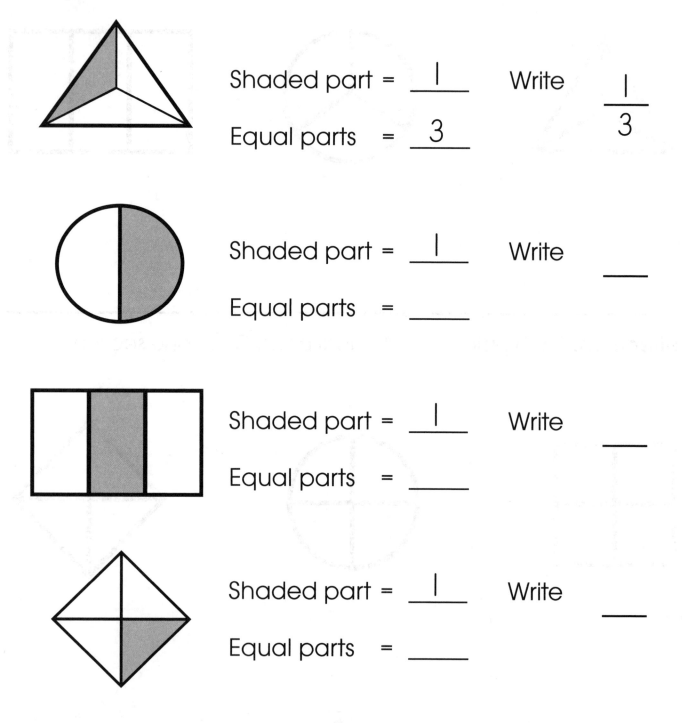

Shaded part = __1__   Write $\frac{1}{3}$

Equal parts = __3__

Shaded part = __1__   Write   ___

Equal parts = ____

Shaded part = __1__   Write   ___

Equal parts = ____

Shaded part = __1__   Write   ___

Equal parts = ____

Review

Directions: Write the missing numbers by counting by tens and fives.

_____ , 20, _____ , _____ , _____ , _____ , 70, _____ , _____ , 100

5, _____ , 15, _____ , _____ , 30, _____ , _____ , _____ , _____

Directions: Color the object with thirds red. Color the object with halves blue. Color the object with fourths green.

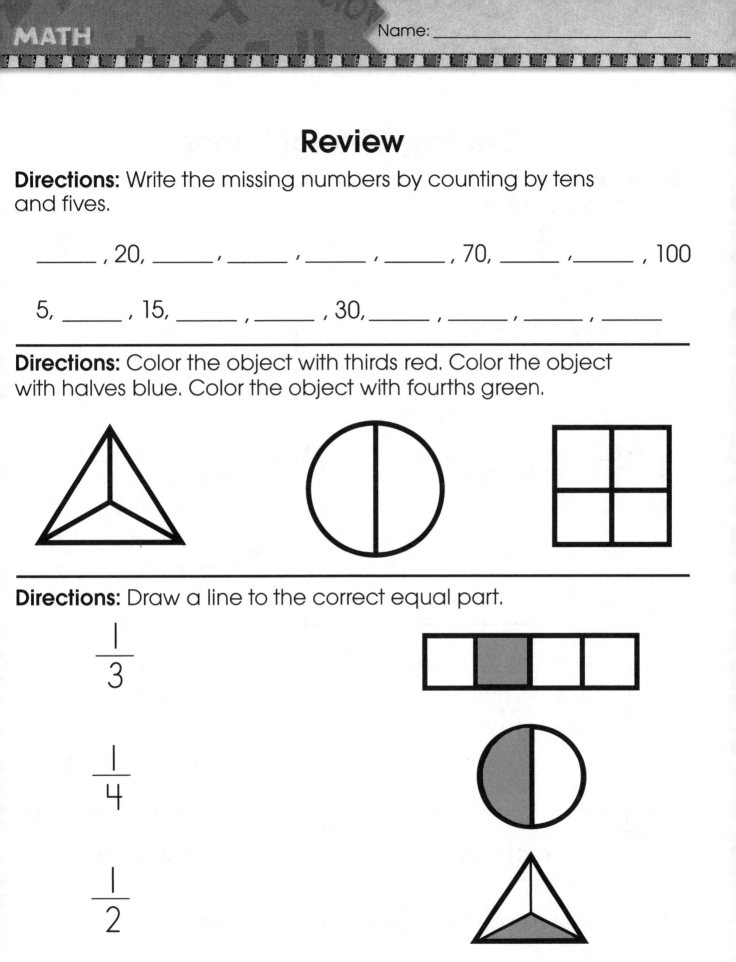

Directions: Draw a line to the correct equal part.

$\frac{1}{3}$

$\frac{1}{4}$

$\frac{1}{2}$

Name: _____

Tracking: Straight Lines

Directions: Draw a straight line from A to B. Use a different color crayon for each line.

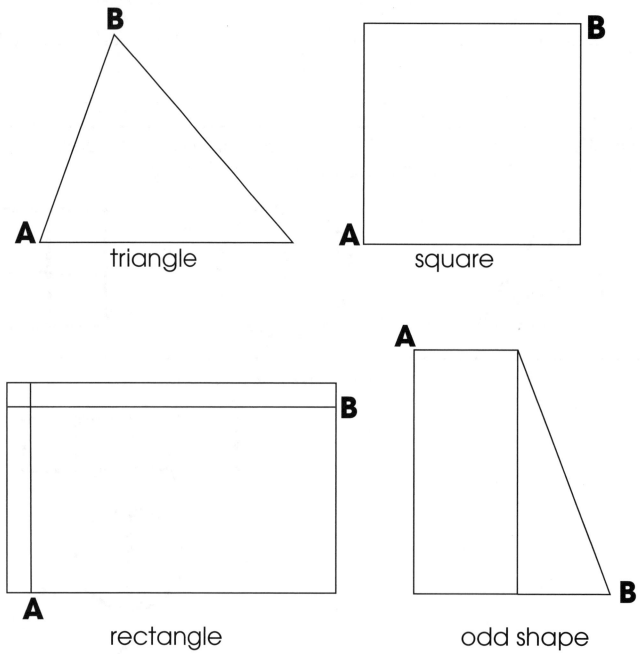

triangle

square

rectangle

odd shape

What shapes do you see hidden in these shapes?

Name: _____

Tracking: Different Paths

Directions: Trace three paths from A to B.

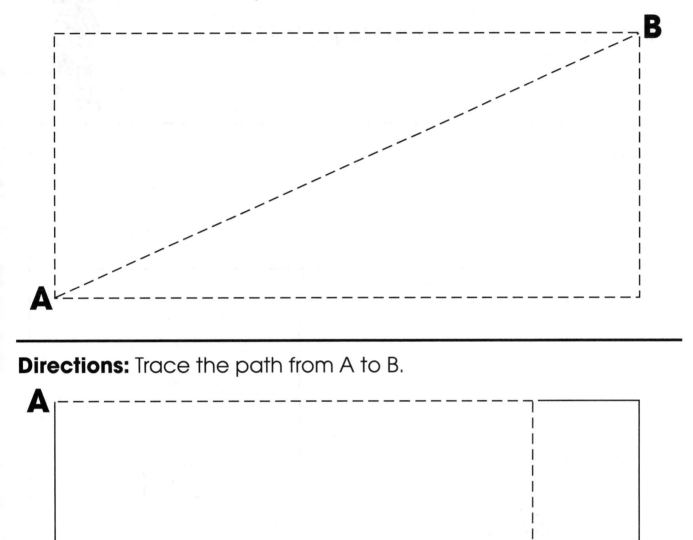

Directions: Trace the path from A to B.

How many corners did you turn?_____

Name: _____

Tracking: Different Paths

Help Megan find Mark.

Directions: Trace a path from Megan to Mark.

How many different paths can she follow to reach him? _____

Name: _____

Tracking: Different Paths

Directions: Use different colors to trace three paths the bear could take to get the honey.

Grade 1 - Comprehensive Curriculum

Time: Hour

The short hand of the clock tells the hour. The long hand tells how many minutes after the hour. When the minute hand is on the **12**, it is the beginning of the hour.

Directions: Look at each clock. Write the time.

Example:

_3_ o'clock

_9_ o'clock

_1_ o'clock

_8_ o'clock

___ o'clock

_5_ o'clock

_2_ o'clock

_10_ o'clock

_12_ o'clock

Name: _____

Time: Hour, Half-Hour

The short hand of the clock tells the hour. The long hand tells how many minutes after the hour. When the minute hand is on the **6**, it is on the half-hour. A half-hour is thirty minutes. It is written **:30**, such as **5:30**.

Directions: Look at each clock. Write the time.

Example:

hour   half-hour

__1__ : __30__

_____ : 30   6 : 30   4 : 20   8 : 30

9 : 30   2 : 30   10 : 30   9 : 30

Grade 1 - Comprehensive Curriculum

Time: Hour, Half-Hour

Directions: Draw the hands on each clock to show the correct time.

2:30

9:00

7:00

4:30

3:00

1:30

Time: Counting by Fives

Directions: Fill in the numbers on the clock face. Count by fives around the clock.

There are 60 minutes in one hour.

Time: Review

Directions: Look at the time on the digital clocks and draw the hands on the clocks.

Directions: Look at each clock. Write the time.

_____o'clock   _____o'clock

Directions: Look at each clock. Write the time.

_____:_____   _____:_____   _____:_____

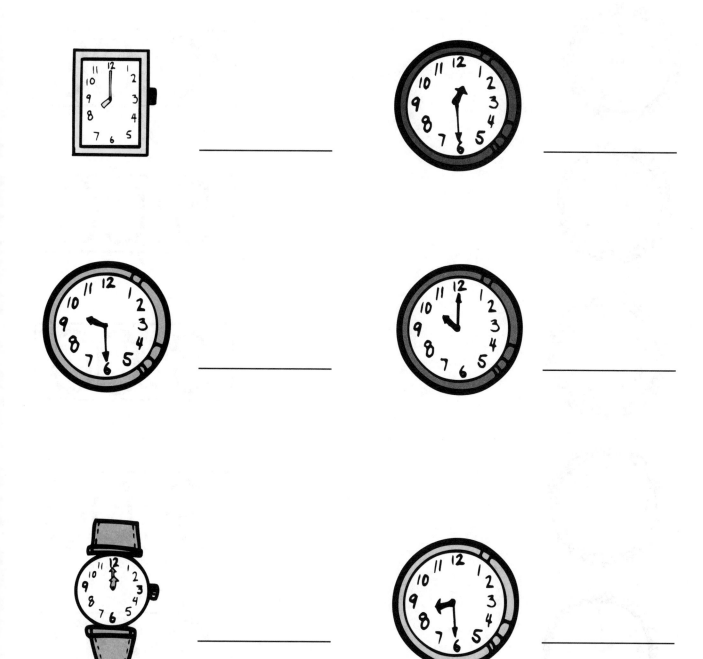

Review: Time

Directions: Tell what time it is on the clocks.

Grade 1 - Comprehensive Curriculum

Name: _____

Review: Time

Directions: Match the time on the clock with the digital time.

Money: Penny and Nickel

A penny is worth one cent. It is written **1¢** or **$.01**. A nickel is worth five cents. It is written **5¢** or **$.05**.

Directions: Count the money and write the answers.

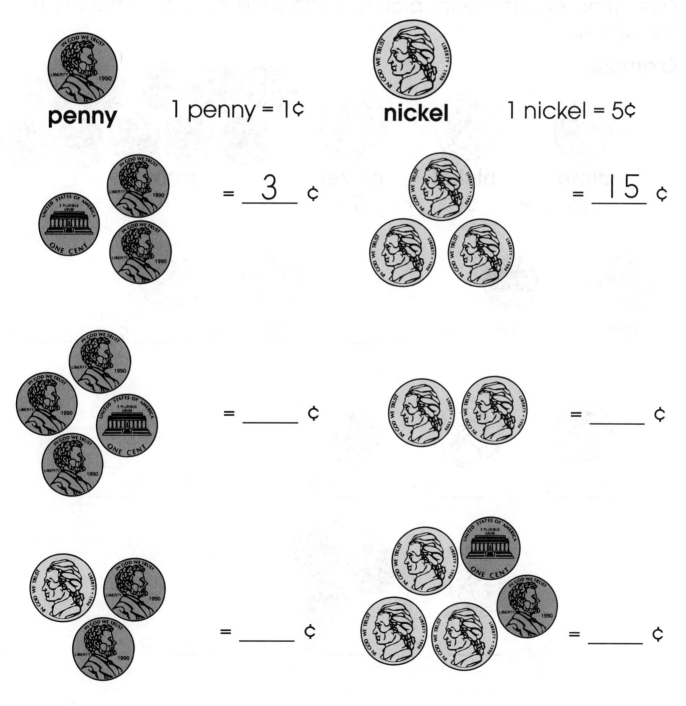

penny   1 penny = 1¢   **nickel**   1 nickel = 5¢

= _3_ ¢   = _15_ ¢

= _____ ¢   = _____ ¢

= _____ ¢   = _____ ¢

Money: Penny, Nickel, Dime

A penny is worth one cent. It is written **1¢** or **$.01**. A nickel is worth five cents. It is written **5¢** or **$.05**. A dime is worth ten cents. It is written **10¢** or **$.10**.

Directions: Add the coins pictured and write the total amounts in the blanks.

Example:

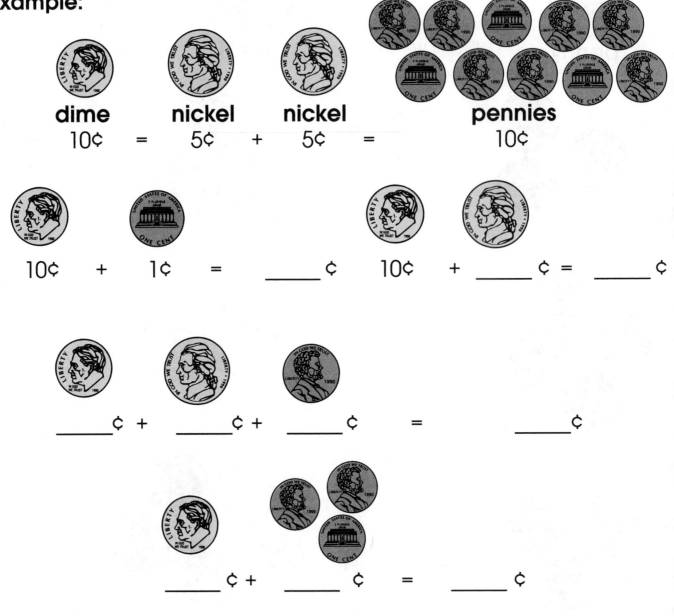

dime   nickel   nickel   pennies

10¢   =   5¢   +   5¢   =   10¢

10¢   +   1¢   =   _____ ¢   10¢   +   _____ ¢   =   _____ ¢

_____ ¢ +   _____ ¢ +   _____ ¢   =   _____ ¢

_____ ¢ +   _____ ¢   =   _____ ¢

Name: _____

Money

Directions: Match the amounts in each purse to the price tags.

Grade 1 - Comprehensive Curriculum

Name: _____

Money: Penny, Nickel, Dime

Directions: Match the correct amount of money with the price of the object.

Review

Directions: What time is it?

_____ o'clock

Directions: Draw the hands on each clock.

2:30

7:30

11:00

Directions: How much money?

= _____ ¢

= _____ ¢

Directions: Add or subtract.

9 + 3 = _____   6 + 8 = _____   15 - 9 = _____

12 - 8 = _____   12 + 2 = _____   7 + 6 = _____

Name: _____

Review

Directions: Follow the instructions.

1. How much money?

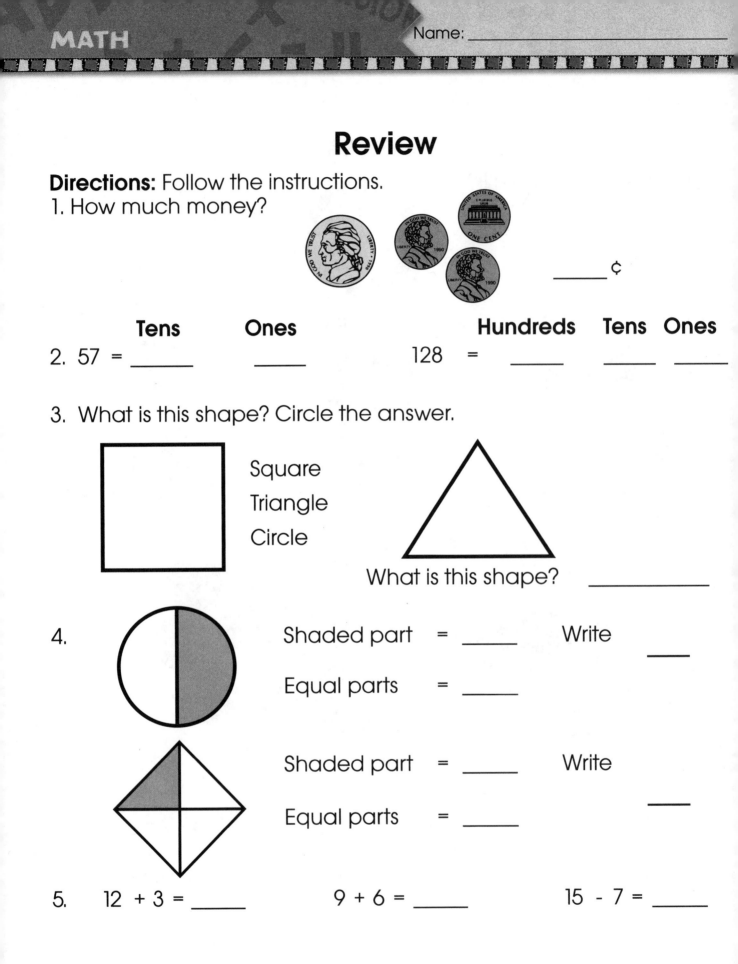

_____ ¢

2.   **Tens   Ones**   **Hundreds   Tens   Ones**

   57 = _____ _____   128 = _____ _____ _____

3. What is this shape? Circle the answer.

Square

Triangle

Circle

What is this shape? _____

4.   Shaded part = _____   Write _____

   Equal parts = _____

   Shaded part = _____   Write

   Equal parts = _____   _____

5.   12 + 3 = _____   9 + 6 = _____   15 - 7 = _____

Measurement

A ruler has 12 inches. 12 inches equal 1 foot.

Directions: Cut out the ruler at the bottom of the page. Measure the objects to the nearest inch.

The screwdriver is _____ inches long.

The pencil is _____ inches long.

The pen is _____ inches long.

The fork is _____ inches long.

Cut ✂ -

| 1 | 2 | 3 | 4 | 5 | 6 | 7 | 8 | 9 | 10 | 11 | 12 |

Page is blank for cutting exercise on previous page.

Abbreviation: A short way of writing words. Examples: Mon., Tues., etc.

Addition: "Putting together" or adding two or more numbers to find the sum.

Alphabetical (ABC) Order: Putting letters or words in the order in which they appear in the alphabet.

Antonyms: Words that are opposites. Example: big and small are opposites.

Asking Sentences: Sentences that ask a question. An asking sentence begins with a capital letter and ends with a question mark.

Beginning Consonants: Consonant sounds that come at the beginning of words.

Beginning Sounds: The sounds you hear first in a word.

Capital Letters: Letters that are used at the beginning of names of people, places, days, months and holidays. Capital letters are also used at the beginning of sentences. These letters (A, B, C, D, E, F, G, H, I, J, K, L, M, N, O, P, Q, R, S, T, U, V, W, X, Y and Z) are sometimes called uppercase or "big" letters.

Circle: A figure that is round. It looks like this: ◯

Classifying: Putting objects, words or ideas that are alike into categories.

Compound Words: Two words that are put together to make one new word. Example: house + boat = houseboat.

Comprehension: Understanding what is seen, heard or read.

Consonant Blends: Two consonant sounds put together.

Consonants: The letters b, c, d, f, g, h, j, k, l, m, n, p, q, r, s, t, v, w, x, y and z. Consonants are all the letters except a, e, i, o and u.

Describing Words: Words that tell more about a person, place or thing.

Diamond: A figure with four sides of the same length. Its corners form points at the top, sides and bottom. It looks like this: ◇

Digits: The symbols used to write numbers: 0, 1, 2, 3, 4, 5, 6, 7, 8 and 9.

Dime: Ten cents. It is written 10¢ or $.10.

Directions: Doing what the instructions say to do.

Ending Consonants: Consonant sounds which come at the end of words.

Ending Sounds: The sounds made by the last letters of words.

Following Directions: Doing what the directions say to do.

Fraction: A number that names part of a whole, such as $\frac{1}{2}$ or $\frac{2}{3}$.

Half-Hour: Thirty minutes. When the long hand of the clock is pointing to the six, the time is on the half-hour. It is written :30, such as 5:30.

Homophones: Words that sound the same but are spelled differently and mean different things. Example: blue and blew.

Hour: Sixty minutes. The short hand of a clock tells the hour. It is written 2:00.

Long Vowels: The letters a, e, i, o and u which say the "long" or letter name sound. Long a is the sound you hear in hay. Long e is the sound you hear in me. Long i is the sound you hear in pie. Long o is the sound you hear in no. Long u is the sound you hear in cute.

Making Inferences: Using logic to figure out what is unspoken but known to be true.

Nickel: Five cents. It is written 5¢ or $.05.

Nouns: Name a person, place or thing.

Opposites: Things that are different in every way.

Ordinal Numbers: Numbers that indicate order in a series, such as first, second or third.

Oval: A figure that is egg-shaped. It looks like this: ⬭

Pattern: A repeated arrangement of pictures, letters or shapes.

Penny: One cent. It is written 1¢ or $.01.

Period: Tells you when to stop reading and is found at the end of sentences. It looks like this: .

Picture Clues: Looking at the pictures to figure out meaning.

Place Value: The value of a digit, or numeral, shown by where it is in the number. For example, in the number 23, 2 has the place value of tens and 3 is ones.

Predicting: Telling what is likely to happen based on available facts.

Rectangle: A figure with four corners and four sides. Sides opposite each other are the same length. It looks like this: ▭

Rhymes: Words with the same ending sounds.

Rhyming Words: Words that sound alike at the end of the word. Example: cat and rat.

Same and Different: Being able to tell how things are alike and not alike.

Sentence: A group of words that tells a complete idea.

Sequencing: Putting numbers in the correct order, such as 7, 8, 9.

Short Vowels: The letters a, e, i, o and u which say the short sound. Short a is the sound you hear in ant. Short e is the sound you hear in elephant. Short i is the sound you hear in igloo. Short o is the sound you hear in octopus. Short u is the sound you hear in umbrella.

Similar: Things that are almost the same.

Square: A figure with four corners and four sides of the same length. It looks like this: ▢

Subtraction: "Taking away" or subtracting one number from another. For example: $10 - 3 = 7$.

Super Silent E: The e that is added to some words which changes the short vowel sound to a long vowel sound. Example: rip + e = ripe.

Synonyms: Words that mean the same thing. Example: small and little.

Telling Sentences: Sentences that tell something. A telling sentence begins with a capital letter and ends with a period.

Tracking: Following a path.

Triangle: A figure with three corners and three sides. It looks like this: △

Verbs: Words that tell what a person or thing can do.

Vowels: The letters a, e, i, o, u and sometimes y.

Page 6

Name, Address, Phone

This book belongs to

Answers will vary.

I live at

Answers will vary.

The city I live in is

Answers will vary.

The state I live in is

Answers will vary.

My phone number is

Answers will vary.

Page 7

Review the Alphabet

Directions: Practice writing the letters.

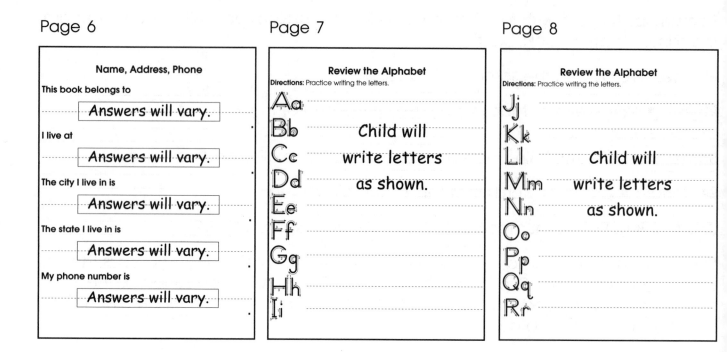

Child will write letters as shown.

Page 8

Review the Alphabet

Directions: Practice writing the letters.

Child will write letters as shown.

Page 9

Review the Alphabet

Directions: Practice writing the letters.

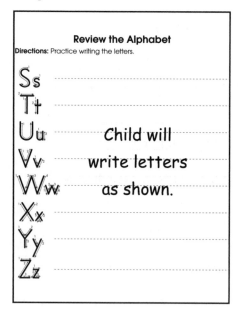

Child will write letters as shown.

Page 10

Letter Recognition

Directions: In each set, match the lower-case letter to the upper-case letter.

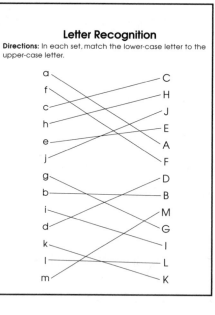

Page 11

Letter Recognition

Directions: In each set, match the lower-case letter to the upper-case letter.

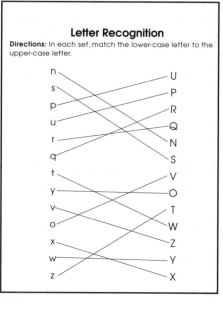

Page 12

Beginning Consonants: Bb, Cc, Dd, Ff

Beginning consonants are the sounds that come at the beginning of words. Consonants are the letters b, c, d, f, g, h, j, k, l, m, n, p, q, r, s, t, v, w, x, y and z.

Directions: Say the name of each letter. Say the sound each letter makes. Circle the letters that make the beginning sound for each picture.

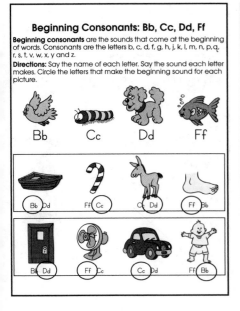

Page 13

Beginning Consonants: Bb, Cc, Dd, Ff

Directions: Say the name of each letter. Say the sound each letter makes. Draw a line from each letter to the picture which begins with that sound.

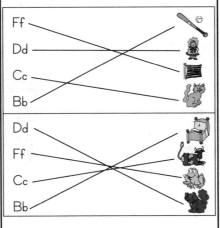

Page 14

Beginning Consonants: Gg, Hh, Jj, Kk

Directions: Say the name of each letter. Say the sound each letter makes. Trace the letter pair that makes the beginning sound in each picture.

Page 15

Beginning Consonants: Gg, Hh, Jj, Kk

Directions: Say the name of each letter. Say the sound each letter makes. Draw a line from each letter pair to the picture which begins with that sound.

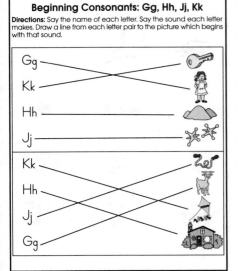

Page 16

Beginning Consonants: Ll, Mm, Nn, Pp

Directions: Say the name of each letter. Say the sound each letter makes. Trace the letters. Then draw a line from each letter pair to the picture which begins with that sound.

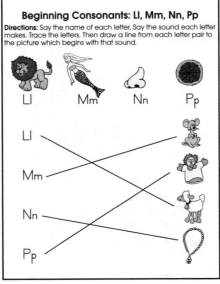

Page 17

Beginning Consonants: Ll, Mm, Nn, Pp

Directions: Say the name of each letter. Say the sound each letter makes. Trace the letter pair that makes the beginning sound in each picture.

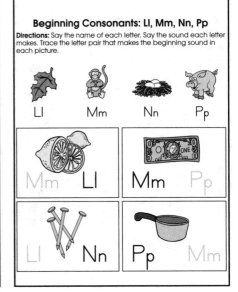

Grade 1 - Comprehensive Curriculum

Page 18

Beginning Consonants: Qq, Rr, Ss, Tt

Directions: Say the name of each letter. Say the sound each letter makes. Trace the letter pair in the boxes. Then color the picture which begins with that sound.

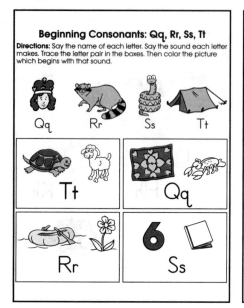

Page 19

Beginning Consonants: Qq, Rr, Ss, Tt

Directions: Say the name of each letter. Say the sound each letter makes. Draw a line from each letter pair to the picture which begins with that sound.

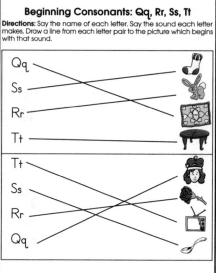

Page 20

Beginning Consonants: Vv, Ww, Xx, Yy, Zz

Directions: Say the name of each letter. Say the sound each letter makes. Trace the letters. Then draw a line from each letter pair to the picture which begins with that sound.

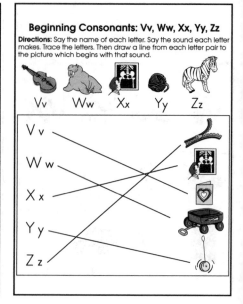

Page 21

Beginning Consonants: Vv, Ww, Xx, Yy, Zz

Directions: Say the name of each letter. Say the sound each letter makes. Then draw a line from each letter pair to the picture which begins with that sound.

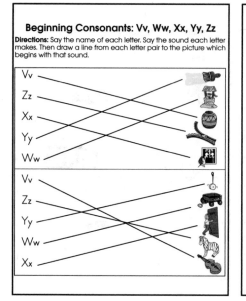

Page 22

Review

Directions: Help Meg, Kent and their dog, Sam, get to the magic castle. Trace each capital consonant letter and write the lower-case consonant next to it. Say the sound each consonant makes.

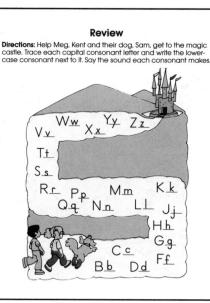

Page 23

Review

Directions: Write the letter that makes the beginning sound for each picture.

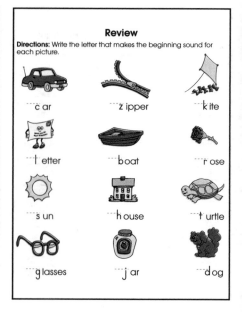

c ar   z ipper   k ite

l etter   boat   r ose

s un   h ouse   t urtle

g lasses   j ar   d og

Page 24

Ending Consonants: b, d, f

Ending consonants are the sounds that come at the end of words.
Directions: Say the name of each picture. Then write the letter which makes the **ending** sound for each picture.

b	f	d
b	d	f
f	d	f
b	d	b

Page 25

Ending Consonants: g, m, n

Directions: Say the name of each picture. Draw a line from each letter to the pictures which end with that sound.

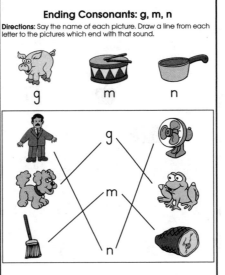

g   m   n

g
m
n

Page 26

Ending Consonants: k, l, p

Directions: Trace the letters in each row. Say the name of each picture. Then color the pictures in each row which end with that sound.

k

l

p

Page 27

Ending Consonants: r, s, t, x

Directions: Say the name of each picture. Then circle the ending sound for each picture.

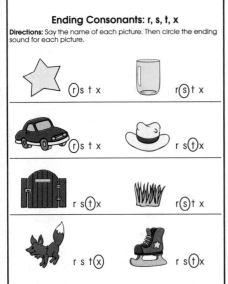

(r) s t x   r (s) t x

(r) s t x   r s (t) x

r s (t) x   r (s) t x

r s t (x)   r s (t) x

Page 28

Beginning and Ending Consonants

Directions: Say the name of each picture. Draw a **blue** circle around the picture if it **begins** with the sound of the letter below it. Draw a **green** triangle around the picture if it **ends** with the sound of the letter below it.

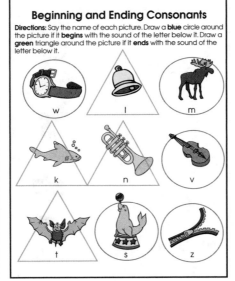

w   l   m

k   n   v

t   s   z

Page 29

Beginning and Ending Consonants

Directions: Say the name of each picture. Draw a triangle around the letter that makes the **beginning** sound. Draw a square around the letter that makes the **ending** sound. Color the pictures.

o △r□ t   f □d△ △w   v t△ b△

x △c□ r   t g △d△   △a△ a k□

l m △n△   x □g△ t△   p □t△ △w△

461

Page 30

Beginning and Ending Consonants

Directions: Say the name of each picture. Write the beginning and ending sounds for each picture.

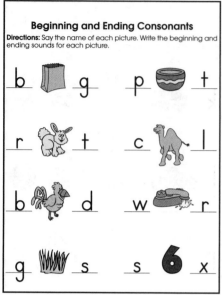

b __g__   p __t__

r __t__   c __l__

b __d__   w __r__

g __s__   s __x__

Page 31

Short Vowels

Vowels are the letters **a, e, i, o** and **u**. Short **a** is the sound you hear in **ant**. Short **e** is the sound you hear in **elephant**. Short **i** is the sound you hear in **igloo**. Short **o** is the sound you hear in **octopus**. Short **u** is the sound you hear in **umbrella**.

Directions: Say the short vowel sound at the beginning of each row. Say the name of each picture. Then color the pictures which have the same short vowel sounds as that letter.

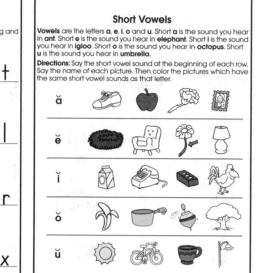

Page 32

Short Vowel Sounds

Directions: In each box are three pictures. The words that name the pictures have missing letters. Write **a, e, i, o** or **u** to finish the words.

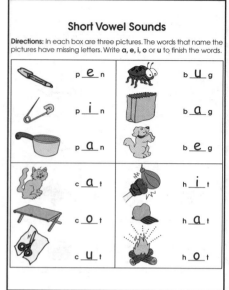

p __e__ n   b __u__ g
p __i__ n   b __a__ g
p __a__ n   b __e__ g

c __a__ t   h __i__ t
c __o__ t   h __a__ t
c __u__ t   h __o__ t

Page 33

Long Vowels

Vowels are the letters **a, e, i, o** and **u**. Long vowel sounds say their own names. Long **a** is the sound you hear in **hay**. Long **e** is the sound you hear in **me**. Long **i** is the sound you hear in **pie**. Long **o** is the sound you hear in **no**. Long **u** is the sound you hear in **cute**.

Directions: Say the long vowel sound at the beginning of each row. Say the name of each picture. Color the pictures in each row that have the same long vowel sound as that letter.

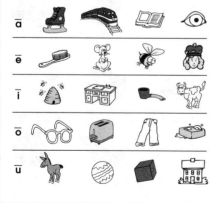

Page 34

Long Vowel Sounds

Directions: Write **a, e, i, o** or **u** in each blank to finish the word. Draw a line from the word to the picture.

c __a__ ke

r __o__ se

k __i__ te

f __ee__ t

m __u__ le

Page 35

Words With a

Directions: Each train has a group of pictures. Write the word that names the pictures. Read your rhyming words.

These trains use the short **a** sound like in the word cat:

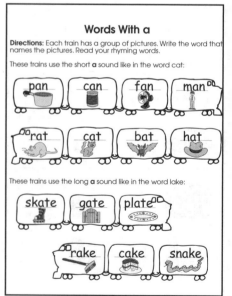

pan   can   fan   man

rat   cat   bat   hat

These trains use the long **a** sound like in the word lake:

skate   gate   plate

rake   cake   snake

Page 36

Short and Long Aa

Directions: Say the name of each picture. If it has the short **a** sound, color it **red**. If it has the long **a** sound, color it **yellow**.

Page 37

Words with e

Directions: Short **e** sounds like the **e** in hen. Long **e** sounds like the **e** in bee. Look at the pictures. If the word has a short **e** sound, draw a line to the **hen** with your **red** crayon. If the word has a long **e** sound, draw a line to the **bee** with your **green** crayon.

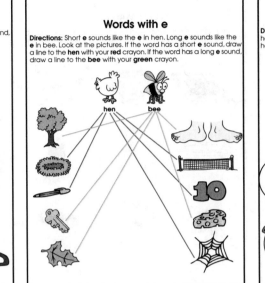

Page 38

Short and Long Ee

Directions: Say the name of each picture. Circle the pictures which have the short **e** sound. Draw a triangle around the pictures which have the long **e** sound.

Page 39

Words with i

Directions: Short **i** sounds like the **i** in pig. Long **i** sounds like the **i** in kite. Draw a circle around the words with the short **i** sound. Draw an **X** on the words with the long **i** sound.

Page 40

Short and Long Ii

Directions: Say the name of each picture. If it has the short **i** sound, color it **yellow**. If it has the long **i** sound, color it **red**.

Page 41

Words With o

Directions: The short **o** sounds like the **o** in dog. Long **o** sounds like the **o** in rope. Draw a line from the picture to the word that names it. Draw a circle around the word if it has a short **o** sound.

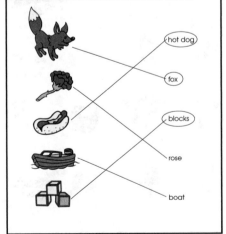

ANSWER KEY

Page 42

Short and Long Oo

Directions: Say the name of each picture. If the picture has the long o sound, write a **green L** on the blank. If the picture has the short o sound, write a **red S** on the blank.

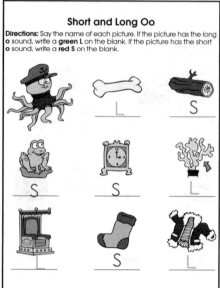

Page 43

Words With u

Directions: The short **u** sounds like the **u** in bug. The long **u** sounds like the **u** in blue. Draw a circle around the words with short **u**. Draw an **X** on the words with long **u**.

Page 44

Short and Long Uu

Directions: Say the name of each picture. If it has the long **u** sound, write a **u** in the **unicorn** column. If it has the short **u** sound, write a **u** in the **umbrella** column.

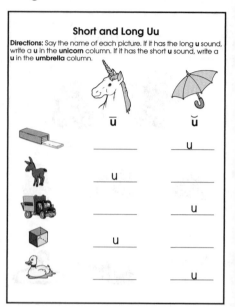

Page 45

Super Silent E

When you add an **e** to the end of some words, the vowel changes from a short vowel sound to a long vowel sound. The **e** is silent.

Example: rip + e = ripe.

Directions: Say the word under the first picture in each pair. Then add an **e** to the word under the next picture. Say the new word.

Page 46

Short and Long Vowels

Directions: Say the name of each picture. Write the vowel on each line that completes the word. Color the short vowel pictures. Circle the long vowel pictures.

Page 47

Short and Long Vowel Sounds

Directions: Cut out the pictures below. If the vowel has a **long** sound glue it on the **long** vowel side. If the vowel has a **short** sound, glue it on the **short** vowel side.

Page 49

Review

Directions: Color all of the vowels black to discover something hidden in the puzzle.

What was hidden?

a spider

Page 50

Review

Directions: Circle the word if it has a long vowel sound.

Remember: A long vowel says its name.

feet
snake
cup
hose
tie
hat
dog
rake
bug
bone
bib
net

Page 51

Review

Directions: Write the vowel on each line that completes the word.

a   e   i   o   u

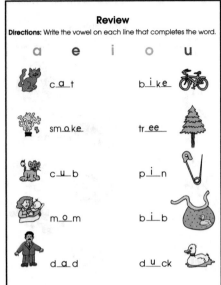

c a t   b i ke

sm o ke   tr ee

c u b   p i n

m o m   b i b

d a d   d u ck

Page 52

Review

Directions: Circle the **long vowel** words with a **red** crayon. Underline the **short vowel** words with a **blue** crayon.

Remember: The vowel is long if:
- There are two vowels in the word. The first vowel is the sound you hear.
- There is a "super silent e" at the end.

cub	red	coat
bite	cube	cage
cat	mean	rake
bit	cot	hen
leaf	feet	key
pen	web	bee
nest	boat	fox
rose	dog	pig

Page 53

My Vowel List

Keep this list handy and add more words to it.

Individual lists will vary.

short a
(ă as in cat)

long a
(ā as in train)

short e
(ĕ as in get)

long e
(ē as in tree)

short i
(ĭ as in pin)

long i
(ī as in ice)

short o
(ŏ as in cot)

long o
(ō as in boat)

short u
(ŭ as in cut)

long u
(ū as in cube)

Page 55

Consonant Blends

Consonant blends are two or more consonant sounds together in a word. The blend is made by combining the consonant sounds.

Example: floor

Directions: The name of each picture begins with a **blend**. Circle the beginning blend for each picture.

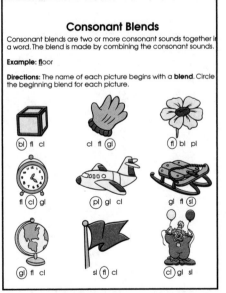

bl fl cl   cl fl gl   fl bl pl

fl cl gl   pl gl cl   gl fl sl

gl fl cl   sl fl cl   cl gl sl

Page 56

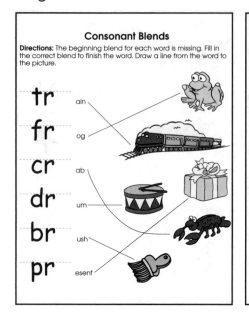

Consonant Blends

Directions: The beginning blend for each word is missing. Fill in the correct blend to finish the word. Draw a line from the word to the picture.

tr — ain
fr — og
cr — ab
dr — um
br — ush
pr — esent

Page 57

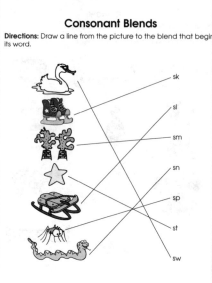

Consonant Blends

Directions: Draw a line from the picture to the blend that begins its word.

sk
sl
sm
sn
sp
st
sw

Page 58

Consonant Blends

Directions: Look at the first picture in each row. Circle the pictures in the row that begin with the same sound.

chair
shell
thumb
wheel

Page 59

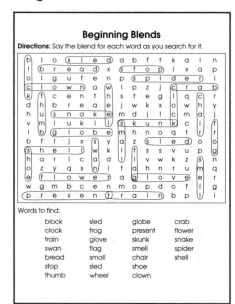

Beginning Blends

Directions: Say the blend for each word as you search for it.

Words to find:

block	sled	globe	crab
clock	frog	present	flower
train	glove	skunk	snake
swan	flag	smell	spider
bread	small	chair	shell
stop	sled	shoe	
thumb	wheel	clown	

Page 60

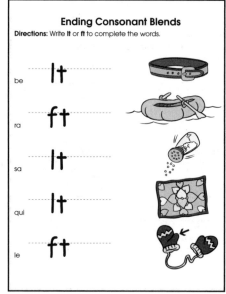

Ending Consonant Blends

Directions: Write **lt** or **ft** to complete the words.

be — lt
ra — ft
sa — lt
qui — lt
le — ft

Page 61

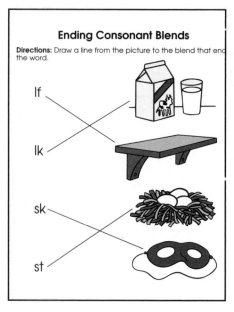

Ending Consonant Blends

Directions: Draw a line from the picture to the blend that ends the word.

lf
lk
sk
st

Page 62

Ending Consonant Blends

Directions: Every juke box has a word ending and a list of letters. Add each of the letters to the word ending to make rhyming words.

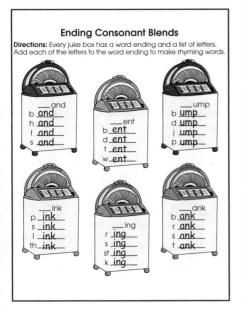

b **and**
h **and**
l **and**
s **and**

___ ent
b **ent**
d **ent**
t **ent**
w **ent**

___ ump
b **ump**
d **ump**
j **ump**
p **ump**

p **ink**
s **ink**
l **ink**
th **ink**

___ ing
r **ing**
s **ing**
st **ing**
k **ing**

___ ank
b **ank**
r **ank**
s **ank**
t **ank**

Page 63

Ending Consonant Blends

Directions: Say the blend for each word as you search for it.

Words to find:

belt	raft	milk	shelf
mask	clasp	nest	band
think	went	lump	crank
ring	blank	shrink	land
bring	tent	dump	sing

Page 64

Review

Directions: Finish each sentence with a word from the word box.

sting	shelf	drank	plant	stamp

1. Tom **drank** his milk.

2. A bee can **sting** you.

3. I put a **stamp** on my letter.

4. The **plant** is green.

5. The book is on the **shelf**

Page 65

Rhyming Words

Rhyming words are words that sound alike at the end of the word. **Cat** and **hat** rhyme.

Directions: Draw a circle around each word pair that rhymes. Draw an **X** on each pair that does not rhyme.

Example:

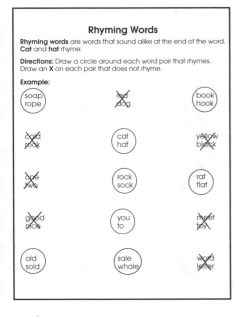

(soap rope)   red dog ✗   (book hook)

cold rock ✗   (cat hat)   yellow black ✗

one two ✗   (rock sock)   (rat flat)

good price ✗   (you to)   meet toy ✗

(old sold)   (sale whale)   word letter ✗

Page 66

Rhyming Words

Rhyming words are words that sound alike at the end of the word.

Directions: Draw a line to match the pictures that rhyme. Write two of your own rhyming word pairs below.

Answers will vary.

Page 67

ABC Order

Directions: Abc order is the order in which letters come in the alphabet. Draw a line to connect the dots. Follow the letters in **abc** order. Then color the picture.

Page 68

ABC Order

Directions: Draw a line to connect the dots. Follow the letters in abc order. Then color the picture.

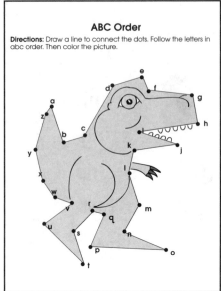

Page 69

ABC Order

Directions: Circle the first letter of each word. Then put each pair of the words in abc order.

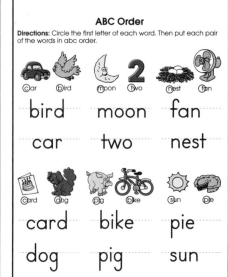

bird   moon   fan

car   two   nest

card   bike   pie

dog   pig   sun

Page 70

ABC Order

Directions: Look at the words in each box. Circle the word that comes first in abc order.

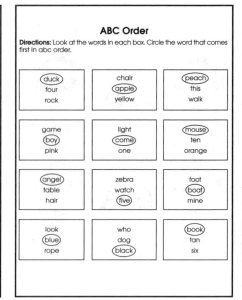

(duck) four rock	chair (apple) yellow	(peach) this walk
game (boy) pink	light (come) one	(mouse) ten orange
(angel) table hair	zebra watch (five)	foot (boat) mine
look (blue) rope	who dog (black)	(book) tan six

Page 71

ABC Order

Directions: Cut out the foods Mom wants to buy when she goes shopping. Glue the words in abc order on the shopping list.

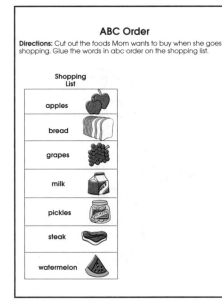

Shopping List

- apples
- bread
- grapes
- milk
- pickles
- steak
- watermelon

Page 73

Sequencing: ABC Order

Directions: Put each group of words in ABC order by numbering them 1, 2, 3.

Example:

cold 1   warm 3   hot 2

small 3   big 1   cute 2

baby 1   sister 3   family 2

doll 2   truck 3   ball 1

man 3   boy 1   grandma 2

Page 74

ABC Order

Directions: Put the words in abc order. Circle the first letter of each word. Then write 1, 2, 3, 4, 5 or 6 on the line next to each animal's name.

skunk 4   dog 2

butterfly 1   zebra 6

tiger 5   fish 3

Page 75

Compound Words

Compound words are two words that are put together to make one new word.

Directions: Look at the pictures and the two words that are next to each other. Put the words together to make a new word. Write the new word.

Example:

house + boat = **houseboat**

side + walk = **sidewalk**

lip + stick = **lipstick**

sand + box = **sandbox**

lunch + box = **lunchbox**

Page 76

Compound Words

Directions: Circle the compound word which completes each sentence. Write each word on the lines.

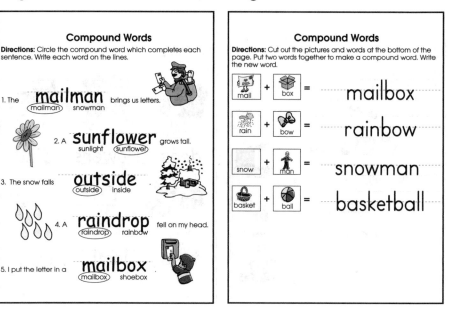

1. The **mailman** (mailman) snowman brings us letters.

2. A **sunflower** sunlight (sunflower) grows tall.

3. The snow falls **outside** (outside) inside

4. A **raindrop** (raindrop) rainbow fell on my head.

5. I put the letter in a **mailbox** (mailbox) shoebox

Page 77

Compound Words

Directions: Cut out the pictures and words at the bottom of the page. Put two words together to make a compound word. Write the new word.

mail + box = **mailbox**

rain + bow = **rainbow**

snow + man = **snowman**

basket + ball = **basketball**

Page 79

Compound Words

Directions: Cut out the cards below. Turn them over. Take turns trying to make compound words. When a compound word is made, the player gets to keep the word.

Cut ✂ -

Possible combinations:

flashlight	snowball
mailbox	houseplant
sunlight	postcard
rainbow	doghouse
inside	familyroom
anything	birthday

Page 81

Names

You are a special person. Your name begins with a capital letter. We put a capital letter at the beginning of people's names because they are special.

Directions: Write your name. Did you remember to use a capital letter?

Answers will vary.

Directions: Write each person's name. Use a capital letter at the beginning.

Ted — **Ted**

Katie — **Katie**

Mike — **Mike**

Tim — **Tim**

Write a friend's name. Use a capital letter at the beginning.

Answers will vary.

Page 82

Names: Days of the Week

The days of the week begin with capital letters.

Directions: Write the days of the week in the spaces below. Put them in order. Be sure to start with capital letters.

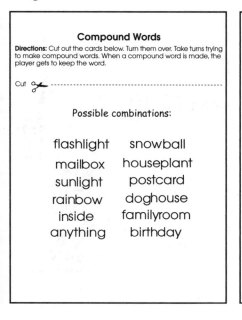

	Sunday
	Monday
Tuesday	Tuesday
Saturday	Wednesday
Monday	
Friday	Thursday
Thursday	
Sunday	Friday
Wednesday	Saturday

Page 83

Names: Months of the Year

The months of the year begin with capital letters.

Directions: Write the months of the year in order on the calendar below. Be sure to use capital letters.

January September	December February	April July	May March	October November	June August

January		July	
February		August	
March		September	
April		October	
May		November	
June		December	

Page 84

More Than One

Directions: An **s** at the end of a word often means there is more than one. Look at each picture. Circle the correct word. Write the word on the line.

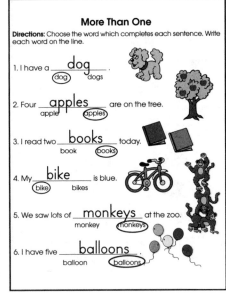

two dog (dogs)

four flower (flowers)

one bikes (bike)

dogs **flowers** **bike**

three (toys) toy

a (lamb) lambs

two cat (cats)

toys **lamb** **cats**

Page 85

More Than One

Directions: Read the nouns under the pictures. Then write each noun under **One** or **More Than One**.

One

barn

wagon

horse

More Than One

cows

pigs

ducks

barn cows ducks wagon horse pigs

Page 86

More Than One

Directions: Circle the correct word to complete each sentence.

Remember: An **s** at the end of a word can mean more than one.

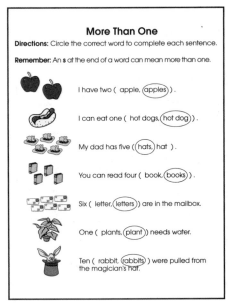

I have two (apple, (apples)).

I can eat one (hot dogs, (hot dog)).

My dad has five ((hats,) hat).

You can read four (book, (books)).

Six (letter, (letters)) are in the mailbox.

One (plants, (plant)) needs water.

Ten (rabbit, (rabbits)) were pulled from the magician's hat.

Page 88

More Than One

Directions: Choose the word which completes each sentence. Write each word on the line.

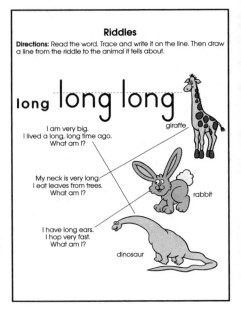

1. I have a ___dog___ (dog) dogs

2. Four ___apples___ are on the tree. apple (apples)

3. I read two ___books___ today. book (books)

4. My ___bike___ is blue. (bike) bikes

5. We saw lots of ___monkeys___ at the zoo. monkey (monkeys)

6. I have five ___balloons___ balloon (balloons)

Page 89

Riddles

Directions: Read the word. Trace and write it on the line. Then draw a line from the riddle to the animal it tells about.

long **long long**

giraffe

I am very big.
I lived a long, long time ago.
What am I?

My neck is very long.
I eat leaves from trees.
What am I?

rabbit

I have long ears.
I hop very fast.
What am I?

dinosaur

Page 90

Riddles

Directions: Read the word and write it on the line. Then read each riddle and draw a line to the picture and word that tells about it.

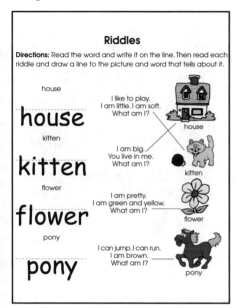

house

house

kitten

kitten

flower

flower

pony

pony

I like to play. I am little. I am soft. What am I? — house

I am big. You live in me. What am I? — kitten

I am pretty. I am green and yellow. What am I? — flower

I can jump. I can run. I am brown. What am I? — pony

Page 91

Riddles

Directions: Write a word from the box to answer each riddle.

| ice cream | book | chair | sun |

There are many words in me. I am fun to read. What am I?

book

I am in the sky in the day. I am hot. I am yellow. What am I?

sun

I am soft and yellow. You can sit on me. What am I?

chair

I am cold. I am sweet. You like to eat me. What am I?

ice cream

Page 92

Picture Clues

Directions: Read the sentence. Circle the word that makes sense. Use the picture clues to help you. Then write the word.

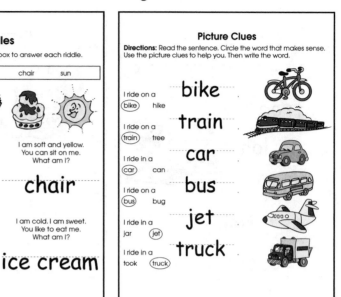

I ride on a (bike) hike — **bike**

I ride on a (train) tree — **train**

I ride in a (car) can — **car**

I ride on a (bus) bug — **bus**

I ride in a jar (jet) — **jet**

I ride in a took (truck) — **truck**

Page 93

Picture Clues

Directions: Read the sentence. Circle the word that makes sense. Use the picture clues to help you. Then write the word.

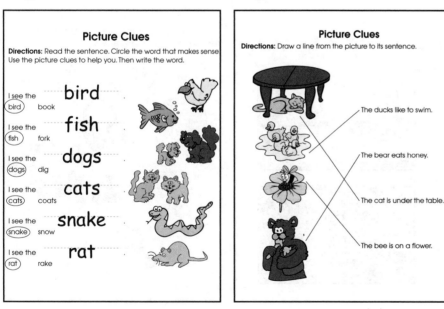

I see the (bird) book — **bird**

I see the (fish) fork — **fish**

I see the (dogs) dig — **dogs**

I see the (cats) coats — **cats**

I see the (snake) snow — **snake**

I see the (rat) rake — **rat**

Page 94

Picture Clues

Directions: Draw a line from the picture to its sentence.

The ducks like to swim.

The bear eats honey.

The cat is under the table.

The bee is on a flower.

Page 95

Picture Clues

Directions: Cut out the pictures below. Glue them next to the sentences.

The sun is yellow.

It is raining.

I can grin.

The bed is broken.

My pen and paper are here.

Cut ✂ ------------------------

Page 97

Comprehension

Directions: Look at the picture. Write the words from the box to finish the sentences.

| frog | log | bird | fish | ducks |

The **frog** can jump.

The turtle is on a **log**.

A **bird** is in the tree.

The boy wants a **fish**.

I see three **ducks**.

Page 98

Comprehension

Directions: Read the poem. Write the correct words in the blanks.

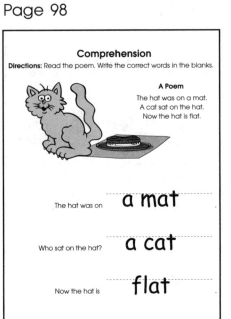

A Poem
The hat was on a mat.
A cat sat on the hat.
Now the hat is flat.

The hat was on **a mat**

Who sat on the hat? **a cat**

Now the hat is **flat**

Page 99

Following Directions: Color the Path

Directions: Color the path the girl should take to go home. Use the sentences to help you.

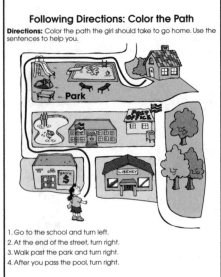

1. Go to the school and turn left.
2. At the end of the street, turn right.
3. Walk past the park and turn right.
4. After you pass the pool, turn right.

Page 100

Following Directions

Directions: Look at the pictures. Follow the directions in each box.

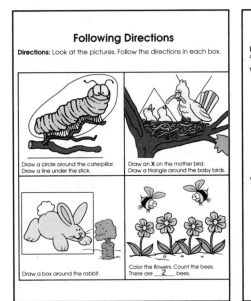

Draw a circle around the caterpillar. Draw a line under the stick.

Draw an **X** on the mother bird. Draw a triangle around the baby birds.

Draw a box around the rabbit.

Color the flowers. Count the bees. There are **2** bees.

Page 101

Classifying

Directions: Classifying is sorting things into groups. Draw a circle around the pictures that answer the question.

What Can Swim?

What Can Fly?

Page 102

Classifying: These Keep Me Warm

Directions: Color the things that keep you warm.

socks

apple

lunch box

earmuffs

cookie

coat

hat

umbrella

gloves

book

Page 103

Classifying: Objects

Help Dan clean up the park.

Directions: Circle the litter. Underline the coins. Draw a box around the balls.

Page 104

Classifying: Things to Drink

Directions: Circle the pictures of things you can drink. Write the names of those things in the blanks.

milk

juice   soda

Page 105

Classifying: Leaves

Directions: Cut out the leaves. Put them into two groups. Glue each group in a box on the top of the page. Write a name for each group.

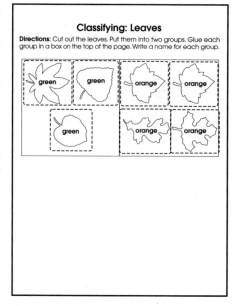

green   green   orange   orange

green   orange   orange

Page 107

Classifying: Things to Chew

Directions: Draw a line from the pictures of things you chew to the plate.

pizza

soup

ice-cream bar

carrot

soda

GULP!

macaroni

gum

corn on the cob

milk

Page 108

Vocabulary

Directions: Read the words. Trace and write them on the lines. Look at each picture. Write **hot** or **cold** on the lines to show if it is hot or cold.

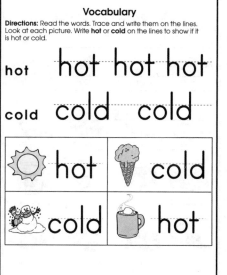

hot   hot hot hot

cold   cold cold

hot   cold

cold   hot

Page 109

Vocabulary

Directions: Read the words. Trace and write them on the lines. Look at each picture and write **day** or **night** on the lines to show if they happen during the day or night.

day   day day

night   night night

night   day

night   day

Page 110

Classifying: Night and Day

Directions: Write the words from the box under the pictures they describe.

stars sun moon rays dark light night day

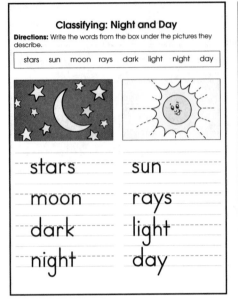

stars	sun
moon	rays
dark	light
night	day

Page 111

Classifying: Clowns and Balloons

Some words describe clowns. Some words describe balloons.

Directions: Read the words. Write the words that match in the correct columns.

float	laughs	hat	string
air	feet	pop	nose

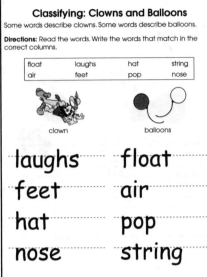

clown   balloons

laughs	float
feet	air
hat	pop
nose	string

Page 112

Similarities: Objects

Directions: Circle the picture in each row that is most like the first picture.

Example:

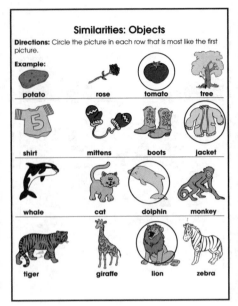

potato rose tomato tree

shirt mittens boots jacket

whale cat dolphin monkey

tiger giraffe lion zebra

Page 113

Similarities: Objects

Directions: Circle the picture in each row that is most like the first picture.

Example:

carrot jacks bread pea

baseball sneakers basketball bat

store school home bakery

kitten dog fox cat

Page 114

Classifying: Food Groups

Directions: Color the meats and eggs blue. Color the fruits and vegetables green. Color the breads tan. Color the dairy foods (milk and cheese) yellow.

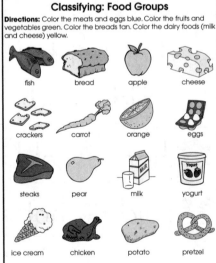

fish bread apple cheese

crackers carrot orange eggs

steaks pear milk yogurt

ice cream chicken potato pretzel

Page 115

Same and Different: These Don't Belong

Directions: Circle the pictures in each row that go together

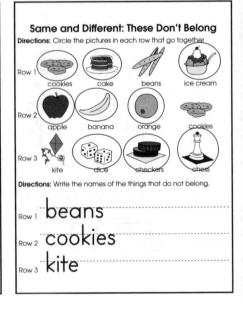

Row 1 cookies cake beans ice cream

Row 2 apple banana orange cookies

Row 3 kite dice shackers chess

Directions: Write the names of the things that do not belong.

Row 1 beans
Row 2 cookies
Row 3 kite

Page 116

Classifying: What Does Not Belong?
Directions: Draw an **X** on the picture that does not belong in each group.

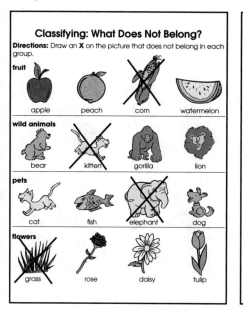

fruit: apple, peach, corn, watermelon
wild animals: bear, kitten, gorilla, lion
pets: cat, fish, elephant, dog
flowers: grass, rose, daisy, tulip

Page 117

Classifying: What Does Not Belong?
Directions: Draw an **X** on the word in each row that does not belong.

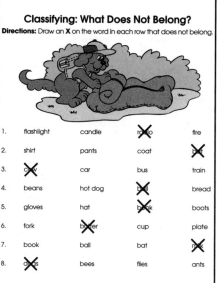

1. flashlight, candle, ~~radio~~, fire
2. shirt, pants, coat, ~~ball~~
3. ~~cow~~, car, bus, train
4. beans, hot dog, ~~ball~~, bread
5. gloves, hat, ~~book~~, boots
6. fork, ~~butter~~, cup, plate
7. book, ball, bat, ~~milk~~
8. ~~dogs~~, bees, flies, ants

Page 118

Classifying: Objects
Directions: Write each word in the correct row at the bottom of the page.

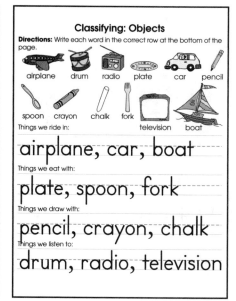

airplane, drum, radio, plate, car, pencil
spoon, crayon, chalk, fork, television, boat

Things we ride in:
airplane, car, boat

Things we eat with:
plate, spoon, fork

Things we draw with:
pencil, crayon, chalk

Things we listen to:
drum, radio, television

Page 119

Classifying: Names, Numbers, Animals, Colors
Directions: Write the words from the box next to the words they describe.

Joe	cat	blue	Tim
two	dog	red	ten
Sue	green	pig	six

Name Words: Joe Tim Sue

Number Words: two ten six

Animal Words: cat dog pig

Color Words: green red blue

Page 120

Classifying: Things That Belong Together
Directions: Circle the pictures in each row that belong together.

Row 1: knife, key, fork, spoon
Row 2: orange, apple, candy, banana
Row 3: beach ball, soccer ball, baseball, apple

Directions: Write the names of the pictures that do not belong.

Row 1: key
Row 2: candy
Row 3: apple

Page 121

Classifying: Why They Are Different
Directions: Look at your answers on page 120. Write why each object does not belong.

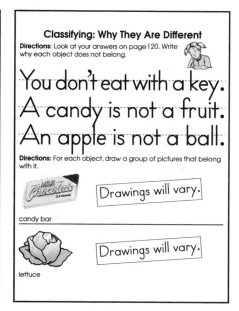

You don't eat with a key.
A candy is not a fruit.
An apple is not a ball.

Directions: For each object, draw a group of pictures that belong with it.

candy bar — Drawings will vary.

lettuce — Drawings will vary.

Page 122

Classifying: What Does Not Belong?

Directions: Circle the two things that do not belong in the picture. Write why they do not belong.

1. Flowers do not grow in snow.
2. Palm trees do not grow in snow.

Page 123

Sequencing: Fill the Glasses

Directions: Follow the instructions to fill each glass. Use crayons to draw your favorite drink in the ones that are full and half-full.

full   half-full   empty

empty   half-full   full

Page 124

Sequencing: Raking Leaves

Directions: Write a number in each box to show the order of the story.

Page 125

Sequencing: Make a Snowman!

Directions: Write the number of the sentence that goes with each picture in the box.

1. Roll a large snowball for the snowman's bottom.
2. Make another snowball and put it on top of the first.
3. Put the last snowball on top.
4. Dress the snowman.

Page 126

Sequencing: A Recipe

Directions: Look at the recipe below. Put each step in order. Write **1, 2, 3** or **4** in the box.

HOW TO MAKE BREAD BUDDIES

3 — Roll dough into balls and shapes. Connect pieces with a drop of water.

1 — Mix 1 cup of water, 1 cup of salt and 3 cups of flour.

2 — Knead the dough.

4 — Have an adult bake your bread buddy for 2-3 hours at 300°. Let it cool. Then paint it!

What kind of bread buddy did you make?

Answers will vary.

Page 127

Sequencing: How Flowers Grow

Directions: Read the story. Then write the steps to grow a flower.

First find a sunny spot. Then plant the seed. Water it. The flower will start to grow. Pull the weeds around it. Remember to keep giving the flower water. Enjoy your flower.

1. Find a sunny spot
2. Plant the seed
3. Water it
4. Pull the weeds
5. Enjoy your flower

Page 128

Sequencing: Make an Ice-Cream Cone

Directions: Number the boxes in order to show how to make an ice-cream cone.

Page 129

Sequencing: Eating a Cone

What if a person never ate an ice-cream cone? Could you tell them how to eat it? Think about what you do when you eat an ice-cream cone.

Directions: Write directions to teach someone how to eat an ice-cream cone.

How to Eat an Ice-Cream Cone

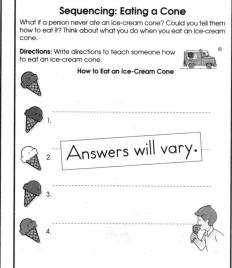

1. _____
2. Answers will vary.
3. _____
4. _____

Page 130

Comprehension: Apples

Directions: Read about apples. Then write the answers.

I like ____. Do you?   Some ____ are red.

Some ____ are green.   Some ____ are yellow.

1. How many kinds of apples does the story tell about?

three

2. Name the kinds of apples.

red   green   yellow

3. What kind of apple do you like best?

Answers will vary.

Page 131

Comprehension: Crayons

Directions: Read about crayons. Then write your answers.

Crayons come in many colors.
Some crayons are dark colors.
Some crayons are light colors.
All crayons have wax in them.

1. How many colors of crayons are there?   (many)
   few

2. Crayons come in dark colors
   and light colors.

3. What do all crayons have in them?

They have wax in them.

Page 132

Comprehension

Directions: Read the story. Write the words from the story that complete each sentence.

Jane and Bill like to play in the rain. They take off their shoes and socks.
They splash in the puddles.
It feels cold!
It is fun to splash!

Jane and Bill like to **play in the rain**

They take off their **shoes and socks**

They splash in **the puddles**

Do you like to splash in puddles?   (Yes)   No

Page 133

Comprehension

Directions: Read the story. Write the words from the story that complete each sentence.

Ben and Sue have a bug.
It is red with black spots.
They call it Spot.
Spot likes to eat green leaves and grass.
The children keep Spot in a box.

Ben and Sue have a **bug**

It is **red** with black spots.

The bug's name is **Spot**

The bug eats **green leaves and grass**

Page 134

Comprehension: Snow Is Cold!

Directions: Read about snow. Circle the answers.

When you play in snow, dress warmly. Wear a coat. Wear a hat. Wear gloves. Do you wear these when you play in snow?

1. Snow is ⸻ warm. **(cold.)**

2. When you play in snow, dress ⸻ **(warmly.)** quickly.

Answers may include:

Directions: List three things to wear when you play in snow.

hat, scarf, gloves or mittens, coat, boots, snowpants, etc.

Page 135

Comprehension: Growing Flowers

Directions: Read about flowers. Then write the answers.

Some flowers grow in pots. Many flowers grow in flower beds. Others grow beside the road. Flowers begin from seeds. They grow into small buds. Then they open wide and bloom. Flowers are pretty!

Answers may include:

1. Name two places flowers grow.

pots, flower beds or beside the road

2. Flowers begin from **seeds**

3. Then flowers grow into small **buds**

4. Flowers then open wide and **bloom**

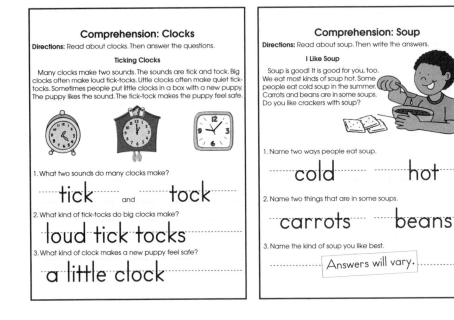

Page 136

Comprehension: Raking Leaves

Directions: Read about raking leaves. Then answer the questions.

I like to rake leaves. Do you? Leaves die each year. They get brown and dry. They fall from the trees. Then we rake them up.

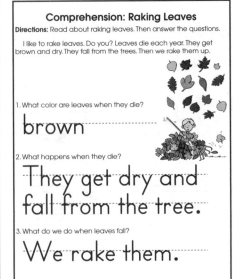

1. What color are leaves when they die?

brown

2. What happens when they die?

They get dry and fall from the tree.

3. What do we do when leaves fall?

We rake them.

Page 137

Comprehension: Clocks

Directions: Read about clocks. Then answer the questions.

Ticking Clocks

Many clocks make two sounds. The sounds are tick and tock. Big clocks often make loud tick-tocks. Little clocks often make quiet tick-tocks. Sometimes people put little clocks in a box with a new puppy. The puppy likes the sound. The tick-tock makes the puppy feel safe.

1. What two sounds do many clocks make?

tick and **tock**

2. What kind of tick-tocks do big clocks make?

loud tick tocks

3. What kind of clock makes a new puppy feel safe?

a little clock

Page 138

Comprehension: Soup

Directions: Read about soup. Then write the answers.

I Like Soup

Soup is good! It is good for you, too. We eat most kinds of soup hot. Some people eat cold soup in the summer. Carrots and beans are in some soups. Do you like crackers with soup?

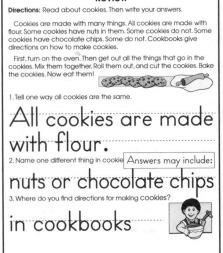

1. Name two ways people eat soup.

cold **hot**

2. Name two things that are in some soups.

carrots **beans**

3. Name the kind of soup you like best.

⸻ Answers will vary.

Page 139

Review

Directions: Read about cookies. Then write your answers.

Cookies are made with many things. All cookies are made with flour. Some cookies have nuts in them. Some cookies do not. Some cookies have chocolate chips. Some do not. Cookbooks give directions on how to make cookies.

First, turn on the oven. Then get out all the things that go in the cookies. Mix them together. Roll them out, and cut the cookies. Bake the cookies. Now eat them!

1. Tell one way all cookies are the same.

All cookies are made with flour.

2. Name one different thing in cookie | Answers may include: |

nuts or chocolate chips

3. Where do you find directions for making cookies?

in cookbooks

Page 140

Review

Directions: Read the story. Then circle the pictures of things that are wet.

Some things used in baking are dry. Some things used in baking are wet. To bake a cake, first mix the salt, sugar and flour. Then add the egg. Now, add the milk. Stir. Put the cake in the oven.

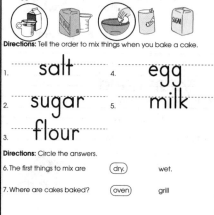

Directions: Tell the order to mix things when you bake a cake.

1. salt
2. sugar
3. flour
4. egg
5. milk

Directions: Circle the answers.

6. The first things to mix are (dry.)   wet.

7. Where are cakes baked?   (oven)   grill

Page 141

Review

Directions: Read how to make no-cook candy. Then answer the questions.

Some candy needs to be cooked on a stove. You do not need to cook this kind of candy. It is easy to make. You will need a large bowl for mixing. You will need five things to make this candy.

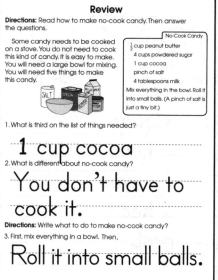

No-Cook Candy
½ cup peanut butter
4 cups powdered sugar
1 cup cocoa
pinch of salt
4 tablespoons milk

Mix everything in the bowl. Roll it into small balls. (A pinch of salt is just a tiny bit.)

1. What is third on the list of things needed?

1 cup cocoa

2. What is different about no-cook candy?

You don't have to cook it.

Directions: Write what to do to make no-cook candy?

3. First, mix everything in a bowl. Then,

Roll it into small balls.

Page 142

Comprehension: The Teddy Bear Song

Do you know the Teddy Bear Song? It is very old!

Directions: Read the Teddy Bear Song. Then answer the questions.

Teddy bear, teddy bear, turn around.
Teddy bear, teddy bear, touch the ground.
Teddy bear, teddy bear, climb upstairs.
Teddy bear, teddy bear, say your prayers.
Teddy bear, teddy bear, turn out the light.
Teddy bear, teddy bear, say, "Good night!"

1. What is the first thing the teddy bear does?

He turns around.

2. What is the last thing the teddy bear does?

He says, "Good night!"

3. What would you name a teddy bear?

Answers will vary.

Page 143

Sequencing: Put Teddy Bear to Bed

Directions: Read the song about the teddy bear again. Write a number in each box to show the order of the story.

Page 144

Comprehension: A New Teddy Bear Song

Directions: Write words to make a new teddy bear song. Act out your new song with your teddy bear as you read it.

Answers will vary.

Teddy bear, teddy bear, turn

Teddy bear, teddy bear, touch the

Teddy bear, teddy bear, climb

Teddy bear, teddy bear, turn out

Teddy bear, teddy bear, say,

Page 145

Comprehension: Balloons

Directions: Read the story. Then answer the questions.

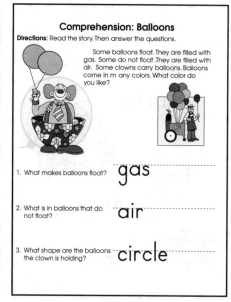

Some balloons float. They are filled with gas. Some do not float. They are filled with air. Some clowns carry balloons. Balloons come in many colors. What color do you like?

1. What makes balloons float?   gas

2. What is in balloons that do not float?   air

3. What shape are the balloons the clown is holding?   circle

Page 146

Comprehension: Balloons

Directions: Read the story about balloons again. Draw a picture for the sentence in each box.

The clown is holding red, yellow and blue balloons filled with air.

The clown is holding purple, orange, green and blue balloons filled with gas.

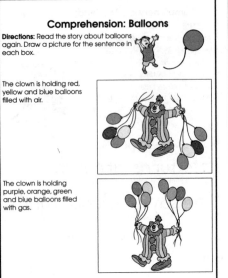

Page 147

Sequencing: Petting a Cat

Directions: Read the story. Then write the answers.

Do you like cats? I do. To pet a cat, move slowly. Hold out your hand. The cat will come to you. Then pet its head. Do not grab a cat! It will run away.

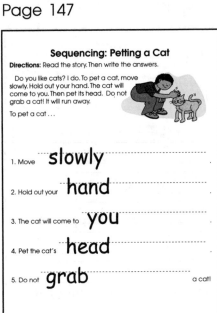

To pet a cat . . .

1. Move **slowly**
2. Hold out your **hand**
3. The cat will come to **you**
4. Pet the cat's **head**
5. Do not **grab**   a cat!

Page 148

Comprehension: Cats

Directions: Read the story about cats again. Then write the answers.

1. What is a good title for the story?

   Answers will vary.

2. The story tells you how to **pet a cat**

3. What part of your body should you pet a cat with?

   your hand

4. Why should you move slowly to pet a cat?

   Answers will vary.

5. Why do you think a cat will run away if you grab it?

   Answers will vary.

Page 149

Comprehension: Cats

Directions: Look at the pictures and read about four cats. Then write the correct name beside each cat.

Fluffy, Blackie and Tiger are playing. Tom is sleeping. Blackie has spots. Tiger has stripes.

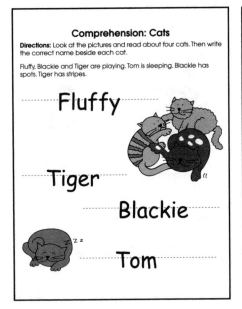

Fluffy

Tiger

Blackie

Tom

Page 150

Same and Different: Cats

Directions: Compare the picture of the cats on page 149 to this picture. Write a word from the box to tell what is different about each cat.

| purple ball | green bow | blue brush | red collar |

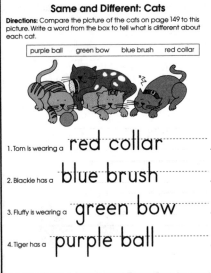

1. Tom is wearing a **red collar**
2. Blackie has a **blue brush**
3. Fluffy is wearing a **green bow**
4. Tiger has a **purple ball**

Page 151

Comprehension: Tigers

Directions: Read about tigers. Then write the answers.

Tigers sleep during the day. They hunt at night. Tigers eat meat. They hunt deer. They like to eat wild pigs. If they cannot find meat, tigers will eat fish.

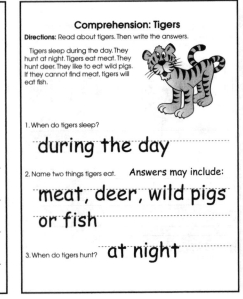

1. When do tigers sleep?

   during the day

2. Name two things tigers eat.   Answers may include:

   meat, deer, wild pigs or fish

3. When do tigers hunt? **at night**

Page 152

Following Directions: Tiger Puzzle

Directions: Read the story about tigers again. Then complete the puzzle.

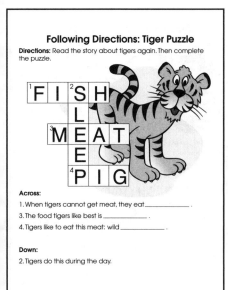

Across:

1. When tigers cannot get meat, they eat _____ .
3. The food tigers like best is _____ .
4. Tigers like to eat this meat: wild _____ .

Down:

2. Tigers do this during the day.

Page 153

Following Directions: Draw a Tiger

Directions: Follow directions to complete the picture of the tiger.

1. Draw black stripes on the tiger's body and tail.
2. Color the tiger's tongue red.
3. Draw claws on the feet.
4. Draw a black nose and two black eyes on the tiger's face.
5. Color the rest of the tiger orange.
6. Draw tall, green grass for the tiger to sleep in.

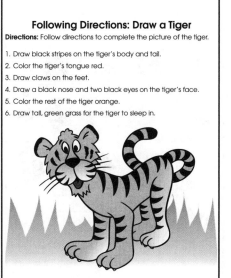

Page 154

Comprehension: How We Eat

Directions: Read the story. Use words from the box to answer the questions.

People eat with spoons and forks. They use a spoon to eat soup and ice cream. They use a fork to eat potatoes. They use a knife to cut their meat. They say, "Thank you. It was good!" when they finish.

| fork | ice cream | knife | soup |

1. What do we use to cut food?

a knife

2. What are two things you can eat with a spoon?

soup   ice cream

3. What do we use to eat meat and potatoes?

fork and knife

Page 155

Classifying: Foods

Directions: Read the questions under each plate. Draw three foods on each plate to answer the questions.

Sample answers:

1. What foods can you cut with a knife?

2. What foods should you eat with a fork?

3. What foods can you eat with a spoon?

Page 156

Comprehension: Write a Party Invitation

Directions: Read about the party. Then complete the invitation.

The party will be at Dog's house. The party will start at 1:00 PM. It will last 2 hours. Write your birthday for the date of the party.

Party Invitation

Where: Dog's house

Date: Answers will vary.

Time It Begins: 1:00 P.M.

Time It Ends: 3:00 P.M.

Answers will vary.

Directions: On the last line, write something else about the party.

Page 157

Sequencing: Pig Gets Ready

Directions: Number the pictures of Pig getting ready for the party to show the order of the story.

What kind of party do you think Pig is going to?   Answers will vary.

Page 158

Comprehension: An Animal Party

Directions: Use the picture for clues. Write words from the box to answer the questions.

bear	cat
dog	elephant
giraffe	hippo
pig	tiger

1. Which animals have bow ties?

cat   **tiger**

2. Which animal has a hat?

bear

3. Which animal has a striped shirt?

pig

Page 159

Classifying: Party Items

Directions: Draw a ☐ around objects that are food for the party. Draw a △ around the party guests. Draw a ◯ around the objects used for fun at the party.

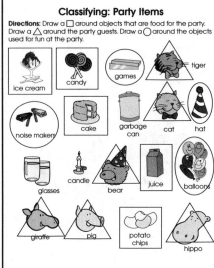

Page 160

Comprehension: Play Simon Says

Directions: Read how to play Simon Says. Then answer the questions.

Simon Says

Here is how to play Simon Says: One kid is Simon. Simon is the leader. Everyone must do what Simon says and does but only if the leader says, "Simon says" first. Let's try it. "Simon says, 'Pat your head.'" "Simon says, 'Pat your nose. Pat your toes.'" Oops! Did you pat your toes? I did not say, "Simon says," first. If you patted your toes, you are out!

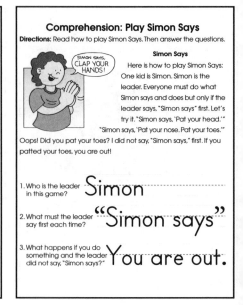

1. Who is the leader in this game? **Simon**

2. What must the leader say first each time? **"Simon says"**

3. What happens if you do something and the leader did not say, "Simon says?" **You are out.**

Page 161

Comprehension: Play Simon Says

Directions: Read each sentence. Look at the picture next to it. Circle the picture if the person is playing Simon Says correctly.

1. Simon says, "Put your hands on your hips."

2. Simon says, "Stand on one leg."

3. Simon says, "Put your hands on your head."

4. Simon says, "Ride a bike."

5. Simon says, "Jump up and down."

6. Simon says, "Pet a dog."

7. Simon says, "Make a big smile."

Page 162

Following Directions: Play Simon Says

Directions: Read the sentences. If Simon tells you to do something, follow the directions. If Simon does not tell you to do something, go to the next sentence.

1. Simon says: Cross out all the numbers 2 through 9.

2. Simon says: Cross out the vowel that is in the word "sun."

3. Cross out the letter "B."

4. Cross out the vowels "A" and "E."

5. Simon says: Cross out the consonants in the word "cup."

6. Cross out the letter "Z."

7. Simon says: Cross out all the "K's."

8. Sim

Answer: Great job!

Page 163

Comprehension: Rhymes

Directions: Read about words that rhyme. Then circle the answers.

Words that rhyme have the same end sounds. "Wing" and "sing" rhyme. "Boy" and "toy" rhyme. "Dime" and "time" rhyme. Can you think of other words that rhyme?

1. Words that rhyme have the same (end sounds.) end letters.

2. "Time" rhymes with "tree." ("dime.")

Directions: Write one rhyme for each word.

wing   Answers will vary.   boy

dime   pink

Page 164

Rhyming Words

Many poems have rhyming words. The rhyming words are usually at the end of the line.

Directions: Complete the poem with words from the box.

My Glue

I spilled my **glue** .

I felt **blue** .

What could I **do** ?

Hey! I have a **clue** !

I'll make it **clean**

The cleanest you've **seen**

No one will **scream**

Wouldn't that be **mean** ?

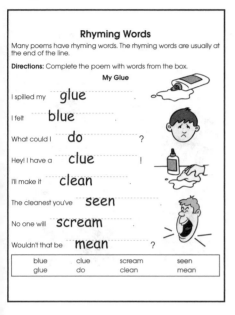

blue	clue	scream	seen
glue	do	clean	mean

Page 165

Classifying: Rhymes

Directions: Cut out the pieces. Read the words. Find two words that rhyme. Put the words together.

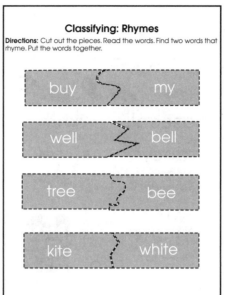

buy — my

well — bell

tree — bee

kite — white

Page 167

Classifying: Rhymes

Directions: Circle the pictures in each row that rhyme.

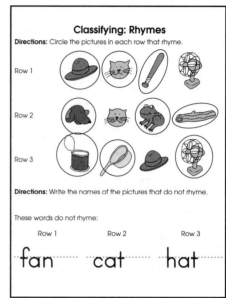

Row 1

Row 2

Row 3

Directions: Write the names of the pictures that do not rhyme.

These words do not rhyme:

Row 1	Row 2	Row 3
fan	cat	hat

Page 168

Comprehension: Babies

Directions: Read about babies. Then write the answers.

Babies are small. Some babies cry a lot. They cry when they are wet. They cry when they are hungry. They smile when they are dry. They smile when they are fed.

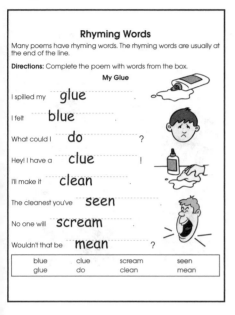

1. Name two reasons babies cry.

hungry **wet**

2. Name two reasons babies smile.

dry **fed**

3. Write a baby's name you like.

Answers will vary.

Page 169

Comprehension: Babies

Directions: Read each sentence. Draw a picture of a baby's face in the box to show if she would cry or smile.

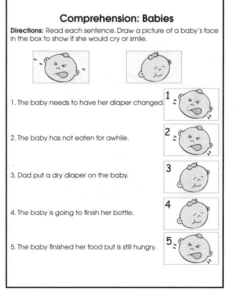

1. The baby needs to have her diaper changed. — 1

2. The baby has not eaten for awhile. — 2

3. Dad put a dry diaper on the baby. — 3

4. The baby is going to finish her bottle. — 4

5. The baby finished her food but is still hungry. — 5

Page 170

Sequencing: Feeding Baby

Directions: Read the sentences. Write a number in each box to show the order of the story.

5 The baby smiles.

3 Mom makes the baby's food.

2 The baby is put in his chair.

1 The baby is crying.

4 Mom feeds the baby.

Page 171

Same and Different: Compare the Twins

Directions: Read the story. Then use the words in the box and the picture to write your answers.

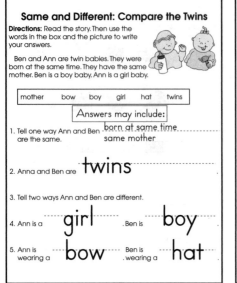

Ben and Ann are twin babies. They were born at the same time. They have the same mother. Ben is a boy baby. Ann is a girl baby.

mother	bow	boy	girl	hat	twins

Answers may include:

1. Tell one way Ann and Ben are the same. **born at same time / same mother**

2. Anna and Ben are **twins**

3. Tell two ways Ann and Ben are different.

4. Ann is a **girl**. Ben is a **boy**

5. Ann is wearing a **bow**. Ben is wearing a **hat**

Page 172

Comprehension: Hats

Directions: Read about hats. Then write your answers.

There are many kinds of hats. Some baseball hats have brims. Some fancy hats have feathers. Some knit hats pull down over your ears. Some hats are made of straw. Do you like hats?

1. Name four kinds of hats.

baseball **knit**
fancy **straw**

Directions: Circle the correct answers.

2. What kind of hats pull down over your ears?

straw hats
(knit hats)

3. What are some hats made of?

(straw)
mud

Page 173

Sequencing: Choosing a Hat

Directions: Write a number in each box to show the order of the story.

Page 174

Following Directions: Draw Hats

Directions: Draw a hat on each person. Read the sentences to know what kind of hat to draw.

1. The first girl is wearing a purple hat with feathers.

2. The boy next to the girl with the purple hat is wearing a red baseball hat.

3. The first boy is wearing a yellow knit hat.

4. The last boy is wearing a brown top hat.

5. The girl next to the boy with the red hat is wearing a blue straw hat.

Page 175

Classifying: Mr. Lincoln's Hat

Abraham Lincoln wore a tall hat. He liked to keep things in his hat so he would not lose them.

Directions: Cut out the pictures of things Mr. Lincoln could have kept in his hat. Glue those pictures on the hat.

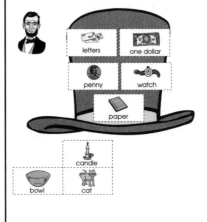

letters one dollar
penny watch
paper

candle
bowl cat

Page 177

Comprehension: Boats

Directions: Read about boats. Then answer the questions.

See the boats! They float on water. Some boats have sails. The wind moves the sails. It makes the boats go. Many people name their sailboats. They paint the name on the side of the boat.

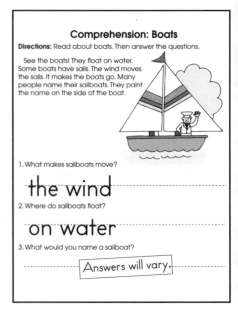

1. What makes sailboats move?

the wind

2. Where do sailboats float?

on water

3. What would you name a sailboat?

Answers will vary.

Page 178

Same and Different: Color the Boats

Directions: Find the three boats that are alike. Color them all the same. One boat is different. Color it differently.

Page 179

Comprehension: A Boat Ride

Directions: Write a sentence under each picture to tell what is happening. Read the story you wrote.

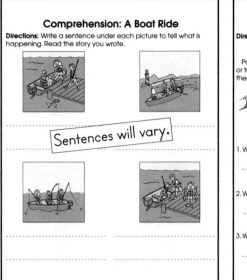

Sentences will vary.

Page 180

Comprehension: Travel

Directions: Read the story. Then answer the questions.

Let's Take a Trip!

Pack your bag. Shall we go by car, plane or train? Let's go to the sea. When we get there, let's go on a sailboat.

Answer may also include sailboat

1. What are three ways to travel?

car   plane   train

2. Where will we go?

to the sea

3. What will we do when we get there?

go on a sailboat

Page 181

Predicting: Words and Pictures

Directions: Complete each story by choosing the correct picture. Draw a line from the story to the picture

1. Shawnda got her books. She went to the bus stop. Shawnda got on the bus.

2. Marco planted a seed. He watered it. He pulled the weeds around it.

3. Abraham's dog was barking. Abraham got out the dog food. He put it in the dog bowl.

Page 182

Predicting: Story Ending

Directions: Read the story. Draw a picture in the last box to complete the story.

That's my ball.   I got it first.

It's mine!   Pictures will vary.

Page 183

Predicting: Story Ending

Directions: Read the story. Draw a picture in the last box to complete the story.

Marco likes to paint.   He likes to help his dad.

Pictures will vary.

He is tired when he's finished.

Page 184

Predicting: Story Ending

Directions: Read each story. Circle the sentence that tells how the story will end.

Ann was riding her bike. She saw a dog in the park. She stopped to pet it. Ann left to go home.

The dog went swimming.

(The dog followed Ann.)

The dog went home with a cat.

Antonio went to a baseball game. A baseball player hit a ball toward him. He reached out his hands.

The player caught the ball.

The ball bounced on a car.

(Antonio caught the ball.)

Page 185

Making Inferences: Baseball

Traci likes baseball. She likes to win. Traci's team does not win.

Directions: Circle the correct answers.

1. Traci likes

football.   soccer.   (baseball.)

2. Traci likes to

(win.)   lose.

3. Traci uses a bat.

Yes   No

4. Traci is

happy.   (sad.)

Page 186

Making Inferences: The Stars

Lynn looks at the stars. She sings a song about them. She makes a wish on them. The stars help Lynn sleep.

Directions: Circle the correct answers.

1. Lynn likes the

moon.   sun.   (stars.)

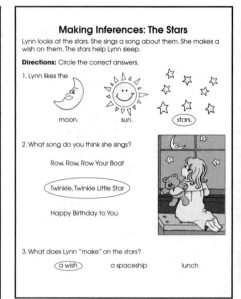

2. What song do you think she sings?

Row, Row, Row Your Boat

(Twinkle, Twinkle Little Star)

Happy Birthday to You

3. What does Lynn "make" on the stars?

(a wish)   a spaceship   lunch

Page 187

Making Inferences: Feelings

Directions: Read each story. Choose a word from the box to show how each person feels.

happy	excited	sad	mad

1. Andy and Sam were best friends. Sam and his family moved far away. How does Sam feel?

sad

2. Deana could not sleep. It was the night before her birthday party. How does Deana feel?

excited

3. Jacob let his baby brother play with his teddy bear. His brother lost the bear. How does Jacob feel?

mad

4. Kia picked flowers for her mom. Her mom smiled when she got them. How does Kia feel?

happy

Page 188

Comprehension: Eating Ice Cream

Directions: Read the story. Write two things Sam could have done so he could have enjoyed eating his ice-cream cone.

It was a hot day. Sam went to the store and got an ice-cream cone. He sat at a table in the sun. Sam watched some friends play ball. Suddenly, his ice cream fell on the sidewalk.

1. _____

Answers will vary.

2. _____

Page 189

Review

Directions: Write a sentence to complete this story.

1. Evan's dog runs away.
2. Evan chases it.
3. The dog runs into a store.
4.

Answers will vary.

Directions: Read this story. Answer the questions.

Lea plays games with her little sister. Sometimes Lea hides from her sister. Her sister calls her name over and over. Lea does not answer. Lea thinks it is funny.

1. Is Lea being nice or mean to her sister? mean

2. Do you think her sister likes Lea to hide? no

3. What would you do if you were Lea's sister?

Answers will vary.

ANSWER KEY

Page 190

Books

Directions: What do you know about books? Use the words in the box below to help fill in the lines.

title	book	author
illustrator	pages	left to right
fun	library	glossary

The name of the book is the **title**.

Left to right is the direction we read.

The person who wrote the words is the **author**.

Reading is **fun**!

There are many books in the **library**.

The person who draws the pictures is the **illustrator**.

The **glossary** is a kind of dictionary in the book to help you find the meanings of words.

Page 192

Nouns

A noun is a word that names a person, place or thing. When you read a sentence, the noun is what the sentence is about.

Directions: Complete each sentence with a noun.

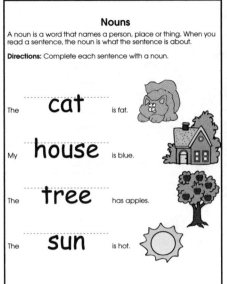

The **cat** is fat.

My **house** is blue.

The **tree** has apples.

The **sun** is hot.

Page 193

Nouns

Directions: Write these naming words in the correct box.

| store | zoo | child | baby | teacher | table |
| cat | park | gym | woman | sock | horse |

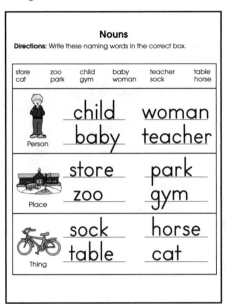

Person: **child baby woman teacher**

Place: **store zoo park gym**

Thing: **sock table horse cat**

Page 194

Things That Go Together

Some nouns name things that go together.

Directions: Draw a line to match the nouns on the left with the things they go with on the right.

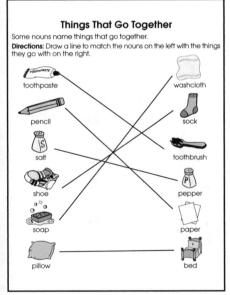

toothpaste, pencil, salt, shoe, soap, pillow — washcloth, sock, toothbrush, pepper, paper, bed

Page 195

Tracking: Things That Go Together

Directions: Draw a line to connect the objects that go together.

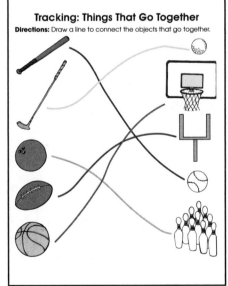

Page 196

Verbs

Verbs are words that tell what a person or a thing can do.
Example: The girl pats the dog.
The word **pats** is the verb. It shows action.
Directions: Draw a line between the verbs and the pictures that show the action.

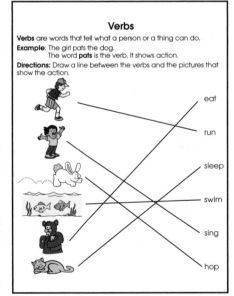

eat, run, sleep, swim, sing, hop

Grade 1 - Comprehensive Curriculum

ANSWER KEY

Page 197

Verbs

Directions:
Look at the picture and read the words. Write an action word in each sentence below.

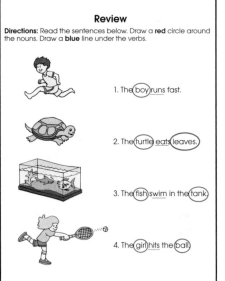

swing   rings   kick   run   talk

1. The two boys like to __talk__ together.
2. The children __kick__ the soccer ball.
3. Some children like to __swing__ on the swing.
4. The girl can __run__ very fast.
5. The teacher __rings__ the bell.

Page 198

Nouns and Verbs

A noun is a person or thing a sentence tells about. A verb tells what the person or thing does.

Directions: Circle the noun in each sentence. Underline the verb.

Example: The (cat) sleeps.

1. (Jill) plays a game on the computer.
2. (Children) swim in the pool.
3. The (car) raced around the track.
4. (Mike) throws the ball to his friend.
5. (Monkeys) swing in the trees.
6. (Terry) laughed at the clown.

Page 199

Review

Directions: Cut out the words below. Glue naming words in the **Nouns** box. Glue action words in the **Verbs** box.

Nouns	Verbs
boy fork	jump sit
cat house	throw swim

Page 201

Review

Directions: Read the sentences below. Draw a **red** circle around the nouns. Draw a **blue** line under the verbs.

1. The (boy) runs fast.
2. The (turtle) eats (leaves.)
3. The (fish) swim in the (tank.)
4. The (girl) hits the (ball.)

Page 202

Words That Describe

Describing words tell us more about a person, place or thing.

Directions: Read the words in the box. Choose the word that describes the picture. Write it next to the picture.

happy   round   sick   cold   long

long
happy
sick
round
cold

Page 203

Words That Describe

Directions: Read the words in the box. Choose the word that describes the picture. Write it next to the picture.

wet   round   funny   soft   sad   tall

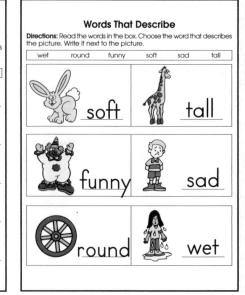

soft   tall

funny   sad

round   wet

Page 204

Words That Describe

Directions: Circle the describing word in each sentence. Draw a line from the sentence to the picture.

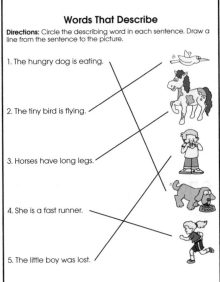

1. The hungry dog is eating.

2. The tiny bird is flying.

3. Horses have long legs.

4. She is a fast runner.

5. The little boy was lost.

Page 205

Words That Describe: Colors and Numbers

Colors and numbers can describe nouns.

Directions: Underline the describing word in each sentence. Draw a picture to go with each sentence.

A yellow moon was in the sky.

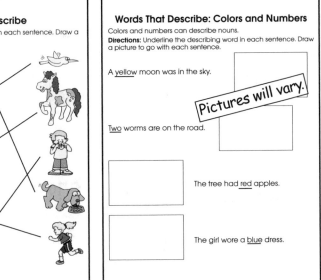

Pictures will vary.

The tree had red apples.

The girl wore a blue dress.

Page 206

Sequencing: Comparative Adjectives

Directions: Look at each group of pictures. Write 1, 2 or 3 under the picture to show where it should be.

Example:

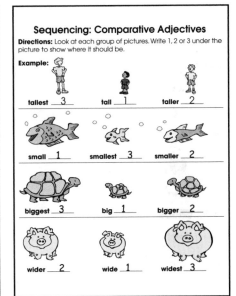

tallest __3__   tall __1__   taller __2__

small __1__   smallest __3__   smaller __2__

biggest __3__   big __1__   bigger __2__

wider __2__   wide __1__   widest __3__

Page 207

Sequencing: Comparative Adjectives

Directions: Look at the pictures in each row. Write 1, 2 or 3 under the picture to show where it should be.

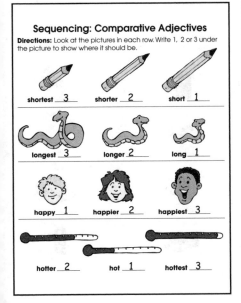

shortest __3__   shorter __2__   short __1__

longest __3__   longer __2__   long __1__

happy __1__   happier __2__   happiest __3__

hotter __2__   hot __1__   hottest __3__

Page 208

Synonyms

Synonyms are words that mean almost the same thing. **Start** and **begin** are synonyms.

Directions: Find the synonyms that describe each picture. Write the words in the boxes below the picture.

small   funny   large   sad   silly   little   big   unhappy

small	large
little	big
sad	silly
unhappy	funny

Page 209

Synonyms

Synonyms are words that mean almost the same thing.

Directions: Read the word in the center of each flower. Find a synonym for each word on a bee at the bottom of the page. Cut out and glue each bee on its matching flower.

fast   shut   cold   tired

Page 211

Similarities: Synonyms

Directions: Circle the word in each row that is most like the first word in the row.

Example:

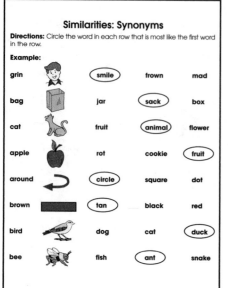

grin		(smile)	frown	mad
bag		jar	(sack)	box
cat		fruit	(animal)	flower
apple		rot	cookie	(fruit)
around		(circle)	square	dot
brown		(tan)	black	red
bird		dog	cat	(duck)
bee		fish	(ant)	snake

Page 212

Synonyms

Synonyms are words that have the same meaning.

Directions: Read each sentence and look at the underlined word. Circle the word that means the same thing. Write the new words.

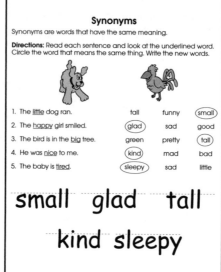

1. The <u>little</u> dog ran. — tall — funny — (small)
2. The <u>happy</u> girl smiled. — (glad) — sad — good
3. The bird is in the <u>big</u> tree. — green — pretty — (tall)
4. He was <u>nice</u> to me. — (kind) — mad — bad
5. The baby is <u>tired</u>. — (sleepy) — sad — little

small   glad   tall
kind sleepy

Page 213

Synonyms

Directions: Read each sentence and look at the underlined word. Circle the word that means the same thing. Write the new words.

1. The boy was <u>mad</u>. — happy — (angry) — pup
2. The <u>dog</u> is brown. — (pup) — cat — rat
3. I like to <u>scream</u>. — soar — mad — (shout)
4. The bird can <u>fly</u>. — (soar) — jog — warm
5. The girl can <u>run</u>. — sleep — (jog) — shout
6. I am <u>hot</u>. — (warm) — cold — soar

angry   pup   shout
soar   jog   warm

Page 214

Similarities: Synonyms

Directions: Read each sentence. Read the word after the sentence. Find the word that is most like it in the sentence and circle it.

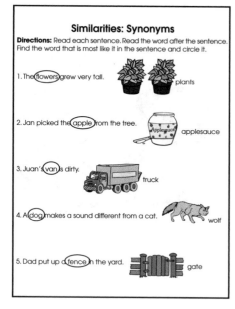

1. The (flowers) grew very tall. — plants

2. Jan picked the (apple) from the tree. — applesauce

3. Juan's (van) is dirty. — truck

4. A (dog) makes a sound different from a cat. — wolf

5. Dad put up a (fence) in the yard. — gate

Page 215

Similarities: Synonyms

Directions: Read the story. Write a word on the line that means almost the same as the word under the line.

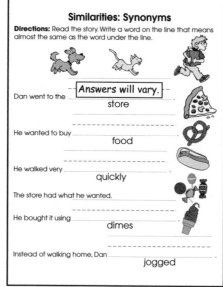

Dan went to the _____ [Answers will vary.]
store

He wanted to buy _____
food

He walked very _____
quickly

The store had what he wanted.

He bought it using _____
dimes

Instead of walking home, Dan _____
jogged

Page 216

Antonyms

Antonyms are words that are opposites. **Hot** and **cold** are antonyms.
Directions: Draw a line between the antonyms.

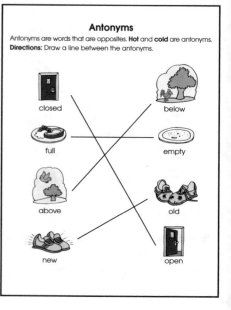

closed — below
full — empty
above — old
new — open

Page 217

Opposites

Directions: Draw lines to connect the words that are opposites.

up — down
over — wet
dry — dirty
clean — under

Page 218

Opposites

Opposites are things that are different in every way.

Directions: Draw a line between the opposites.

day — night
happy — sad
big — little
open — closed
front — back

Page 219

Antonyms

Directions: Find the two words that are opposites. Cut out the balloon basket and glue it on the proper balloon.

Page 221

Opposites

Directions: Circle the picture in each row that is the opposite of the first picture.

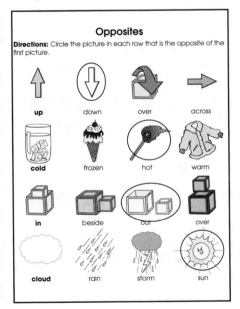

up   down   over   across

cold   frozen   hot   warm

in   beside   out   over

cloud   rain   storm   sun

Page 222

Opposites

Directions: Read each clue. Write the answers in the puzzle.

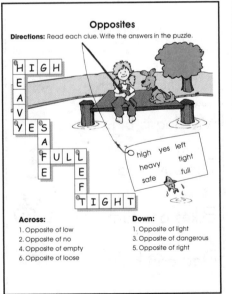

high yes left
heavy tight
safe full

Across:
1. Opposite of low
2. Opposite of no
4. Opposite of empty
6. Opposite of loose

Down:
1. Opposite of light
3. Opposite of dangerous
5. Opposite of right

Page 223

Opposites

Directions: Cut out the pieces. Read the words. Find the pair of words that are opposites and put the pieces together. On the blank pieces, write your own pair of opposites.

tall
short

fast
slow

sad
glad

hot
cold

few
many

Page 225

Opposites

Directions: Circle the two words in each sentence that are opposites.

1. (Cold) ice cream is good on a (hot) day.

2. Sam took off his (wet) socks and put on (dry) ones.

3. Do you like to run (fast) or (slow)?

4. The dog is (black) and the cat is (white).

5. The elephant looked really (big) next to the (small) mouse.

6. The (tiny) seed grew into a (large) plant.

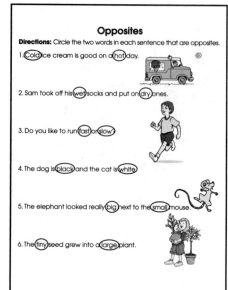

Page 226

Homophones

Homophones are words that **sound** the same but are spelled differently and mean something different. **Blew** and **blue** are homophones.

Directions: Look at the word pairs. Choose the word that describes the picture. Write the word on the line next to the picture.

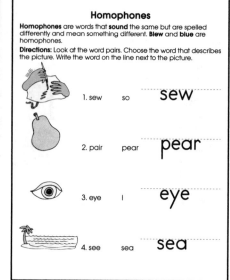

1. sew   so   sew

2. pair   pear   pear

3. eye   I   eye

4. see   sea   sea

Page 227

Homophones

Directions: Read each sentence. Underline the two words that sound the same but are spelled differently and mean something different.

1. Tom <u>ate</u> <u>eight</u> grapes.

2. Becky <u>read</u> Little <u>Red</u> Riding Hood.

3. I went <u>to</u> buy <u>two</u> dolls.

4. Five <u>blue</u> feathers <u>blew</u> in the wind.

5. <u>Would</u> you get <u>wood</u> for the fire?

Page 228

Following Directions: Days of the Week

Calendars show the days of the week in order. Sunday comes first. Saturday comes last. There are five days in between. An **abbreviation** is a short way of writing words. The abbreviations for the days of the week are usually the first three or four letters of the word followed by a period.

Example: Sunday — Sun.

Directions: Write the days of the week in order on the calendar. Use the abbreviations.

Day 1	Day 2	Day 3
Sunday	Monday	Tuesday
Sun.	Mon.	Tues.
Day 4	Day 5	Day 6
Wednesday	Thursday	Friday
Wed.	Thurs.	Fri.
	Day 7	
	Saturday	
	Sat.	

Page 229

Sentences

Sentences begin with capital letters.

Directions: Read the sentences and write them below. Begin each sentence with a capital letter.

Example: the cat is fat.

The cat is fat.

my dog is big.

My dog is big.

the boy is sad.

The boy is sad.

bikes are fun!

Bikes are fun!

dad can bake.

Dad can bake.

Page 230

Word Order

If you change the order of the words in a sentence, you can change the meaning of the sentence.

Directions: Read the sentences. Draw a circle around the sentence that describes the picture.

Example:

(The fox jumped over the dogs.)
The dogs jumped over the fox.

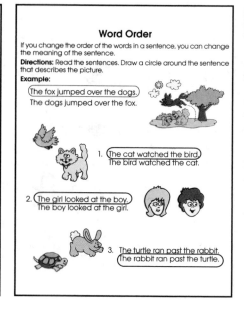

1. (The cat watched the bird.)
The bird watched the cat.

2. (The girl looked at the boy.)
The boy looked at the girl.

3. The turtle ran past the rabbit.
(The rabbit ran past the turtle.)

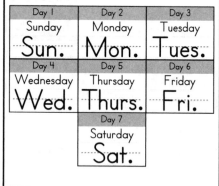

Page 231

Word Order

Word order is the order of words in a sentence which makes sense.
Directions: Cut out the words and put them in the correct order.
Glue each sentence on another sheet of paper.

I   like   to   ride   my   bike.

It   is   hot   and   sunny.

I   can   drink   water.

My   mom   plays   with   me.

The   dog   can   do   tricks.

Can   you   go   to   the   store?

Page 233

Word Order

Directions: Look at the picture. Put the words in order. Write the sentences on the lines below.

1. We made lemonade. some
2. good. It was
3. We the sold lemonade.
4. cost It five cents.
5. fun. We had

1. We made some lemonade.
2. It was good.
3. We sold the lemonade.
4. It cost five cents.
5. We had fun.

Page 234

Word Order

Directions: Look at the picture. Put the words in the right order. Write the sentences on the lines below.

1. a Jan starfish. has
2. and Bill to Peg swim. like
3. The shining. sun is
4. sand. the in Jack plays
5. cold. water The is

1. Jan has a starfish.
2. Bill and Peg like to swim.
3. The sun is shining.
4. Jack plays in the sand.
5. The water is cold.

Page 235

Review

Directions: Put the words in the right order to make a sentence. Write the sentences on the lines below.

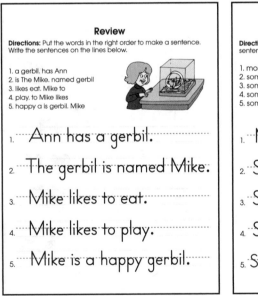

1. a gerbil. has Ann
2. is The Mike. named gerbil
3. likes eat. Mike to
4. play. to Mike likes
5. happy a is gerbil. Mike

1. Ann has a gerbil.
2. The gerbil is named Mike.
3. Mike likes to eat.
4. Mike likes to play.
5. Mike is a happy gerbil.

Page 236

Telling Sentences

Directions: Read the sentences and write them below. Begin each sentence with a capital letter. End each sentence with a period.

1. most children like pets
2. some children like dogs
3. some children like cats
4. some children like snakes
5. some children like all animals

1. Most children like pets.
2. Some children like dogs.
3. Some children like cats.
4. Some children like snakes.
5. Some children like all animals.

Page 237

Telling Sentences

Directions: Read the sentences and write them below. Begin each sentence with a capital letter. End each sentence with a period.

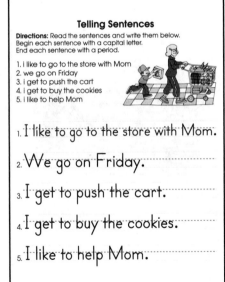

1. i like to go to the store with Mom
2. we go on Friday
3. i get to push the cart
4. i get to buy the cookies
5. i like to help Mom

1. I like to go to the store with Mom.
2. We go on Friday.
3. I get to push the cart.
4. I get to buy the cookies.
5. I like to help Mom.

Page 238

Asking Sentences

Directions: Write the first word of each asking sentence. Be sure to begin each question with a capital letter. End each question with a question mark.

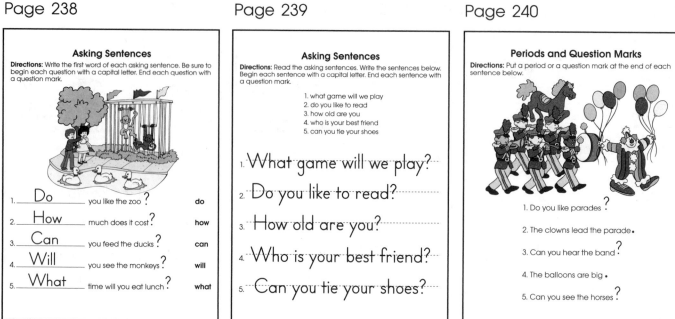

1. __Do__ you like the zoo ?   **do**
2. __How__ much does it cost ?   **how**
3. __Can__ you feed the ducks ?   **can**
4. __Will__ you see the monkeys ?   **will**
5. __What__ time will you eat lunch ?   **what**

Page 239

Asking Sentences

Directions: Read the asking sentences. Write the sentences below. Begin each sentence with a capital letter. End each sentence with a question mark.

1. what game will we play
2. do you like to read
3. how old are you
4. who is your best friend
5. can you tie your shoes

1. What game will we play?
2. Do you like to read?
3. How old are you?
4. Who is your best friend?
5. Can you tie your shoes?

Page 240

Periods and Question Marks

Directions: Put a period or a question mark at the end of each sentence below.

1. Do you like parades ?
2. The clowns lead the parade .
3. Can you hear the band ?
4. The balloons are big .
5. Can you see the horses ?

Page 241

Review

Directions: Look at the picture. In the space below, write one telling sentence about the picture. Then write one asking sentence about the picture.

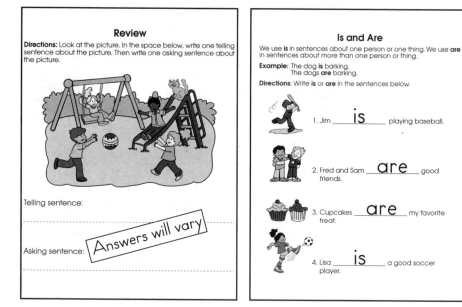

Telling sentence:

Asking sentence: *Answers will vary*

Page 242

Is and Are

We use **is** in sentences about one person or one thing. We use **are** in sentences about more than one person or thing.

Example: The dog **is** barking.
The dogs **are** barking.

Directions: Write **is** or **are** in the sentences below.

1. Jim __is__ playing baseball.
2. Fred and Sam __are__ good friends.
3. Cupcakes __are__ my favorite treat.
4. Lisa __is__ a good soccer player.

Page 243

Is and Are

Directions: Write **is** or **are** in the sentences below.
Example: Lisa __is__ sleeping.

1. Cats and dogs __are__ good pets.
2. Bill __is__ my best friend.
3. Apples __are__ good to eat.
4. We __are__ going to the zoo.
5. Pedro __is__ coming to my house.
6. When __are__ you all going to the zoo?

ANSWER KEY

Page 244

Vocabulary

Directions: Read the words. Trace and write them on the lines. Circle the word which completes each sentence. Write the word on the lines.

you and me you and me

you and me

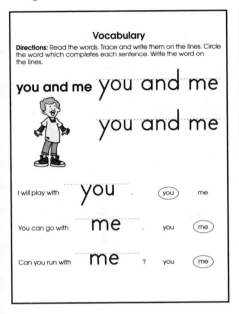

I will play with you . (you) me

You can go with me . you (me)

Can you run with me ? you (me)

Page 245

Vocabulary

Directions: Read the words. Trace and write them on the lines. Then circle the word which completes each sentence. Write it on the line.

over over over

under under under

The kite is under the tree. over (under)

The kite is over the tree. (over) under

Page 246

Vocabulary

Directions: Read the words. Trace and write them on the lines. Then circle the word which completes each sentence. Write it on the line.

above above above

below below below

The fish is below the water. above (below)

The fish is above the water. (above) below

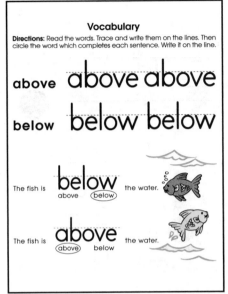

Page 247

Vocabulary

Directions: Read and trace the words. Then circle the word which completes each sentence. Write it on the line.

inside inside

outside outside

The dog is inside his house. (inside) outside

The dog is outside his house. inside (outside)

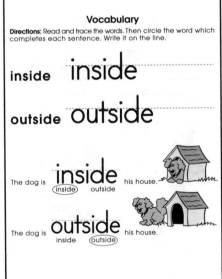

Page 248

Vocabulary

Directions: Read the words. Trace and write them on the lines. Then circle the word which completes each sentence. Write it on the line.

up up up up up

down down down

The flag is up the pole. (up) down

The flag is down the pole. up (down)

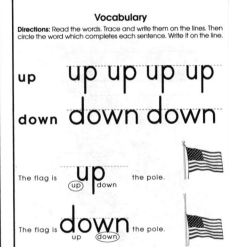

Page 250

Color Names

Directions: Trace the letters to write the name of each color. Then write the name again by yourself.

Example:

orange orange
blue blue
green green
yellow yellow
red red
brown brown

Grade 1 - Comprehensive Curriculum

Page 251

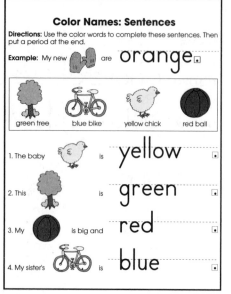

Color Names: Sentences

Directions: Use the color words to complete these sentences. Then put a period at the end.

Example: My new 🧤 are orange.

green tree   blue bike   yellow chick   red ball

1. The baby 🐤 is   yellow.

2. This 🌳 is   green.

3. My ⚫ is big and   red.

4. My sister's 🚲 is   blue.

Page 252

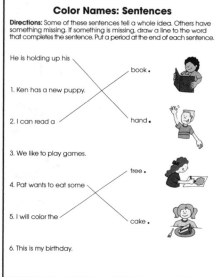

Color Names: Sentences

Directions: Some of these sentences tell a whole idea. Others have something missing. If something is missing, draw a line to the word that completes the sentence. Put a period at the end of each sentence.

He is holding up his — hand.

1. Ken has a new puppy.

2. I can read a — book.

3. We like to play games.

4. Pat wants to eat some — cake.

5. I will color the — tree.

6. This is my birthday.

Page 253

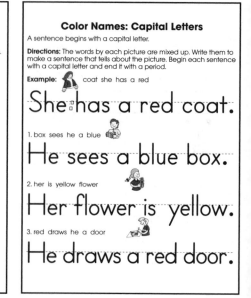

Color Names: Capital Letters

A sentence begins with a capital letter.

Directions: The words by each picture are mixed up. Write them to make a sentence that tells about the picture. Begin each sentence with a capital letter and end it with a period.

Example: coat she has a red

She has a red coat.

1. box sees he a blue

He sees a blue box.

2. her is yellow flower

Her flower is yellow.

3. red draws he a door

He draws a red door.

Page 254

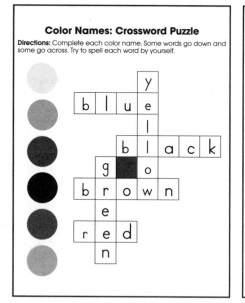

Color Names: Crossword Puzzle

Directions: Complete each color name. Some words go down and some go across. Try to spell each word by yourself.

Page 255

Color the Eggs

Directions: Read the words. Color the picture with the correct colors.

Page 256

Finish the Pictures

Directions: Read the words. Finish the pictures.

a red ball   a black hat

a yellow sun   a pink kite

an orange balloon   a blue umbrella

ANSWER KEY

Page 257

Animal Names

Directions: Fill in the missing letters for each word.

Example:

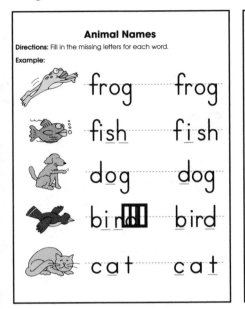

frog   frog

fish   fi_sh

dog   d_og

bir_d   bird

ca_t   c_at

Page 258

Animal Names

Directions: The letters in the name of each animal are mixed up. Write each word correctly.

Example:

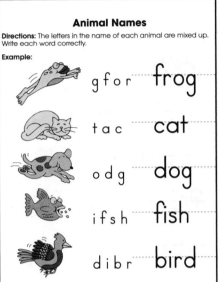

g f o r   frog

t a c   cat

o d g   dog

i f s h   fish

d i b r   bird

Page 259

Animal Names: Beginning Sounds

Directions: Say the name of each animal. Write the beginning sound under its name. Find two pictures in each row that begin with the same sound as the animal. Write the same first letter under them.

Example:

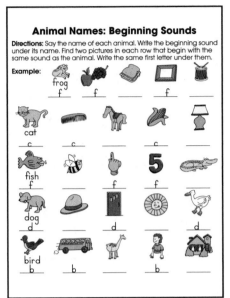

frog   f   f   f

cat   c   c   c

fish   f   f   f

dog   d   d   d

bird   b   b   b

Page 260

Animal Names: Sentences

A **sentence** tells about something.

Directions: These sentences tell about animals. Write the word that completes each sentence.

Example:

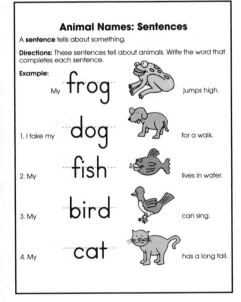

My   frog   jumps high.

1. I take my   dog   for a walk.

2. My   fish   lives in water.

3. My   bird   can sing.

4. My   cat   has a long tail.

Page 261

Animal Names: Sentences

Directions: Finish writing the name of each animal on the line. Draw a line from the first part of the sentence to the part which completes it. Put a period at the end of each sentence.

Example:

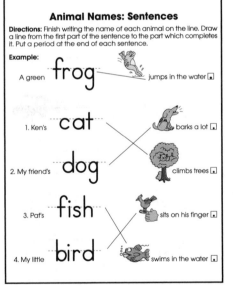

A green   frog   jumps in the water.

1. Ken's   cat   barks a lot.

2. My friend's   dog   climbs trees.

3. Pat's   fish   sits on his finger.

4. My little   bird   swims in the water.

Page 262

Review

Directions: Use the words in the pictures to write a sentence about each animal. Put a period at the end of each sentence.

Example: The   eats bugs.

The frog eats bugs.

The cat drinks milk.

The bird eats seeds.

The dog jumps out.

The fish meet.

Page 263

Things That Go

Directions: Trace the letters to write the name of each thing. Write each name again by yourself. Then color the pictures.

Example:

car   car

truck   truck

train   train

bike   bike

plane   plane

Page 264

Things That Go

Directions: Fill in the missing letters for each word.

Example:

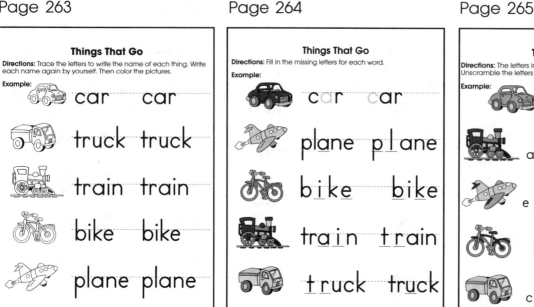

car   car

plane   plane

bike   bike

train   train

truck   truck

Page 265

Things That Go

Directions: The letters in the name of each thing are mixed up. Unscramble the letters and write each word correctly below.

Example:

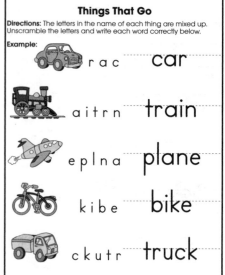

r a c   car

a i t r n   train

e p l n a   plane

k i b e   bike

c k u t r   truck

Page 266

Things That Go: Beginning Sounds

Directions: Say the name of each thing. Write the beginning sound under its name. Find two pictures in each row that begin with the same sound as the first picture. Write the same first letter under them.

Example:

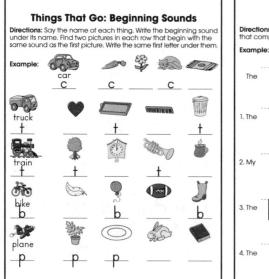

car
c   c   c

truck
t   t   t

train
t   t   t

bike
b   b   b

plane
p   p   p

Page 267

Things That Go: Sentences

Directions: These sentences tell about things that go. Write the word that completes each sentence.

Example:

The   car   is in the garage.

1. The   truck   was at the farm.

2. My   bike   had a flat tire.

3. The   plane   flew high.

4. The   train   went fast.

Page 268

Things That Go: Sentences

Directions: Finish writing the names of the things that go. Draw a line from the first part of the sentence to the part which completes it. Put a period at the end of each sentence.

Example:

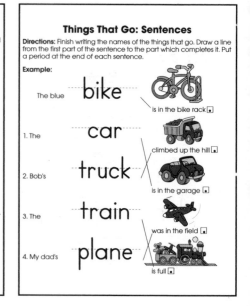

The blue   bike   is in the bike rack.

1. The   car   climbed up the hill.

2. Bob's   truck   is in the garage.

3. The   train   was in the field.

4. My dad's   plane   is full.

Page 269

Things That Go: Sentences

Directions: Draw a line from the first part of each sentence to the part which completes it. Put a period at the end of each sentence.

Example:

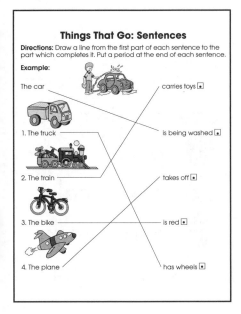

The car — carries toys •

1. The truck — is being washed •

2. The train — takes off •

3. The bike — is red •

4. The plane — has wheels •

Page 270

Review

Directions: Use the words in the pictures to write a sentence about each thing that goes. Put a period at the end of each sentence.

Example:

The [ ] is red — The car is red.

The [ ] flies — The plane flies.

The [ ] has apples — The truck has apples.

The [ ] has wheels — The bike has wheels.

The [ ] goes fast — The train goes fast.

Page 271

Clothing Words

Directions: Trace the letters to write the name of each clothing word. Then write each name again by yourself.

Example:

shirt — shirt
pants — pants
jacket — jacket
socks — socks
shoes — shoes
dress — dress
hat — hat

Page 272

Clothing Words: Beginning Sounds

Directions: Circle the words that begin with the same sound.

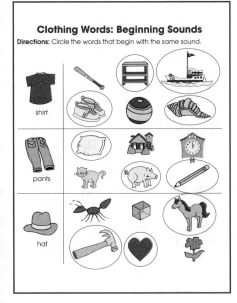

shirt

pants

hat

Page 273

Clothing Words: Sentences

Directions: Some of these sentences tell a whole idea. Others have something missing. If something is missing, draw a line to the word that completes the sentence. Put a period at the end of each sentence.

Example:

She is wearing a polka-dot — holes •

1. The baseball player wore a — dress •

2. His pants were torn.

3. The socks had — hat •

4. The jacket had blue buttons.

5. The shoes were brown.

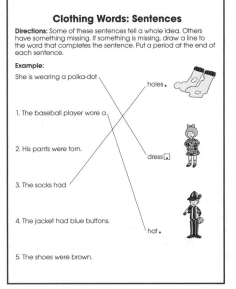

Page 274

Clothing Words: Sentences

Directions: The words by each picture are mixed up. Write them to make a sentence that tells about the picture. Begin each sentence with a capital letter and end it with a period.

Example: is shirt a drying

A shirt is drying.

1. ties his shoes he

He ties his shoes.

2. red wear I a jacket

I wear a red jacket.

3. blue are pants his

His pants are blue.

Page 275

Clothing Words: Sentences

Directions: Use the clothing words to complete these sentences. Then put a period at the end.

Example:

Mike is wearing a **hat .**

1. Put on your socks before your **shoes .**

2. When it's cold, wear a **jacket .**

3. The little girl liked to wear a pink **dress .**

4. He wore jeans with the **shirt .**

5. The man wore a suit coat and **pants .**

6. The clown wore long, striped **socks .**

Page 276

Review

Directions: Write three sentences that tell about this picture. Begin each sentence with a capital letter and end it with a period.

Answers may include:

1. **They are shopping.**

2. **A woman is working.**

3. **She sells shirts.**

Page 277

Food Names

Directions: Trace the letters to write the name of each food word. Write each name again by yourself. Then color the pictures.

Example:

bread bread

cookie cookie

apple apple

cake cake

milk milk

egg egg

Page 278

Food Names: Beginning Sounds

Directions: Write the food names that answer the questions.

| egg | milk | ice cream | apple | cookie | cake |

1. Which food words start with the same sounds as the pictures?

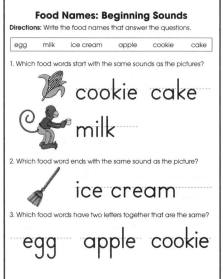

cookie   cake

milk

2. Which food word ends with the same sound as the picture?

ice cream

3. Which food words have two letters together that are the same?

egg   apple   cookie

Page 279

Food Names: Asking Sentences

An **asking sentence** asks a question. Asking sentences end with a question mark.

Directions: Write each sentence on the line. Begin each sentence with a capital letter. Put a period at the end of the telling sentences and a question mark at the end of the asking sentences.

Example: do you like cake

Do you like cake?

1. the cow has spots

The cow has spots.

2. is that cookie good

Is that cookie good?

3. she ate the apple

She ate the apple.

Page 280

Food Names: Asking Sentences

Directions: Change each telling sentence into an asking sentence by moving the words. Put a question mark at the end of each question.

Example: The girl is eating.

Is the girl eating?

1. He is sharing.

Is he sharing?

2. He is drinking.

Is he drinking?

3. She is baking.

Is she baking?

Page 281

Food Names: Asking Sentences

Directions: Use the food names to answer each question.

1. Which one can you drink? **milk**
2. Which one do you have to keep very cold? **ice cream**
3. Which one grows on trees? **apple**
4. Which one do you put birthday candles on? **cake**
5. Which one do people sometimes eat in the morning? **eggs**
6. Which one do you like best? Answers will vary.

Page 282

Food Names: Sentences

Directions: In each sentence, write a word in the first blank to tell who is doing something. Write one of the food names in the second blank. Then draw a picture to go with each sentence.

The **mother** is making **a cake.**

Answers may include:

1. The **boy** is eating **apples.**

Pictures will vary.

2. The **girl** is buying **milk.**

Page 283

Food Names: Completing a Story

Directions: Write the food names in the story.

Kim got up in the morning.

"Do you want an **egg** ?" her mother asked.

"Yes, please," Kim said.

"May I have some **milk** , too?"

"Okay," her mother said.

"How about some **ice cream** ?" Kim asked with a smile.

Her mother laughed. "Not now," she said.

She put an **apple** in Kim's lunch.

"Do you want a **cookie** or some **cake** today?"

"Both!" Kim said.

Page 284

Review

Directions: Write two telling sentences and one asking sentence about this picture. Use the food, color and animal words you know.

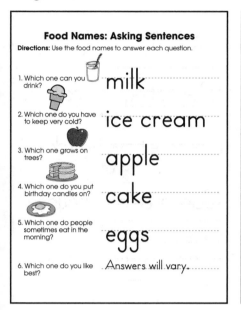

Answers may include:

Two telling sentences:

1. The cat is gray.
2. The egg is cracked.

One asking sentence:

Is the girl angry?

Page 285

Number Words

Directions: Trace the letters to write the name of each number. Write the numbers again by yourself. Then color the number pictures.

Example:
Colors will vary.

1	one	one
2	two	two
3	three	three
4	four	four
5	five	five
6	six	six
7	seven	seven
8	eight	eight
9	nine	nine
10	ten	ten

Page 286

Number Words: Asking Sentences

Directions: Write each sentence on the line. Begin each sentence with a capital letter. Put a period at the end of the telling sentences and a question mark at the end of the asking sentences.

Example: may I eat two cookies

May I eat two cookies?

1. I see five flowers

I see five flowers.

2. is one cat yellow

Is one cat yellow?

3. are there six eggs

Are there six eggs?

Page 287

Number Words: Asking Sentences

Directions: Use a number word to answer each question.

| one | five | seven | three | eight |

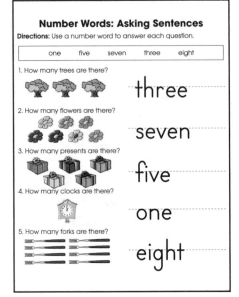

1. How many trees are there?

three

2. How many flowers are there?

seven

3. How many presents are there?

five

4. How many clocks are there?

one

5. How many forks are there?

eight

Page 288

Number Words: Asking Sentences

Directions: Use the number words to answer each question.

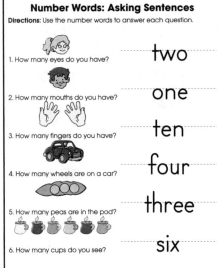

1. How many eyes do you have?

two

2. How many mouths do you have?

one

3. How many fingers do you have?

ten

4. How many wheels are on a car?

four

5. How many peas are in the pod?

three

6. How many cups do you see?

six

Page 289

Number Words: Asking Sentences

Directions: Change each telling sentence into an asking sentence by moving the words. Put a question mark at the end of each question.

Example: He ate one cookie.

Is he eating one cookie?

1. She has two dogs.

Does she have two dogs?

2. Three balls can bounce.

Can three balls bounce?

3. One balloon is red.

Is one balloon red?

Page 290

Review

Directions: Write two telling sentences and one asking sentence about this picture. Use the number words you know.

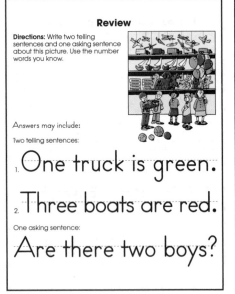

Answers may include:

Two telling sentences:

1. One truck is green.

2. Three boats are red.

One asking sentence:

Are there two boys?

Page 291

Action Words

Action words tell things we can do.

Directions: Trace the letters to write each action word. Then write the action word again by yourself.

Example:

sleep   sleep

run   run

make   make

ride   ride

play   play

stop   stop

Page 292

Action Words

Directions: Circle the word that is spelled correctly. Then write the correct spelling in the blank.

Example: seep / (sleep) / slep

sleep

paly / pay / (play)

play

seee / cee / (see)

see

rum / (run) / runn

run

(jump) / jumb / junp

jump

mack / maek / (make)

make

Page 293

Action Words

Directions: Read each sentence and write the correct words in the blanks.

Example:

go
sleep   I will **go** to bed and **sleep** all night.

1.
see
jump   The girls **see** the frogs **jump**

2.
sit
run   After the boys **run** , they **sit** and rest.

3.
stop
play   They **stop** at the park so they can **play**

4.
ride
make   They will **make** a car to **ride** in.

Page 294

Action Words: Beginning and Ending Sounds

Directions: Write the action words that answer the questions.

| sit | run | make | see | jump | stop | play | ride |

1. Which words begin with the same sound as  ?

see   sit   stop

2. Which words begin with the same sound as

run   ride

3. Which words begin with the same sound as each of these words?

play   jump   make

4. Which words end with the same sound as these?

jump   make   sit

Page 295

Action Words: More Than One

To show more than one of something, add **s** to the end of the word.

Example: one cat   two cats

Directions: In each sentence, add **s** to show more than one. Then write the action word that completes each sentence.

| sit | jump | stop | ride |

Example:

The frog **s sleep** in the sun.

1. The boy **s sit** on the fence.

2. The car **s stop** at the sign.

3. The girl **s swim** in the water.

4. The dog **s sit** in the wagon.

Page 296

Action Words: Asking Sentences

Directions: Write an asking sentence about each picture. Begin each sentence with **can**. Add an action word. Begin each asking sentence with a capital letter and end it with a question mark.

Example:
I with you can

Can I sit with you?

she can

Can she cook?

with you can I

Can I play with you?

can she fast

Can she run fast?

Page 297

Review

Directions: Write three telling sentences and one asking sentence about this picture. Put an action word in each sentence.

Answers may include:

Three telling sentences:

1. **The children play.**

2. **She flies a kite.**

3. **The dogs run.**

One asking sentence:

Is the sun shining?

Page 298

Sense Words

Directions: Circle the word that is spelled correctly. Then write the correct spelling in the blank.

Example:

tast
(taste)
tste   **taste**

(touch)
tuch
touh   **touch**

smel
smll
(smell)   **smell**

her
(hear)
har   **hear**

(see)
se
sea   **see**

Page 299

Sense Words: Sentences

Directions: Read each sentence and write the correct words in the blanks.

Example:

taste
mouth   I can **taste** things with my **mouth**

touch
hands   1. I can **touch** things with my **hands**

nose
smell   2. I can **smell** things with my **nose**

hear
ears   3. I can **hear** with my **ears**

see
eyes   4. I can **see** things with my **eyes**

Page 300

Sense Words: Beginning Sounds

Directions: Use the sense words in the box to answer each question.

| smell | see | taste | hear | touch |

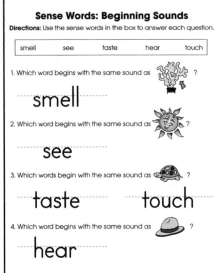

1. Which word begins with the same sound as ?

smell

2. Which word begins with the same sound as ?

see

3. Which words begin with the same sound as ?

taste   **touch**

4. Which word begins with the same sound as ?

hear

Page 301

Sense Words: More Than One

Directions: In each sentence, add **s** to show more than one. Then write the sense word that completes each sentence.

Example: The dog **s** **taste** the food.

| see | touch | smell | hear |

1. The flower **s** **smell** good.

2. I can **see** five bird **s**.

3. The girl **s** **hear** the bells ring.

4. The boy **s** wanted to **touch** the cactus.

Page 302

Sense Words: Asking Sentences

Directions: Write an asking sentence about each picture. Begin each sentence with **can**. Add a sense word. Begin each asking sentence with a capital letter and end it with a question mark.

Example: can rose I a

Can I smell a rose?

1.   can I the dog

Can I touch the dog?

2.   can I pie the

Can I taste the pie?

3.   can he car the

Can he see the car?

4.   he can bell the

Can he hear the bell?

Page 303

Review

Directions: Write three telling sentences and one asking sentence about this picture. Use a sense word in each sentence.

Answers may include:
Three telling sentences:

1. We see the beach.

2. We hear the waves.

3. We touch the sand.

One asking sentence:

Do you see a bird?

Page 304

Weather Words: Beginning Sounds

Directions: Say the sound of the letter at the beginning of each row. Find the pictures in each row that begin with the same letter. Write the letter under the pictures.

Example:

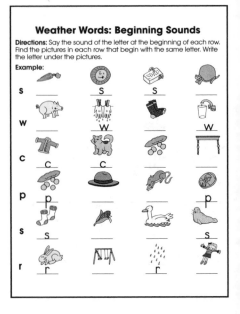

s   S   S
w   W   W
c   C   C
p   p   p
s   S   S
r   r   r

Page 305

Weather Words: Sentences

Directions: Write the weather word that completes each sentence. Put a period at the end of the telling sentences and a question mark at the end of the asking sentences.

Example:
Do flowers grow in the **sun** **?**

| rain | water | wet | hot |

1. The sun makes me **hot** **.**

2. When it rains, the grass gets **wet** **.**

3. Do you think it will **rain** on our picnic **?**

4. Should you drink the **water** from the rain **?**

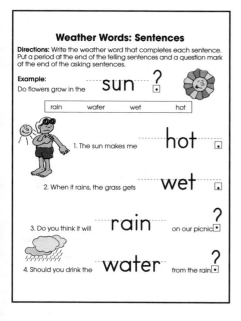

Page 306

Weather Words: Sentences

Directions: Read the sentence parts below. Draw a line from the first part of the sentence to the second part that completes it.

Example: When I'm cold, ——— I put on my coat.
I take off my shoes.

1. When it rains, ——— we ride our bikes to the park.
we play games inside.

2. I like snow ——— because I can eat lunch.
because I can make a snowman.

3. When the sun comes out, ——— the grass grows fast.
the grass gets wet.

4. At night, the rain ——— makes ice on my windows.
helps me go to sleep.

Page 307

Weather Words: Completing a Story

Directions: Write the missing words to complete the story. The first letter of each word is written for you.

"Please may I go outside?" I asked.

"It's too **cold**," my father told me. "Maybe later the sun will come out." Later, the sun did come out. Then it began to **rain** again. "May I go out now?" I asked again. Dad looked out the window. "You will get **wet**," he said. "But I want to see if the **rain** helped our flowers grow," I said. "You mean you want to play in the **water**," Dad said with a smile. How did Dad know that?

Page 308

Weather Words: Sentences

Directions: Read the two sentences on each line and draw a line between them. Then write each sentence again on the lines below. Begin each sentence with a capital letter and end each one with a period or a question mark.

Example: will it rain|the sky is dark
Will it rain?
The sky is dark.

1. she fell in the pond|she got wet
She fell in the pond.
She got wet.

2. do you like my hat|it is red
Do you like my hat?
It is red.

Page 309

Review

Directions: Write a telling sentence about each of these pictures. Then write an asking sentence about one of the pictures. Use the weather words and other words you know.

Answers may include:
Telling sentences:

1. ## They are cold.
2. ## Rain can be fun.

Asking sentence:

Is it still snowing?

Page 310

My World

Directions: Fill in the missing letters for each word.

tree   tree
grass   grass
flower   flower
pond   pond
sand   sand
sky   sky

Page 311

My World

Directions: The letters in the words below are mixed up. Unscramble the letters and write each word correctly.

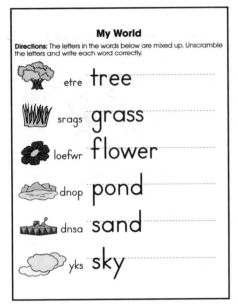

etre **tree**

srags **grass**

loefwr **flower**

dnop **pond**

dnsa **sand**

yks **sky**

Page 312

My World: Beginning Sounds

Directions: Say the name of each picture. Write the beginning sound under its name. Find two pictures in each row that begin with the same sound as the first picture. Write the same first letter under them.

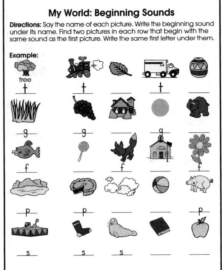

Page 313

My World: Sentences

Directions: Write the word that completes each sentence. Put a period at the end of the telling sentences and a question mark at the end of the asking sentences.

Example: Does the sun shine on the **flowers** ?

| tree | grass | pond | sand | sky |

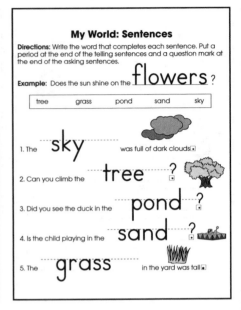

1. The **sky** was full of dark clouds▪

2. Can you climb the **tree** ?▫

3. Did you see the duck in the **pond** ?▫

4. Is the child playing in the **sand** ?▫

5. The **grass** in the yard was tall▪

Page 314

My World: Sentences

Directions: Read the two sentences on each line and draw a line between them. Then write each sentence again on the lines below. Begin each sentence with a capital letter, and end each one with a period or a question mark.

Example: the tree has leaves|can we rake some

The tree has leaves.

Can we rake some?

1. the lake is fun|we swim in it

The lake is fun.

We swim in it.

2. the sky is so blue|isn't it pretty

The sky is so blue.

Isn't it pretty?

Page 315

Review

Directions: Write three telling sentences about the picture. Then write an asking sentence about the picture. Use the words that tell about your world and other words you know.

Answers may include:
Telling sentences:

1. **The grass is green.**

2. **There are two trees.**

3. **The pool is pink.**

Asking sentence:

Is the sky clear?

Page 316

The Parts of My Body: Sentences

Directions: Write the word that completes each sentence. Put a period at the end of the telling sentences and a question mark at the end of the asking sentences.

Example: I wear my hat on my **head**▪

| arms | legs | feet | hands |

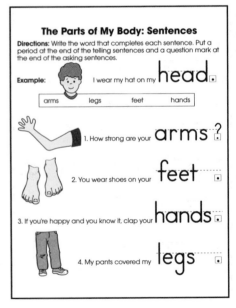

1. How strong are your **arms** ?

2. You wear shoes on your **feet** ▪

3. If you're happy and you know it, clap your **hands** ▪

4. My pants covered my **legs** ▪

Page 317

The Parts of My Body: Beginning Sounds

Directions: Say the sound of the letter at the beginning of each row. Find the pictures in each row that begin with the same letter. Write the letter under the pictures.

Example:

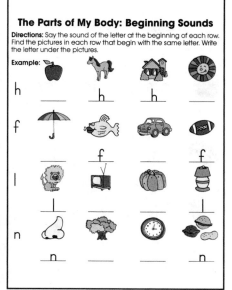

h

h   h

f

f   f

l

l

n

n   n

Page 318

The Parts of My Body: Sentences

Directions: Read the sentence parts below. Draw a line from the first part of the sentence to the second part that completes it.

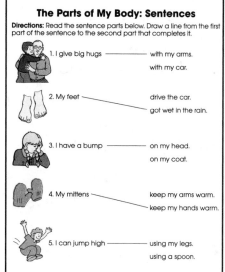

1. I give big hugs ——— with my arms.
    with my car.

2. My feet   drive the car.
    got wet in the rain.

3. I have a bump ——— on my head.
    on my coat.

4. My mittens   keep my arms warm.
    keep my hands warm.

5. I can jump high ——— using my legs.
    using a spoon.

Page 319

The Parts of My Body: Sentences

Directions: Read the two sentences on each line and draw a line between them. Then write each sentence again on the lines below. Begin each sentence with a capital letter, and end each one with a period or a question mark.

Example: wash your hands|they are dirty

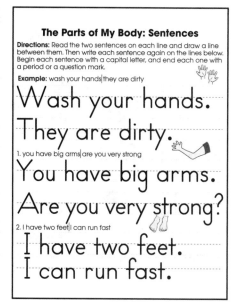

Wash your hands.

They are dirty.

1. you have big arms|are you very strong

You have big arms.

Are you very strong?

2. I have two feet|I can run fast

I have two feet.

I can run fast.

Page 320

Review

Directions: Write a telling sentence about each of these pictures. Then write an asking sentence about one of the pictures. Use the words that name the parts of your body and other words you know.

Answers may include:

Telling sentences:

1. He has strong arms.

2. His nose is a carrot.

Asking sentence:

Are his hands cold?

Page 321

Opposite Words

Some words are opposites. **Opposites** are things that are different in every way. **Dark** and **light** are opposites.

Directions: Trace the letters to write each word. Then write the word again by yourself.

Example:

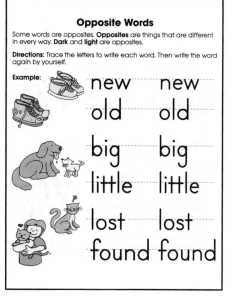

new   new
old   old
big   big
little   little
lost   lost
found   found

Page 322

Opposite Words

Directions: Circle one word in each sentence that is not spelled correctly. Then write the word correctly.

| dark | found | old | first | lost |

Example:

The house is (little).

1. Are those your (olde) shoes?

2. I (fond) your book.

3. She is (frist) in line.

4. She (losst) her lunch.

5. I am afraid of the (drak).

little
old
found
first
lost
dark

Page 323

Opposite Words: Beginning and Ending

Directions: Write the opposite words that answer the questions.

| dark | found | old | light | new | first | lost | last |

1. Which words begin with the same sound as  ?

light   lost   last

2. Which words begin with the same sound as ___ ?

found   first

3. Which words begin with the same sound as each of these words?

dark   9   new

4. Which two words end with the same sound as ___ ?

old   found

Page 324

Opposite Words: Sentences

Directions: Read the sentence by the first picture. Then look at the next picture. Write a sentence that tells about it.

Example: The dog is little.

The dog is big.

| found | new | first | lost | old | last |

1. His book is lost.

His book is found.

2. The dog eats first.

The fish eats last.

3. I like my old shirt.

I like my new shirt.

Page 325

Opposite Words: Sentences

Directions: Read the sentence about the first picture. Write another sentence about the picture beside it. Use the opposite words.

Example: This apple is little.

This apple is big.

| dark | old | first | new | light | last |

1. This coat is light.

This coat is dark.

2. This woman is first.

This woman is last.

3. This car is old.

This car is new.

Page 326

Opposite Words: Sentences

Directions: Write opposite words to complete these sentences.

Example:

The rain made my little flower grow big

| dark | first | found | last | light | lost |

1. Kim ate the dark candy first

and the light candy last .

2. All day John looked for his lost shoe.

Then his father called, "John, come here! I found your shoe."

3. When I get up, it is dark outside. By the time I go to school, it is light .

Page 327

Review

Directions: Look at the pictures in each row. Write one sentence about the last picture in each row. Begin each sentence with a capital letter and end it with a period.

Answers may include:

The cake is gone.

The barn is red.

Page 328

More Action Words

Directions: Fill in the missing letters for each word.

Example:

paint   paint

catch   catc h

color   colo r

eat   e at

grow   g r ow

fly   f l y

ANSWER KEY

Page 329

More Action Words: Beginning and Ending Sounds

Words that **rhyme** have the same ending sound.

Directions: Write the words that answer the questions.

catch   fly   eat   grow   buy   color

1. Which words begin with the same sound as 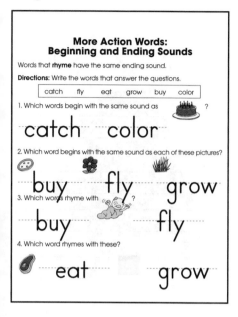 ?

catch   color

2. Which word begins with the same sound as each of these pictures?

buy   fly   grow

3. Which words rhyme with ?

buy   fly

4. Which word rhymes with these?

eat   grow

Page 330

More Action Words: Sentences

Directions: Write a sentence that tells about the picture. Use the words next to the picture. Remember to begin each sentence with a capital letter and end it with a period.

Example: likes boy to paint the

The boy likes to paint.

1. boy see grow the

See the boy grow.

2. bird the can fly

The bird can fly.

3. she will color

She will color.

Page 331

More Action Words: Sentences

Directions: Put the two sentences together to make one new sentence.

Example: The ball is red. The ball is blue.

The ball is red and blue.

1. I eat apples. I eat cookies.

I eat apples and cookies.

2. We buy milk. We buy eggs.

We buy milk and eggs.

Page 332

Review

Directions: Use the action words you know to write sentences that tell about these pictures. Write a question about the last picture.

Example: Answers may include:

The flowers grow.

The dog runs fast.

They eat apples.

Write a question about this picture.

Do you like cake?

Page 333

People Words

Directions: Trace the letters to write each word. Then write the word again by yourself.

girl   girl
boy   boy
man   man
woman   woman
people   people
children   children

Page 334

People Words

Directions: Write a people word in each sentence to tell who is doing something.

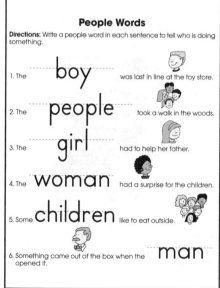

1. The boy was last in line at the toy store.

2. The people took a walk in the woods.

3. The girl had to help her father.

4. The woman had a surprise for the children.

5. Some children like to eat outside.

6. Something came out of the box when the man opened it.

Grade 1 - Comprehensive Curriculum

Page 335

People Words

Sometimes we use other words in place of people names. For **boy** or **man**, we can use the word **he**. For **girl** or **woman**, we can use the word **she**. For two or more people, we can use the word **they**.

Directions: Write the words **he**, **she** or **they** in these sentences.

Example: The boy likes cookies. **He** likes cookies.

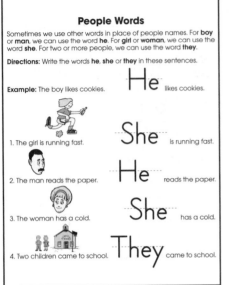

1. The girl is running fast. **She** is running fast.

2. The man reads the paper. **He** reads the paper.

3. The woman has a cold. **She** has a cold.

4. Two children came to school. **They** came to school.

Page 336

People Words: Sentences

Directions: Write the people word that completes each sentence.

| people | man | girl | children | boy | woman |

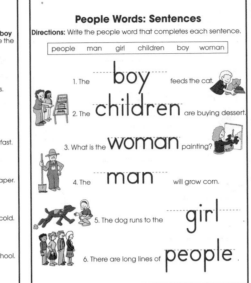

1. The **boy** feeds the cat.

2. The **children** are buying dessert.

3. What is the **woman** painting?

4. The **man** will grow corn.

5. The dog runs to the **girl**

6. There are long lines of **people**

Page 338

Number Recognition

Directions: Write the numbers 1-10. Color the bear.

1 2 3 4 5 6 7 8 9 10

Page 339

Number Recognition 1, 2, 3, 4, 5

Directions: Use the color codes to color the parrot.

Color:
1's red
2's blue
3's yellow
4's green
5's orange

Page 340

Number Recognition 6, 7, 8, 9, 10

Directions: Use the code to color the carousel horse.

Color:
6's purple
7's yellow
8's black
9's pink
10's brown

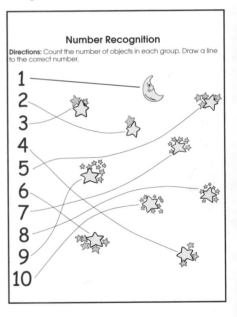

Page 341

Number Recognition

Directions: Count the number of objects in each group. Draw a line to the correct number.

1
2
3
4
5
6
7
8
9
10

Page 342

Counting

Directions: How many are there of each shape? Write the answers in the boxes. The first one is done for you.

Page 343

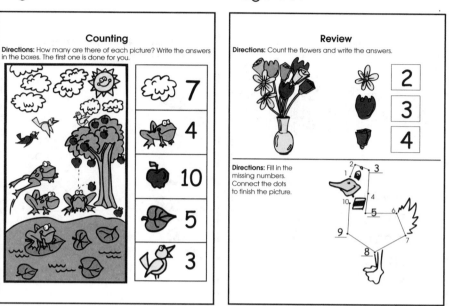

Counting

Directions: How many are there of each picture? Write the answers in the boxes. The first one is done for you.

Page 344

Review

Directions: Count the flowers and write the answers.

Directions: Fill in the missing numbers. Connect the dots to finish the picture.

Page 345

Number Recognition

Directions: Cut out the pieces. Mix them up and match the number with the picture.

Page 347

Number Word Find

Directions: Find the number words 0 through 12 hidden in the box.

Words to find:

zero	four	eight	eleven
one	five	nine	twelve
two	six	ten	
three	seven		

Page 348

Number Words

Directions: Number the buildings from one to six.

Directions: Draw a line from the word to the number.

two — 1
five — 3
six — 5
four — 6
one — 2
three — 4

Page 349

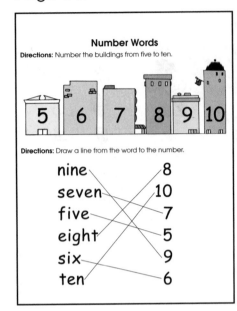

Number Words

Directions: Number the buildings from five to ten.

5 6 7 8 9 10

Directions: Draw a line from the word to the number.

nine — 8
seven — 10
five — 7
eight — 5
six — 9
ten — 6

Page 350

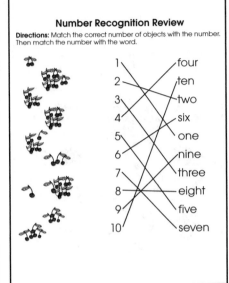

Number Recognition Review

Directions: Match the correct number of objects with the number. Then match the number with the word.

1 — four
2 — ten
3 — two
4 — six
5 — one
6 — nine
7 — three
8 — eight
9 — five
10 — seven

Page 351

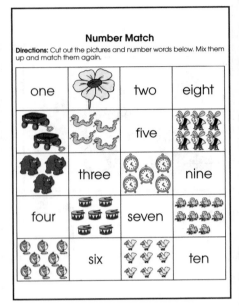

Number Match

Directions: Cut out the pictures and number words below. Mix them up and match them again.

one		two	eight
		five	
	three		nine
four		seven	
	six		ten

Page 353

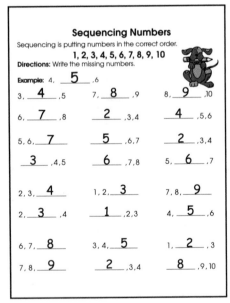

Sequencing Numbers

Sequencing is putting numbers in the correct order.
1, 2, 3, 4, 5, 6, 7, 8, 9, 10

Directions: Write the missing numbers.

Example: 4, _5_ ,6

3, _4_ ,5   7, _8_ ,9   8, _9_ ,10
6, _7_ ,8   _2_ ,3,4   _4_ ,5,6
5,6, _7_   _5_ ,6,7   _2_ ,3,4
_3_ ,4,5   _6_ ,7,8   5, _6_ ,7
2,3, _4_   1,2, _3_   7,8, _9_
2, _3_ ,4   _1_ ,2,3   4, _5_ ,6
6,7, _8_   3,4, _5_   1, _2_ ,3
7,8, _9_   _2_ ,3,4   _8_ ,9,10

Page 354

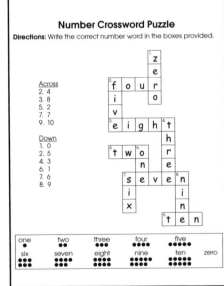

Number Crossword Puzzle

Directions: Write the correct number word in the boxes provided.

Across
2. 4
3. 8
5. 2
7. 7
9. 10

Down
1. 0
2. 5
4. 3
6. 1
7. 6
8. 9

Page 355

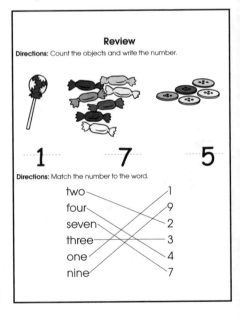

Review

Directions: Count the objects and write the number.

1   7   5

Directions: Match the number to the word.

two — 1
four — 9
seven — 2
three — 3
one — 4
nine — 7

Page 356

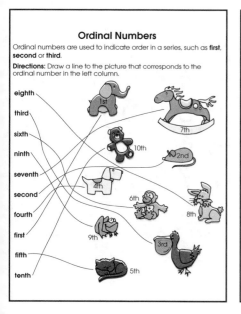

Ordinal Numbers

Ordinal numbers are used to indicate order in a series, such as **first**, **second** or **third**.

Directions: Draw a line to the picture that corresponds to the ordinal number in the left column.

eighth — 1st
third
sixth
ninth — 10th
seventh — 2nd
second — 4th
fourth — 6th
first — 9th — 8th
fifth — 3rd
tenth — 5th

Page 357

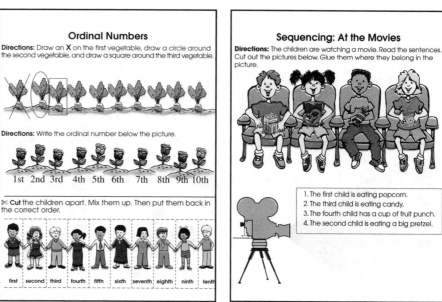

Ordinal Numbers

Directions: Draw an **X** on the first vegetable, draw a circle around the second vegetable, and draw a square around the third vegetable.

Directions: Write the ordinal number below the picture.

1st 2nd 3rd 4th 5th 6th 7th 8th 9th 10th

✂ **Cut** the children apart. Mix them up. Then put them back in the correct order.

first second third fourth fifth sixth seventh eighth ninth tenth

Page 359

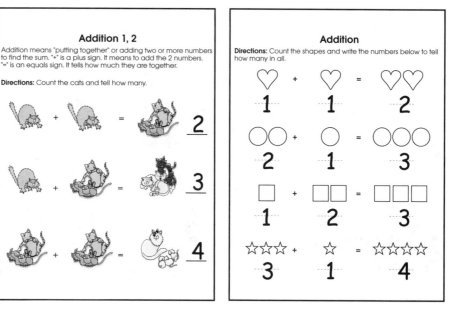

Sequencing: At the Movies

Directions: The children are watching a movie. Read the sentences. Cut out the pictures below. Glue them where they belong in the picture.

1. The first child is eating popcorn.
2. The third child is eating candy.
3. The fourth child has a cup of fruit punch.
4. The second child is eating a big pretzel.

Page 361

Sequencing: Standing in Line

Directions: These children are waiting to see a movie. Look at them and follow the instructions.

1. Color the person who is first in line yellow.
2. Color the person who is last in line brown.
3. Color the person who is second in line pink.
4. Circle the person who is at the end of the line.

Page 362

Addition 1, 2

Addition means "putting together" or adding two or more numbers to find the sum. "+" is a plus sign. It means to add the 2 numbers. "=" is an equals sign. It tells how much they are together.

Directions: Count the cats and tell how many.

+ = **2**

+ = **3**

+ = **4**

Page 363

Addition

Directions: Count the shapes and write the numbers below to tell how many in all.

♡ + ♡ = ♡♡
1   1   2

○○ + ○ = ○○○
2   1   3

□ + □□ = □□□
1   2   3

☆☆☆ + ☆ = ☆☆☆☆
3   1   4

Page 364

Addition

Directions: Draw the correct number of dots next to the numbers in each problem. Add up the number of dots to find your answer.

Example:

$$\begin{array}{r} 3 \\ +2 \\ \hline 5 \end{array}$$

$$2 + 2 = \underline{4}$$

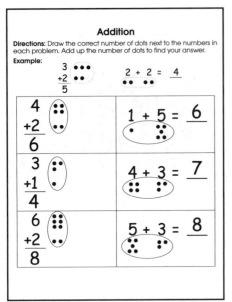

$\begin{array}{r} 4 \\ +2 \\ \hline 6 \end{array}$	$1 + 5 = \underline{6}$
$\begin{array}{r} 3 \\ +1 \\ \hline 4 \end{array}$	$4 + 3 = \underline{7}$
$\begin{array}{r} 6 \\ +2 \\ \hline 8 \end{array}$	$5 + 3 = \underline{8}$

Page 365

Addition 3, 4, 5, 6

Directions: Practice writing the numbers and then add. Draw dots to help, if needed.

3 3 3 3

4 4 4 4

5 5 5 5

6 6 6 6

$$\begin{array}{r} 2 \\ +4 \\ \hline 6 \end{array} \qquad \begin{array}{r} 1 \\ +4 \\ \hline 5 \end{array}$$

$$\begin{array}{r} 3 \\ +2 \\ \hline 5 \end{array} \qquad \begin{array}{r} 1 \\ +2 \\ \hline 3 \end{array}$$

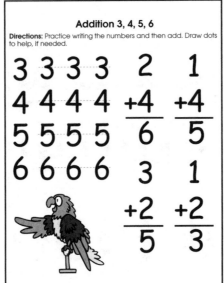

Page 366

Addition 4, 5, 6, 7

Directions: Practice writing the numbers and then add. Draw dots to help, if needed.

4 4 4 4

5 5 5 5

6 6 6 6

7 7 7 7

$$\begin{array}{r} 2 \\ +5 \\ \hline 7 \end{array} \qquad \begin{array}{r} 3 \\ +1 \\ \hline 4 \end{array}$$

$$\begin{array}{r} 4 \\ +1 \\ \hline 5 \end{array} \qquad \begin{array}{r} 2 \\ +4 \\ \hline 6 \end{array}$$

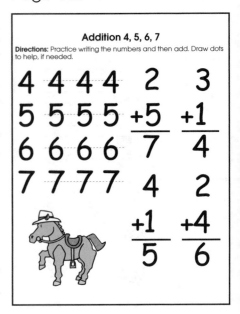

Page 367

Addition 6, 7, 8

Directions: Practice writing the numbers and then add. Draw dots to help, if needed.

6 6 6 6

7 7 7 7

8 8 8 8

$$\begin{array}{r} 3 \\ +4 \\ \hline 7 \end{array} \qquad \begin{array}{r} 5 \\ +1 \\ \hline 6 \end{array}$$

$$\begin{array}{r} 2 \\ +6 \\ \hline 8 \end{array} \qquad \begin{array}{r} 4 \\ +4 \\ \hline 8 \end{array}$$

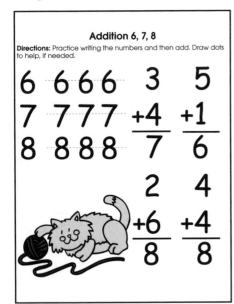

Page 368

Addition 7, 8, 9

Directions: Practice writing the numbers and then add. Draw dots to help, if needed.

7 7 7 7

8 8 8 8

9 9 9 9

$$\begin{array}{r} 8 \\ +1 \\ \hline 9 \end{array} \qquad \begin{array}{r} 3 \\ +5 \\ \hline 8 \end{array}$$

$$\begin{array}{r} 2 \\ +7 \\ \hline 9 \end{array} \qquad \begin{array}{r} 6 \\ +1 \\ \hline 7 \end{array}$$

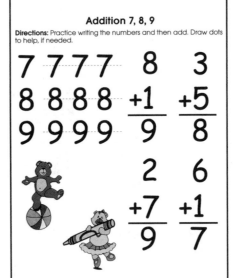

Page 369

Addition Table

Directions: Add across and down with a friend. Fill in the spaces.

+	0	1	2	3	4	5
0	0	1	2	3	4	5
1	1	2	3	4	5	6
2	2	3	4	5	6	7
3	3	4	5	6	7	8
4	4	5	6	7	8	9
5	5	6	7	8	9	10

Do you notice any number patterns in the Addition Table?

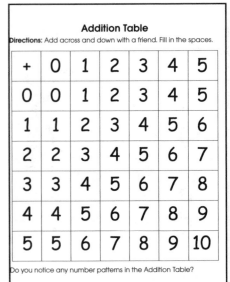

Page 370

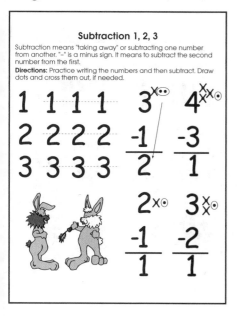

Subtraction 1, 2, 3

Subtraction means "taking away" or subtracting one number from another. "–" is a minus sign. It means to subtract the second number from the first.
Directions: Practice writing the numbers and then subtract. Draw dots and cross them out, if needed.

Page 371

Subtraction 3, 4, 5, 6

Directions: Practice writing the numbers and then subtract. Draw dots and cross them out, if needed.

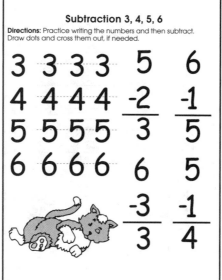

Page 372

Subtraction

Directions: Draw the correct number of dots next to the numbers in each problem. Cross out the ones subtracted to find your answer.

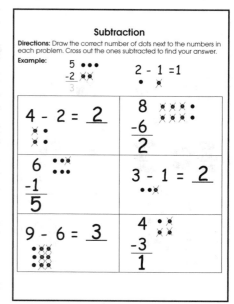

Page 373

Review

Directions: Trace the numbers. Work the problems.

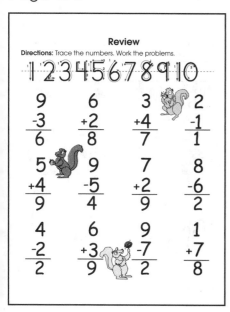

Page 374

Zero

Directions: Write the number.

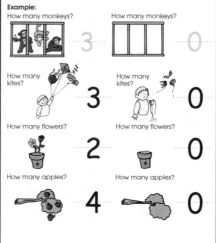

Page 375

Zero

Directions: Write the number that tells how many.

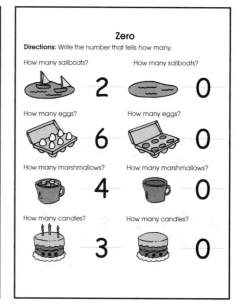

ANSWER KEY

Page 376

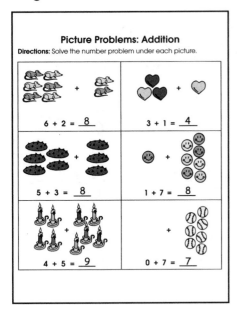

Picture Problems: Addition

Directions: Solve the number problem under each picture.

6 + 2 = __8__   3 + 1 = __4__

5 + 3 = __8__   1 + 7 = __8__

4 + 5 = __9__   0 + 7 = __7__

Page 377

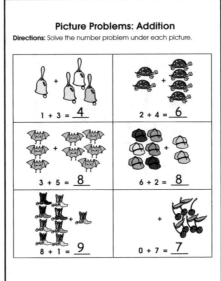

Picture Problems: Addition

Directions: Solve the number problem under each picture.

1 + 3 = __4__   2 + 4 = __6__

3 + 5 = __8__   6 + 2 = __8__

8 + 1 = __9__   0 + 7 = __7__

Page 378

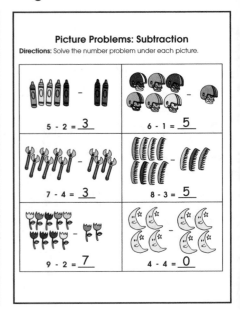

Picture Problems: Subtraction

Directions: Solve the number problem under each picture.

5 - 2 = __3__   6 - 1 = __5__

7 - 4 = __3__   8 - 3 = __5__

9 - 2 = __7__   4 - 4 = __0__

Page 379

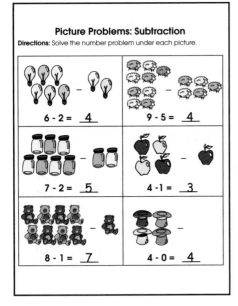

Picture Problems: Subtraction

Directions: Solve the number problem under each picture.

6 - 2 = __4__   9 - 5 = __4__

7 - 2 = __5__   4 - 1 = __3__

8 - 1 = __7__   4 - 0 = __4__

Page 380

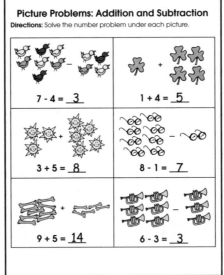

Picture Problems: Addition and Subtraction

Directions: Solve the number problem under each picture.

7 - 4 = __3__   1 + 4 = __5__

3 + 5 = __8__   8 - 1 = __7__

9 + 5 = __14__   6 - 3 = __3__

Page 381

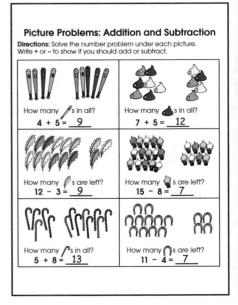

Picture Problems: Addition and Subtraction

Directions: Solve the number problem under each picture.
Write + or – to show if you should add or subtract.

How many 🦴s in all?
4 + 5 = __9__

How many 🍫s in all?
7 + 5 = __12__

How many 🍗s are left?
12 - 3 = __9__

How many 🍷s are left?
15 - 8 = __7__

How many 🍬s in all?
5 + 8 = __13__

How many ∩s are left?
11 - 4 = __7__

ANSWER KEY

Page 382

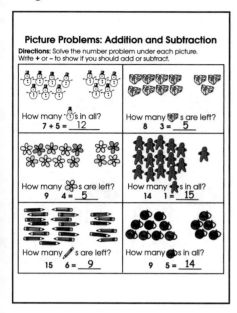

Picture Problems: Addition and Subtraction

Directions: Solve the number problem under each picture. Write + or – to show if you should add or subtract.

How many ☃'s in all? 7 + 5 = 12

How many 🦋 s are left? 8 – 3 = 5

How many 🌼 s are left? 9 – 4 = 5

How many 🍪 s in all? 14 + 1 = 15

How many ✏ s are left? 15 – 6 = 9

How many 🍎 s in all? 9 + 5 = 14

Page 383

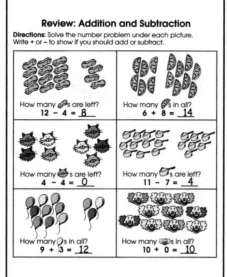

Review: Addition and Subtraction

Directions: Solve the number problem under each picture. Write + or – to show if you should add or subtract.

How many 🥜 s are left? 12 – 4 = 8

How many 🍊 s in all? 6 + 8 = 14

How many 🐱 s are left? 4 – 4 = 0

How many 🥄 s are left? 11 – 7 = 4

How many 🎈 s in all? 9 + 3 = 12

How many 🐑 s in all? 10 + 0 = 10

Page 384

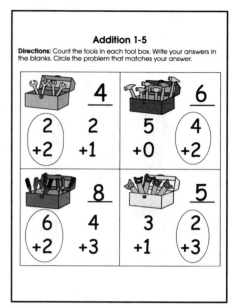

Addition 1-5

Directions: Count the tools in each tool box. Write your answers in the blanks. Circle the problem that matches your answer.

4 — 2+2 (circled) — 2+1

6 — 5+0 — 4+2 (circled)

8 — 6+2 (circled) — 4+3

5 — 3+1 — 2+3 (circled)

Page 385

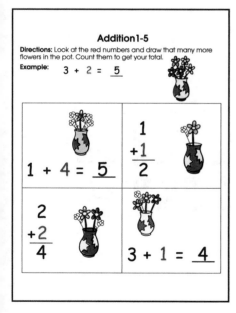

Addition 1-5

Directions: Look at the red numbers and draw that many more flowers in the pot. Count them to get your total.

Example: 3 + 2 = 5

1 + 4 = 5

1 + 1 / 2

2 + 2 / 4

3 + 1 = 4

Page 386

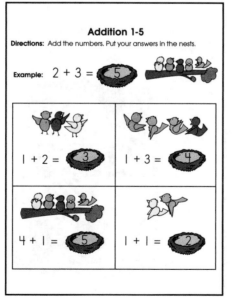

Addition 1-5

Directions: Add the numbers. Put your answers in the nests.

Example: 2 + 3 = 5

1 + 2 = 3

1 + 3 = 4

4 + 1 = 5

1 + 1 = 2

Page 387

Addition 6-10

Directions: Add the numbers. Put your answers in the doghouses.

Example: 4 + 2 = 6

2 + 6 = 8

7 + 3 = 10

6 + 1 = 7

4 + 5 = 9

6 + 2 = 8

7 + 2 = 9

Page 388

Subtraction 1-5

Directions: Subtract the red numbers by crossing out that many flowers in the pot. Count the ones not crossed out to get the total.

Example:

2 - 1 = _1_

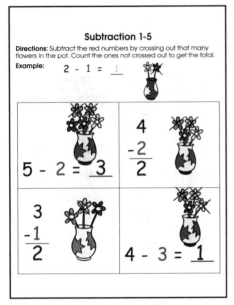

5 - 2 = _3_

$\begin{array}{r} 4 \\ -2 \\ \hline 2 \end{array}$

$\begin{array}{r} 3 \\ -1 \\ \hline 2 \end{array}$

4 - 3 = _1_

Page 389

Subtraction 1-5

Directions: Count the fruit in each bowl. Write your answers on the blanks. Circle the problem that matches your answer.

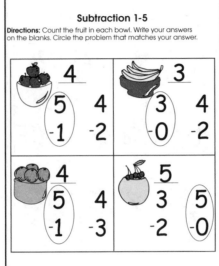

$\begin{array}{r} 4 \\ 5 \\ -1 \end{array}$ 4 -2

$\begin{array}{r} 3 \\ 3 \\ -0 \end{array}$ 4 -2

$\begin{array}{r} 4 \\ 5 \\ -1 \end{array}$ 4 -3

$\begin{array}{r} 5 \\ 3 \\ -2 \end{array}$ 5 -0

Page 390

Subtraction 6-10

Directions: Count the flowers. Write your answer on the blank. Circle the problem that matches your answer.

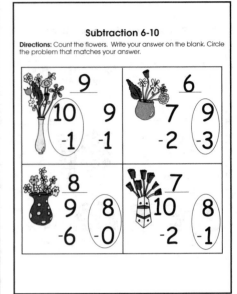

$\begin{array}{r} 9 \\ 10 \\ -1 \end{array}$ 9 -1

$\begin{array}{r} 6 \\ 7 \\ -2 \end{array}$ 9 -3

$\begin{array}{r} 8 \\ 9 \\ -6 \end{array}$ 8 -0

$\begin{array}{r} 7 \\ 10 \\ -2 \end{array}$ 8 -1

Page 391

Addition and Subtraction

Directions: Solve the problems. Remember, addition means "putting together" or adding two or more numbers to find the sum. Subtraction means "taking away" or subtracting one number from another.

1 + 3 = _4_   4 - 3 = _1_   4 + 5 = _9_

6 + 1 = _7_   7 - 2 = _5_   8 - 4 = _4_

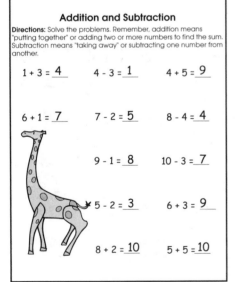

9 - 1 = _8_   10 - 3 = _7_

5 - 2 = _3_   6 + 3 = _9_

8 + 2 = _10_   5 + 5 = _10_

Page 392

Addition and Subtraction

Remember, addition means "putting together" or adding two or more numbers to find the sum. Subtraction means "take away" or subtracting one number from another.

Directions: Solve the problems. From your answers, use the code to color the quilt.

Color:
6 = blue
7 = yellow
8 = green
9 = red
10 = orange

Page 393

Place Value: Tens and Ones

The place value of a digit, or numeral, is shown by where it is in the number. For example, in the number **23**, **2** has the place value of **tens**, and **3** is ones.

Directions: Count the groups of ten crayons and write the number by the word **tens**. Count the other crayons and write the number by the word **ones**.

Example:

+ = _1_ ten + _1_ one

+ = _2_ tens + _3_ ones

+ = _4_ tens + _8_ ones

+ = _7_ tens + _2_ ones

6 tens + 3 ones = _63_	5 tens + 1 one = _51_
3 tens + 8 ones = _38_	9 tens + 7 ones = _97_
4 tens + 5 ones = _45_	2 tens + 8 ones = _28_

Page 394

Place Value: Tens and Ones

Directions: Count the groups of ten blocks and write the number by the word tens. Count the other blocks and write the number by the word ones.

Example:

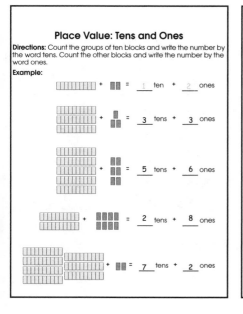

= _1_ ten + _2_ ones

= _3_ tens + _3_ ones

= _5_ tens + _6_ ones

= _2_ tens + _8_ ones

= _7_ tens + _2_ ones

Page 395

Place Value: Tens and Ones

Directions: Write the answers in the correct spaces.

	tens	ones		
3 tens, 2 ones	3	2	=	32
3 tens, 7 ones	3	7	=	37
9 tens, 1 one	9	1	=	91
5 tens, 6 ones	5	6	=	56
6 tens, 5 ones	6	5	=	65
6 tens, 8 ones	6	8	=	68
2 tens, 8 ones	2	8	=	28
4 tens, 9 ones	4	9	=	49
1 ten, 4 ones	1	4	=	14
8 tens, 2 ones	8	2	=	82
4 tens, 2 ones	4	2	=	42

28 = _2_ tens, _8_ ones
64 = _6_ tens, _4_ ones
56 = _5_ tens, _6_ ones
72 = _7_ tens, _2_ ones
38 = _3_ tens, _8_ ones
17 = _1_ ten, _7_ ones
63 = _6_ tens, _3_ ones
12 = _1_ ten, _2_ ones

Page 396

Review: Place Value

The place value of each digit, or numeral, is shown by where it is in the number. For example, in the number **123**, **1** has the place value of **hundreds**, **2** is **tens** and **3** is **ones**.

Directions: Count the groups of crayons and add.

Example:

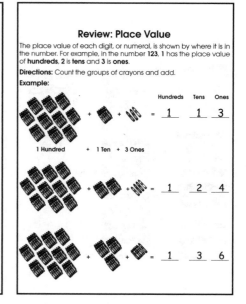

	Hundreds	Tens	Ones
1 Hundred + 1 Ten + 3 Ones =	1	1	3
=	1	2	4
=	1	3	6

Page 397

Counting by Fives

Directions: Count by fives to draw the path to the playground.

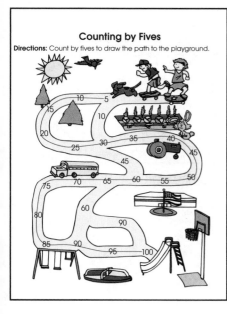

Page 398

Counting by Fives

Directions: Use tally marks to count by fives. Write the number next to the tallies.

Example: A tally mark stands for one = I. Five tally marks look like this = 卌

卌	_5_
卌 卌	_10_
卌 卌 卌	_15_
卌 卌 卌 卌	_20_
卌 卌 卌 卌 卌	_25_
卌 卌 卌 卌 卌 卌	_30_

卌 卌 卌 卌 卌 卌 卌	_35_
卌 卌 卌 卌 卌 卌 卌 卌	_40_
卌 卌 卌 卌 卌 卌 卌 卌 卌	_45_
卌 卌 卌 卌 卌 卌 卌 卌 卌 卌	_50_

Page 399

Counting by Tens

Directions: Count in order by tens to draw the path the boy takes to the store.

Page 400

Counting by Tens

Directions: Use the groups of 10's to count to 100.

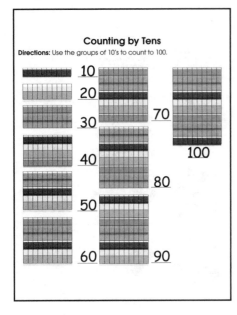

10
20
30
40
50
60
70
80
90
100

Page 401

Addition: 10-15

Directions: Circle groups of ten crayons. Add the remaining ones to make the correct number.

		tens	ones
	+ =	3	9
	+ =	5	7
	+ =	4	6
	+ =	6	7
	+ =	7	8
	+ =	9	6

6 + 6 = 12   8 + 4 = 12   9 + 5 = 14

Page 402

Subtraction: 10-15

Directions: Count the crayons in each group. Put an **X** through the number of crayons being subtracted. How many are left?

		-	5	=	10
		-	4	=	7
		-	7	=	6
		-	6	=	8
		-	5	=	7
		-	8	=	6

13 - 8 = 5   11 - 5 = 6   12 - 9 = 3
14 - 7 = 7   10 - 7 = 3   13 - 3 = 10
15 - 9 = 6   11 - 8 = 3   12 - 10 = 2

Page 403

Shapes: Square

A square is a figure with four corners and four sides of the same length. This is a square □.

Directions: Find the squares and circle them.

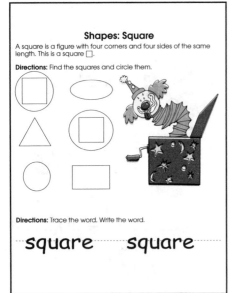

Directions: Trace the word. Write the word.

square   square

Page 404

Shapes: Circle

A circle is a figure that is round. This is a circle ○.

Directions: Find the circles and put a square around them.

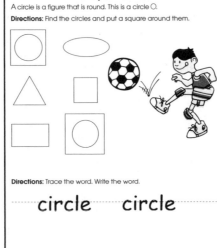

Directions: Trace the word. Write the word.

circle   circle

Page 405

Shapes: Square and Circle

Directions: Practice drawing squares. Trace the samples and make four of your own.

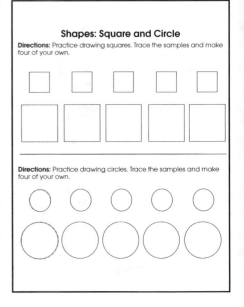

Directions: Practice drawing circles. Trace the samples and make four of your own.

Page 406

Shapes: Triangle

A triangle is a figure with three corners and three sides. This is a triangle △.

Directions: Find the triangles and put a circle around them.

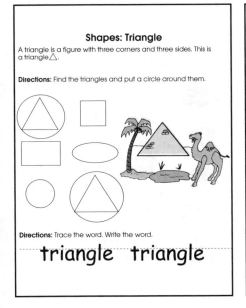

Directions: Trace the word. Write the word.

triangle   triangle

Page 407

Shapes: Rectangle

A rectangle is a figure with four corners and four sides. Sides opposite each other are the same length. This is a rectangle ▢.

Directions: Find the rectangles and put a circle around them.

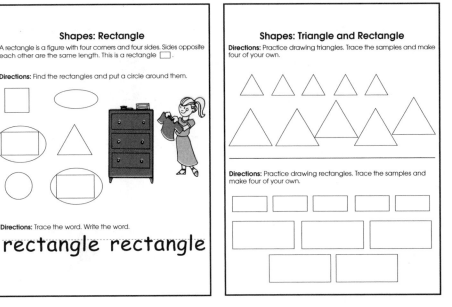

Directions: Trace the word. Write the word.

rectangle rectangle

Page 408

Shapes: Triangle and Rectangle

Directions: Practice drawing triangles. Trace the samples and make four of your own.

Directions: Practice drawing rectangles. Trace the samples and make four of your own.

Page 409

Patterns: Rectangles

Directions: In each picture, there is more than one rectangle. Trace each rectangle with a different color crayon. Under each picture, write how many rectangles you found.

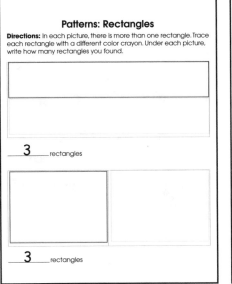

 3 rectangles

 3 rectangles

Page 410

Patterns: Triangles

Directions: In each picture there is more than one triangle. Trace each triangle with a different color crayon. Under each picture, write how many triangles you found.

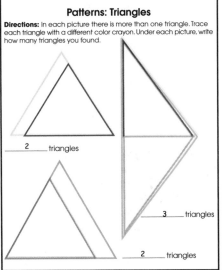

 2 triangles

 3 triangles

 2 triangles

Page 411

Shapes: Oval and Diamond

An oval is an egg-shaped figure. A diamond is a figure with four sides of the same length. Its corners form points at the top, sides and bottom. This is an oval ◯. This is a diamond ◇.

Directions: Color the ovals red. Color the diamonds blue.

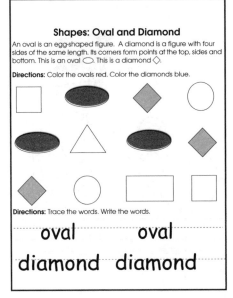

Directions: Trace the words. Write the words.

oval   oval

diamond diamond

Grade 1 - Comprehensive Curriculum

Page 412

Shapes: Oval and Diamond

Directions: Practice drawing ovals. Trace the samples and make four of your own.

Directions: Practice drawing diamonds. Trace the samples and make four of your own.

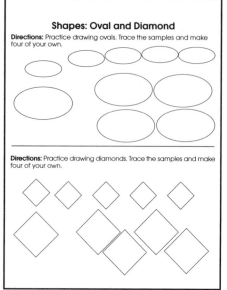

Page 413

Following Directions: Shapes and Colors

Directions: Color the squares ☐ purple.

Directions: Color the heart ♡ blue.

Directions: Color the diamonds ◇ yellow.

Directions: Color the star ☆ red.

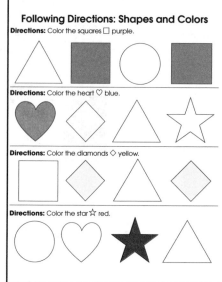

Page 414

Shape Review

Directions: Color the shapes in the picture as shown.

black
red
orange
yellow
blue
green

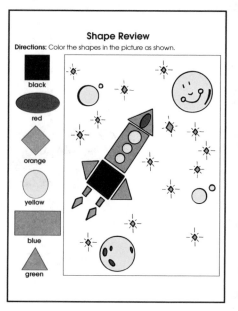

Page 415

Shape Review

Directions:
Trace the circles — red
Trace the squares — blue
Trace the rectangles — yellow
Trace the triangles — green
Trace the ovals — purple
Trace the diamonds — orange

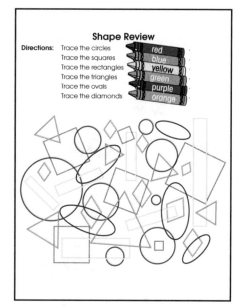

Page 416

Classifying: Stars

Help Bob find the stars.

Directions: Color all the stars blue.

How many stars did you and Bob find? __10__

Page 417

Classifying: Shapes

Mary and Rudy are taking a trip into space. Help them find the stars, moons, circles and diamonds.

Directions: Color the shapes.
Use yellow for ☆'s.   Use blue for ☾'s.
Use red for ○'s.   Use purple for ◇'s.

How many stars? __5__   How many moons? __5__
How many circles? __4__   How many diamonds? __4__

Page 418

Classifying: Shapes

Directions: Look at the shapes. Answer the questions.

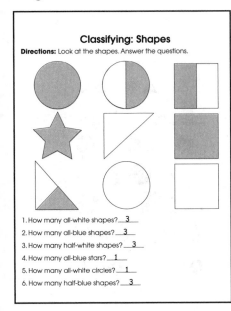

1. How many all-white shapes? __3__
2. How many all-blue shapes? __3__
3. How many half-white shapes? __3__
4. How many all-blue stars? __1__
5. How many all-white circles? __1__
6. How many half-blue shapes? __3__

Page 419

Same and Different: Shapes

Directions: Color the shape that looks the same as the first shape in each row.

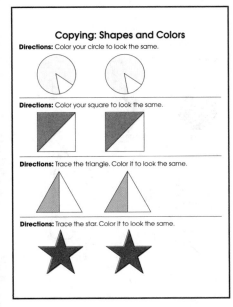

Page 420

Same and Different: Shapes

Directions: Draw an **X** on the shapes in each row that do not match the first shape.

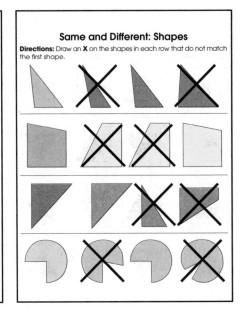

Page 421

Copying: Shapes and Colors

Directions: Color your circle to look the same.

Directions: Color your square to look the same.

Directions: Trace the triangle. Color it to look the same.

Directions: Trace the star. Color it to look the same.

Page 422

Copying: Shapes and Colors

Directions: Color the second shape the same as the first one. Then draw and color the shape two more times.

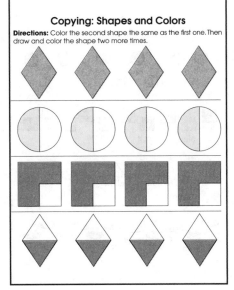

Page 423

Patterns: Shapes

Directions: Draw a line from the box on the left to the box on the right with the same shape and color pattern.

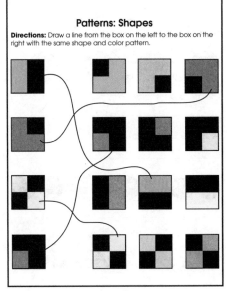

Page 424

Patterns: Shapes

Directions: Draw a line from the box on the left to the box on the right with the same shape and color pattern.

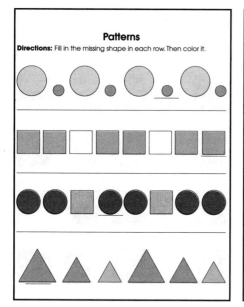

Page 425

Patterns: Find and Copy

Directions: Circle the shape in the middle box that matches the one on the left. Draw another shape with the same pattern in the box on the right.

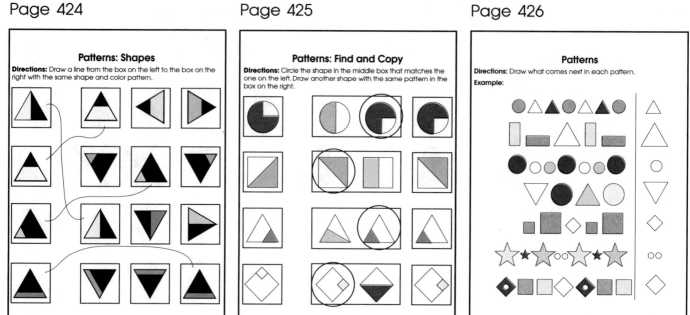

Page 426

Patterns

Directions: Draw what comes next in each pattern.

Example:

Page 427

Patterns

Directions: Fill in the missing shape in each row. Then color it.

Page 428

Patterns

Directions: Color to complete the patterns.

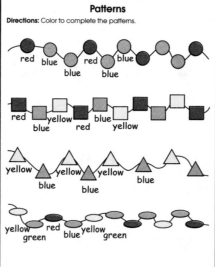

red   blue
   blue
red   blue
   blue

red   blue   blue
   blue   red   yellow
   yellow

yellow   yellow   yellow
   blue   blue   blue

yellow   red   blue   yellow   green
   green

Page 429

Fractions: Whole and Half

A fraction is a number that names part of a whole, such as $\frac{1}{2}$ or $\frac{3}{4}$.

Directions: Color half of each object.

Example:

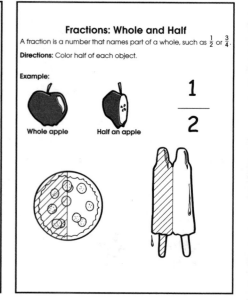

Whole apple   Half an apple

$$\frac{1}{2}$$

Page 430

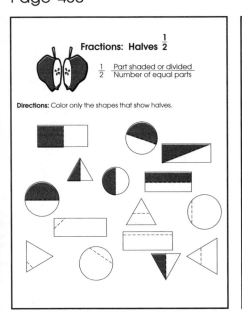

Fractions: Halves $\frac{1}{2}$

$\frac{1}{2}$ Part shaded or divided
    Number of equal parts

Directions: Color only the shapes that show halves.

Page 431

Fractions: Thirds $\frac{1}{3}$

Directions: Circle the objects that have 3 equal parts.

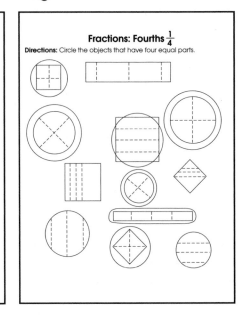

Page 432

Fractions: Fourths $\frac{1}{4}$

Directions: Circle the objects that have four equal parts.

Page 433

Fractions: Thirds and Fourths

Directions: Each object has 3 equal parts. Color one section.

Directions: Each object has 4 equal parts. Color one section.

Page 434

Review: Fractions

Directions: Count the equal parts, then write the fraction.

Example:

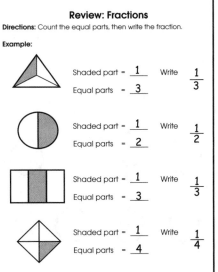

Shaded part = __1__   Write $\frac{1}{3}$
Equal parts = __3__

Shaded part = __1__   Write $\frac{1}{2}$
Equal parts = __2__

Shaded part = __1__   Write $\frac{1}{3}$
Equal parts = __3__

Shaded part = __1__   Write $\frac{1}{4}$
Equal parts = __4__

Page 435

Review

Directions: Write the missing numbers by counting by tens and fives.

__10__ , 20, __30__ , __40__ , __50__ , __60__ , 70, __80__ , __90__ , 100

5, __10__ , 15, __20__ , __25__ , 30, __35__ , __40__ , __45__ , __50__

Directions: Color the object with thirds red. Color the object with halves blue. Color the object with fourths green.

Directions: Draw a line to the correct equal part.

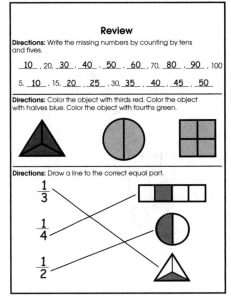

$\frac{1}{3}$

$\frac{1}{4}$

$\frac{1}{2}$

Page 436

Tracking: Straight Lines

Directions: Draw a straight line from A to B. Use a different color crayon for each line.

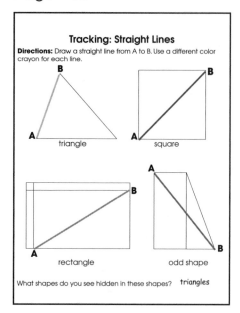

triangle   square

rectangle   odd shape

What shapes do you see hidden in these shapes?   triangles

Page 437

Tracking: Different Paths

Directions: Trace three paths from A to B.

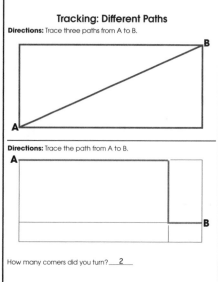

Directions: Trace the path from A to B.

How many corners did you turn?   2

Page 438

Tracking: Different Paths

Help Megan find Mark.

Directions: Trace a path from Megan to Mark.

Paths may vary.

How many different paths can she follow to reach him?   8

Page 439

Tracking: Different Paths

Directions: Use different colors to trace three paths the bear could take to get the honey.

Page 440

Time: Hour

The short hand of the clock tells the hour. The long hand tells how many minutes after the hour. When the minute hand is on the **12**, it is the beginning of the hour.

Directions: Look at each clock. Write the time.

Example:

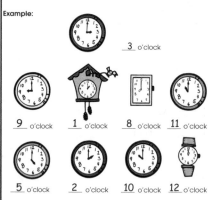

3 o'clock

9 o'clock   1 o'clock   8 o'clock   11 o'clock

5 o'clock   2 o'clock   10 o'clock   12 o'clock

Page 441

Time: Hour, Half-Hour

The short hand of the clock tells the hour. The long hand tells how many minutes after the hour. When the minute hand is on the **6**, it is on the half-hour. A half-hour is thirty minutes. It is written **:30**, such as **5:30**.

Directions: Look at each clock. Write the time.

Example:

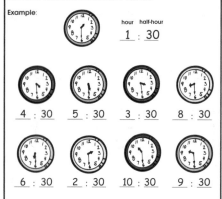

hour   half-hour
1 : 30

4 : 30   5 : 30   3 : 30   8 : 30

6 : 30   2 : 30   10 : 30   9 : 30

Page 442

Time: Hour, Half-Hour

Directions: Draw the hands on each clock to show the correct time.

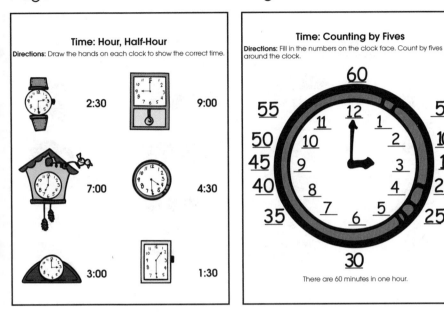

2:30

9:00

7:00

4:30

3:00

1:30

Page 443

Time: Counting by Fives

Directions: Fill in the numbers on the clock face. Count by fives around the clock.

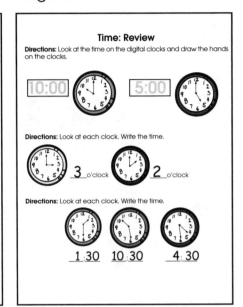

60
55
5
50
10
45
15
40
20
35
25
30

There are 60 minutes in one hour.

Page 444

Time: Review

Directions: Look at the time on the digital clocks and draw the hands on the clocks.

10:00   5:00

Directions: Look at each clock. Write the time.

_3_ o'clock   _2_ o'clock

Directions: Look at each clock. Write the time.

_1:30_   _10:30_   _4:30_

Page 445

Review: Time

Directions: Tell what time it is on the clocks.

8:00   12:30

9:30   10:00

12:00   8:30

Page 446

Review: Time

Directions: Match the time on the clock with the digital time.

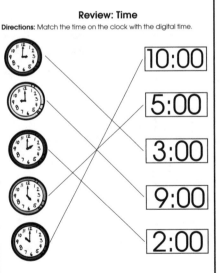

10:00

5:00

3:00

9:00

2:00

Page 447

Money: Penny and Nickel

A penny is worth one cent. It is written **1¢** or **$.01**. A nickel is worth five cents. It is written **5¢** or **$.05**.

Directions: Count the money and write the answers.

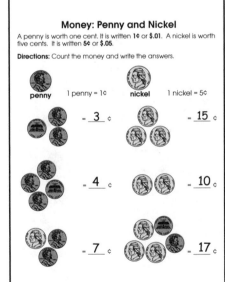

penny   1 penny = 1¢   nickel   1 nickel = 5¢

= _3_ ¢   = _15_ ¢

= _4_ ¢   = _10_ ¢

= _7_ ¢   = _17_ ¢

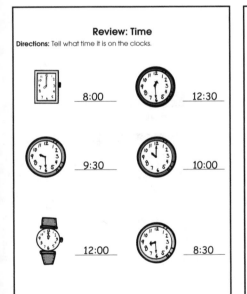

Page 448

Money: Penny, Nickel, Dime

A penny is worth one cent. It is written 1¢ or $.01. A nickel is worth five cents. It is written 5¢ or $.05. A dime is worth ten cents. It is written 10¢ or $.10.

Directions: Add the coins pictured and write the total amounts in the blanks.

Example:

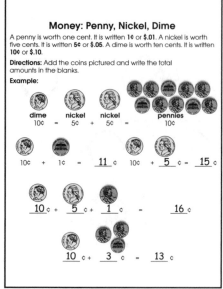

dime   nickel   nickel   pennies
10¢ = 5¢   +   5¢   10¢

10¢ + 1¢ = __11__ ¢   10¢ + __5__ ¢ = __15__ ¢

__10__¢ + __5__¢ + __1__ ¢ = __16__ ¢

__10__ ¢+ __3__ ¢ = __13__ ¢

Page 449

Money

Directions: Match the amounts in the purse to the price tags.

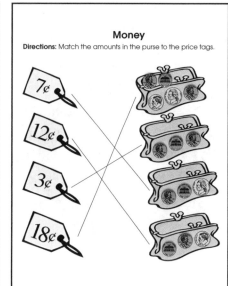

Page 450

Money: Penny, Nickel, Dime

Directions: Match the correct amount of money with the price of the object.

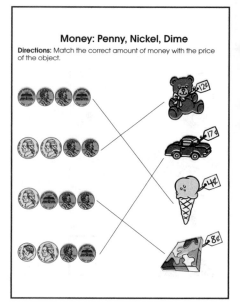

Page 451

Review: Money

Directions: What time is it?

__3__ o'clock

Directions: Draw the hands on each clock.

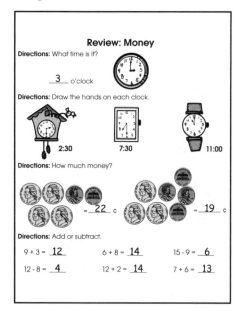

2:30   7:30   11:00

Directions: How much money?

= __22__ ¢   = __19__ ¢

Directions: Add or subtract.

9 + 3 = __12__   6 + 8 = __14__   15 - 9 = __6__

12 - 8 = __4__   12 + 2 = __14__   7 + 6 = __13__

Page 452

Review

Directions: Follow the instructions.
1. How much money?

__8__ ¢

2. 57 =
Tens	Ones
5	7

128 =
Hundreds	Tens	Ones
1	2	8

3. What is this shape? Circle the answer.

(Square)
Triangle
Circle

What is this shape? __triangle__

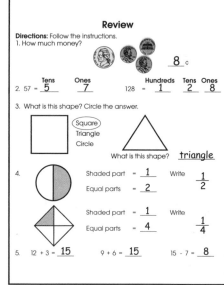

4. Shaded part = __1__   Write $\frac{1}{2}$
    Equal parts = __2__

    Shaded part = __1__   Write $\frac{1}{4}$
    Equal parts = __4__

5. 12 + 3 = __15__   9 + 6 = __15__   15 - 7 = __8__

Page 453

Measurement

A ruler has 12 inches. 12 inches equal 1 foot.

Directions: Cut out the ruler at the bottom of the page. Measure the objects to the nearest inch.

The screwdriver is __9__ inches long.

The pencil is __8__ inches long.

The pen is __6__ inches long.

The fork is __7__ inches long.

ADDITION

Make your own "plus" sign. Glue two toothpicks or popsicle sticks together. Then your child can create groups of objects on either side of the "plus" sign to add.

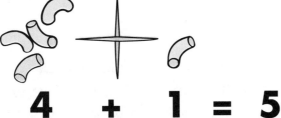

4 + 1 = 5

Use dry beans or other small objects to practice counting. Have your child divide ten beans into two separate groups and combine them by adding. Have your child write the number problem on paper and read it to you.

3 + 4 = 7

Look through magazines with your child. Encourage him/her to create addition problems from the pictures. For example: "One Mommy plus two children equals three!"

ALPHABETICAL (ABC) ORDER

Write three or four words (names of family members, color words, objects found in the kitchen) on a sheet of paper. Space them so they can be cut out and rearranged in random order. Have your child move them around so that they are in the correct order. At first, you will need to be careful not to include two words that begin with the same letter. As your child masters ABC order, however, you can show him/her how to use the second letter of a word when doing alphabetical order. Words such as "brown" and "blue" both begin with the letter "b," so your child would need to look at the "r" and the "l" to help him/her determine which word would come first.

Give your child a copy of your weekly grocery list, and let him/her rewrite it for you in alphabetical order.

Grade 1 - Comprehensive Curriculum

Show your child a dictionary. Lead him/her to discover that the words are listed in alphabetical order. Purchase an inexpensive picture dictionary for your child to use in his/her writing, and encourage him/her to "look up" words he/she wants to spell correctly.

CLASSIFYING

Classifying involves putting objects, words or ideas that are alike into categories. Objects can be classified in more than one way. For example, hats could be sorted by size, color or season worn. If your child creates a category you had not considered, praise him/her for thinking creatively.

Your child could sort the clothing in his/her closet. He/she could sort it according to the season each item is worn, by color, type of clothing or even likes and dislikes. You can also have your child help you sort laundry.

At the grocery store, talk about the layout of the store and how items are arranged. For example, fruits are together, vegetables are together, cooking supplies are together, soups are together, etc. Talk about why items would be arranged in groups like that. What would happen if they were not arranged in groups? Have your child help you find what you need by having him/her decide what section of the store it would be in. After finding the item, talk about alternate places the item could be found.

When planning a family vacation, collect travel brochures on possible destinations and sites to see. Have your child classify the brochures according to location, activity or places you may or may not want to visit. Use these groupings to plan your trip.

Recycling is a good way to practice classifying. Label recycling containers clearly (paper, plastic, glass, metal). Your child's job can be to sort the recyclables and put them in the correct containers.

Let your child help you organize the kitchen cupboards, a closet or dresser drawer. Food could be organized into food groups. Clothes and shoes could be sorted by season or color.

Help your child take a poll while riding in the car. Decide on a topic (color of cars, types of vehicles seen, color of houses, etc.). Have your child draw columns on a sheet of paper and label the columns. Each time you or your child spots an object that belongs in a category, have him/her make a tally mark in that column.

Encourage your child to help you as you prepare meals in the kitchen. Talk about the places where kitchen utensils are kept—silverware, glasses, plates, etc. As you dry the dishes or empty the dishwasher, your child can sort the forks, spoons and knives or the plates and glasses. Helping to sort and fold the laundry is another practical way to reinforce this skill.

Arrange an assortment of "like" objects, such as buttons, safety pins, paper clips (all used to fasten things) or chalk, pens, markers (things used to write with), and have your child find something that also belongs in that grouping. You could also arrange an assortment of "like" materials with one object that doesn't belong and have your child remove the wrong one.

COLORS

Fill six clear plastic glasses half full with water. Have your child experiment with mixing drops of food coloring into each cup. Talk about the colors created and how they were created. Help your child record his/her findings. For example, red + yellow = orange.

COMPOUND WORDS

Look for compound words in newspapers and magazines or write compound words on cards, and cut them apart for your child. Challenge your child to match the word parts, glue them together and illustrate them.

COMPREHENSION

Your child can make a poster for a book or movie. Have him/her include the important events, the most exciting parts, his/her favorite part and reasons why someone else should view or read it.

Comprehension involves understanding what is seen, heard or read. To help your child with this skill, talk about a book, picture, movie or television program. Ask your child if he/she likes it and the reasons why or why not. By listening to what he/she says, you can tell whether the book, etc. was understood. If your child does not fully understand part of it, discuss that section further. Reread the book or watch the program again, if possible.

Watch the news with your child and discuss the job of a news reporter. After your child understands what reporters do, create your own newscast. You can be the reporter, and your child can pretend to be a character from a book or movie. Make up the questions together, based on a book he/she has read or a movie he/she has watched. Use the questions for an "interview." If you have a video camera, record your interview, and play it back for your child to watch.

After reading a book, have your child create a book cover for it. The picture should tell about the book and include a brief summary on the back. If the book belongs to your child, he/she could use the cover on the book.

Find a comic strip without words or use a comic strip from the newspaper and cut off the words. Have your child look at the pictures and create words to go along with them. If your child has difficulty writing, you may want to write what he/she says.

CONSONANTS/VOWELS

Have your child write the names of family members and graph the number of consonants and vowels in each person's name. Then ask questions to help your child interpret the graph. For example: "Whose name has the most vowels?" "The most consonants?" "Whose name has the most letters?"

Play "Letter Bingo" or "Word Bingo" with your child. Cut pictures from magazines and glue them on a Bingo board. Start by calling out beginning consonant sounds. For example, "Cover words that start with the letter 't.'" You can make the game more difficult by asking your child to identify words by both their beginning and ending sound, as in "Cover the word that begins with a 't' and ends with a 'd.'"

Have your child brainstorm a list of words that have the short a sound (or whatever vowel you're working on) in the beginning or middle. Looking at pictures in books or magazines may help spark ideas.

COUNTING

Have your child write his/her name. Have him/her count the number of letters in his/her name and the number of times each letter appears. Have your child do the same with your name and other family members' names.

Buy or make a calendar for your child to keep in his/her room. Have your child number the calendar. Put stickers on or draw pictures to mark special days. Have your child cross out each day.

Play the card game "War" with your child. Each player needs an equal number of cards. Explain the value of face cards to your child. Each player places a card facedown and turns it over at the same time. The player with the higher number gets to keep both cards.

FOLLOWING DIRECTIONS

Give your child a set of three directions to follow. For example, you could say, "Go to the refrigerator and get a carrot stick. Put it on a small plate. Take it to your father in the garage." You may be able to increase the steps in the sequence, but do not make the skill so difficult that your child gets frustrated. Then reverse your roles! Have your child give you a set of directions to follow. This change is not only fun for him/her, it is also good practice in giving clear directions.

When playing a new game, read the directions with your child. Then have him/her explain how to play the game. When a friend visits, let your child explain the rules of the game.

Write a note for your child, giving step-by-step directions on how to do something. If he/she cannot read yet, use pictures to show what needs to be done. Encourage your child to follow the directions to complete the task.

FRACTIONS

Let your child help you cut pie or pizza into equal slices.

Peel an orange. Separate the sections and talk about "fractions" as parts of a whole.

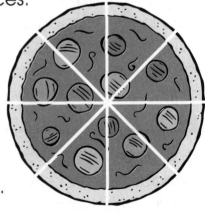

Pick clovers. Talk about equal parts as you pull off the petals.

Fold a sheet of paper into four equal sections. Have your child shade three sections blue and one brown. Explain that $\frac{1}{4}$ of the Earth is water and $\frac{1}{4}$ is land.

LETTER SOUNDS

Write each consonant letter on a large index card. Choose four to eight of the cards and lay them out on a table. Say a word that begins with one of the letters and have your child identify the beginning sound. (At first, avoid naming words that begin with blends and digraphs such as frog or shop.) Repeat with other consonant letters.

To help your child develop his/her skill in recognizing beginning and ending sounds, play a game of "I Spy" together. Say, for example, "I see something in this room that starts with the sound of 't,'" or "I spy something that ends with the same sound as 'top.'" Your child should respond with an appropriate object. You can make the game more challenging by using consonant blends, as in "Can you spy something that begins with the same beginning blend as 'glove'?"

Make up letter riddles. Example: "I'm thinking of an animal that hops and whose name begins with 'r.'" Have your child guess the answer.

LETTER SOUNDS AND ABC ORDER

Create an ABC scavenger hunt for your child. Provide your child with a list of words and pictures representing each of the 26 letters of the alphabet. For example:

a   apple
b   ball
c   cat
d   doll

Let him/her collect the items for the scavenger hunt from around your home or neighborhood and label them.

LETTER RECOGNITION AND FORMATION

Use glue to "write" the capital and lowercase letters of the alphabet. After the glue dries, encourage your child to trace the letters with his/her fingers. Then encourage him/her to identify the letters with his/her eyes closed!

Using white liquid glue, have your child "write" words in large letters on drawing paper. Then have your child place thick yarn in the glue to form each letter of the word. When the words dry, your child can trace them with his/her fingers while spelling the words.

On a trip to the beach, encourage your child to write the entire alphabet in the sand before the waves wash the letters away!

MAKING INFERENCES

Talk about daily events with your child. Ask your child questions about what he/she thinks might happen next or how a person might have felt about an event. Ask your child how he/she arrived at that answer.

Use questions to encourage your child to think about why people do things. For example, "Why do you think that man is scraping the paint off the house?" "Why do you think we are buying chicken at the store today?" Based upon what your child sees, he/she can come up with information without being told.

MEASUREMENT

Purchase a plastic or wooden ruler for your child. Let him/her measure various objects around the house. Record his/her findings and talk about length.

MONEY

Practice counting by fives with nickels and by tens with dimes.

Let your child label canned goods in your home with "prices." He/she will gain valuable practice counting and exchanging money by playing "store."

Give your child small amounts of money to purchase items when you go shopping. Encourage your child to count his/her change after each transaction.

Encourage your child to create other combinations of money for the same amount. For example, ten cents can be made with one dime, two nickels, ten pennies or one nickel and five pennies.

NUMBER RECOGNITION

Have your child read the numbers on the license plates of other vehicles as you drive around town. This will not only reinforce number recognition but letter recognition as well!

Safety Tip: Make sure your child knows his/her address. Have your child write his/her address (with your assistance) and keep it with him/her:

> My Child
> 12345 Oak Street
> Any City, Any State 12345

Help your child memorize his/her phone number as well. Have him/her practice writing it and dialing it on the phone.

NUMBER WORDS

Play hopscotch with your child. Instead of using numbers, write the number words in each hopscotch grid.

PATT RNS

Patterns can also be made from beads, blocks, paper clips, pencils and any other small objects, either alone or combined (blue block, red block, blue block, red block, . . . pencil, paper clip, paper clip, pencil . . .). Begin a pattern with objects and have your child continue the pattern.

PLAC VALUE (TENS AND ONES)

Rubber band or glue ten toothpicks together to represent "tens" and let your child practice counting by tens.

Let your child practice "trading" with pennies, dimes and a dollar to reinforce the concept of ones, tens and hundreds. Roll a die and let your child take as many pennies from the "pot" as the die indicates. When he/she has ten pennies, he/she can trade them in for a dime. Continue playing and trading pennies for dimes. When your child gets ten dimes, he/she can trade them in for a dollar!

PREDICTING

When reading a story to your child, pause often and ask, "What do you think will happen next?" This can also be done with videotapes.

You can also help your child practice predicting by giving clues about where you are going. For example, you might say that you are going to visit someone who lives in a white house. If your child needs more information, give additional clues.

RHYMING WORDS

Read familiar nursery rhymes to your child, and leave out the last line. For example:

> Jack and Jill
> Went up the ____ .

SAME AND DIFFERENT, SIMILARITIES, OPPOSITES

Play a game with your child by giving him/her a clue, such as, "Can you bring me something that looks like a book?" or "Can you find a shirt that is the opposite of white?"

In the car, you can play "I Spy." Take turns with your child finding things that are opposite or similar, then give your child a clue such as, "I spy a sign that is the opposite of go." Have your child guess the object.

Give your child two similar objects such as a baseball and a balloon. Ask him/her to tell you ways the two are alike and ways they are different. Do the same with objects that are not very much alike, such as a ball and a toy truck. Again, ask your child to tell you how they are alike and different.

SEQUENCING

A daily activity like setting the table can help your child practice sequencing. Develop an order in which objects should be put on the table. You can also have your child put away toys according to size, such as from smallest to largest. Words could be put into alphabetical order.

After reading a story, ask your child to retell the story in his/her own words. Listen to see if he/she orders the events correctly. If not, relate an event in the story and ask your child to tell you what happened next.

Talk to your child about order and sequencing in everyday life. Make lists together.

> Example: 1. Go to the bank.
> 2. Go to the grocery store.

SHAPES

Encourage your child to look at the different shapes of traffic signs and road signs. What shapes does your child see?

Shapes are part of our everyday lives. What shapes does your child see in his/her home, yard, etc.? List the shapes and objects. Add more as you find them.

Purchase or make a geoboard. To make a geoboard, pound sixteen 2-inch nails an equal distance apart into a 1-inch thick piece of wood. Pull rubber bands over the nails to create various geometric shapes. Talk with your child about the shapes he/she has created.

When going for a walk, have your child look around for shapes in the environment. For example, the front of a house might be a square, etc. Suggest a shape for your child to find.

Cut a long piece of yarn or string for your child. He/she can use it to make shapes. Draw a shape on a sheet of paper and have your child put the yarn on top of it to trace it. Then have him/her make the shape without tracing it first. Do this with other shapes.

SPELLING

Purchase magnetic alphabet letters and let your child practice spelling words and reading them to you. You can spell a word for your child, leaving out the vowel, as in "c _ t." Have your child add a vowel to complete the word.

Have your child write words on an index card with a black marker. Using a different colored crayon or marker to write the word again, have him/her "shadow" the first spelling. Let your child repeat this using several colors to create a "rainbow" effect.

Have your child spell words with alphabet soup letters, alphabet cereal letters or alphabet pasta letters.

Let your child spell words with bread dough letters. To make bread dough, help your child mix together the ingredients listed below.

$3\frac{3}{4}$ cups whole wheat flour
2 cups buttermilk
$\frac{1}{4}$ cup wheat germ
2 teaspoons baking soda
1 cup molasses
1 cup raisins

On wax paper, have your child roll out each piece of dough like a snake. Then help him/her form each piece into a letter of the alphabet. Place the letters on a greased cookie sheet and bake at 350 degrees for 20 minutes or until golden brown.

STORY ORDER

Encourage your child to tell you about his/her day. Write each event of your child's day on a separate strip of paper as he/she relates them to you. Then cut the strips apart, and challenge him/her to rearrange the events in the correct order.

TRACKING

To practice tracking, your child can make a road out of blocks, cardboard or paper. Then he/she can "drive" a toy car on the road.

If your child has a bike or tricycle, you can set up a course for him/her to follow. This could also be done on in-line skates or a skateboard. He/she can practice tracking by following a jogging path. Mazes also provide practice in tracking. Provide a city map or draw one of your own. Point out where you are and where you are going. Let your child help find the shortest route to follow.

WRITING

Fold a sheet of construction paper into a large cube-shaped block. Before folding, write a word on each side of the cube. Have your child throw the block, read the word that is faceup and write a sentence using the word.